SOCCER FOCUS

Also by John Moynihan:

The Soccer Syndrome
Not All a Ball – Fragments of Autobiography
Park Football
Football Fever
Soccer
The Chelsea Story
The West Ham Story

Other SPORTSPAGES titles:

Roger Angell	*Five Seasons*
	The Summer Game
Derek Birley	*The Willow Wand*
Thomas Boswell	*How Life Imitates The World Serie*
	Why Time Begins On Opening Da
Jeff Connor	*Wide-Eyed and Legless*
Ken Dryden	*The Game*
Matthew Engel &	*The Sportspages Almanac*
Ian Morrison	
Gordon Forbes	*A Handful of Summers*
Paul Gallico	*Farewell To Sport*
Arthur Hopcraft	*The Football Man*
AJ Liebling	*The Sweet Science*
Henry Longhurst	*Only On Sundays*
George Plimpton	*The Bogey Man*
	Paper Lion
John Syer	*Team Spirit*
	Sporting Body, Sporting Mind
Sam Toperoff	*Sugar Ray Leonard*
Colin Ward	*Steaming In*

SOCCER
FOCUS

REFLECTIONS ON
A CHANGING GAME

John Moynihan

Foreword by David Miller

SPORTS PAGES

SIMON & SCHUSTER

A SPORTSPAGES BOOK

First published in Great Britain by
Simon & Schuster Ltd in 1989

SPORTSPAGES
The Specialist Sports Bookshop
Caxton Walk
94–96 Charing Cross Road
London WC2H 0JG

Simon & Schuster Ltd
West Garden Place
Kendal Street
London W2 2AQ

Simon & Schuster of Australia Pty Ltd
Sydney

British Library Cataloguing-in-Publication Data available
ISBN 0–671–69709–9

Typeset in Palatino 10.5/12pt by Selectmove Ltd, London
Printed and bound in Great Britain by
Billing & Sons Ltd, Worcester

Contents

Acknowledgements

The author would like to thank many friends and colleagues who witnessed some of these scenes good and bad, triumphant and tragic. They include Brian Glanville, Geoffrey Green, Alan Hoby, Donald Saunders, David Miller, Frank Keating, James Lawton, Patrick Barclay, David Emery, Norman Fox, Patrick Collins, Ken Montgomery, Alex Montgomery, Brian Madley, David Barnes, Reg Drury, Hugh McIlvanney, John Watt, Robert Oxby, Rob Hughes, Ken Gallacher, Philip Evans, Ken Jones, David Lacey, Jeff Powell, Ian Wooldridge, Eamon McCabe, Chris Smith, Con O'Houlihan, Eamonn Dunphy, Peter Ball, Julie Welch, Ron Atkin, Martin Green, Struan Rodger, Peter Doherty, John Hinds, Gilda Hinds, Nicholas Monck, the late Tony White, Simon Barnes, Derek Wallis, Sue Mott, Joe Melling, James Mossop, Albert Sewell, Harry Harris, Bob Harris, Peter Corrigan, Colin Gibson, Chris Davies, Nigel Clarke, Steve Curry, David Meek, Robert Keetch, Malcolm Brody, Brian Moore, Clive White, Steve Tongue, Brian Scovell, Peter Jones, Ken Goldman, Stuart Jones, Byron Butler, Barry Davies, John Motson, Brian James, Peter Backman, Michael Hart, Dennis and Pat Signy – and members of the Football Writers' Association.

Also my sincere thanks to past and present members of the *Sunday Telegraph* sportsroom, including the late Roger Fowler Wright, Trevor Bond, David Grice, Paul and Jean Ward-Smith, Richard Rayment, Jack Rollin, and my special comrade-in-arms Colin Malam for the many years working together in partnership.

And special gratitude to Alex Granditsch, who overcame her prejudice in favour of tennis to wear out a car tyre or two ferrying this often harassed football follower to and from airports.

*This book is dedicated in memory of my late mother
ELINOR BELLINGHAM SMITH, the East Anglian artist
and a firm Ispwich supporter*

— and once again for Brian Glanville.

List of Illustrations

All illustrations are reproduced by courtesy of Bob Thomas, unless otherwise indicated.

Foreword

In his epilogue John Moynihan writes: 'It is sad that I should find myself typing the conclusion of this book at the time of Hillsborough, when it is difficult to imagine the game surviving as an entertainment. But it will.' Football will indeed survive, and mostly because of the unostentatious but passionate affection among millions of followers such as John. It is an affection, and an infection, which usually overtakes us when we are boys. It overtook John in childhood when he lived down the King's Road in London, a stone's throw from Chelsea's football ground, and for the past 40 years or so he has imagined himself, in that fantasy world occupied for so much of the time by those addicted to football, to be Tommy Lawton, that famous centre forward of Everton, Chelsea, Notts County and England. John has delighted in this alter ego, whatever the limitations of his own enthusiastic and enduring efforts on park pitches from Yorkshire to Brittany, and that enthusiasm has also delighted his many friends and has coloured his distinctive writing upon the game.

John is an unusual person, and his writing, too, is unusual. This is to be expected of the only child of two distinguished artists. There is in him, and his observations of football, a sensitivity that is equally rare on the terraces and in what was until recently termed Fleet Street. This book, like those which have preceded it during the past 20 years, is marked by a feel for mood and emotion among both players and spectators. Events both famous and ordinary are recorded with an eye and an ear for detail that are rare among those whose job it is to write about the business of kicking a ball.

On an anonymous day in 1983, John goes to watch Jimmy Melia, that good-humoured former Liverpool player, putting

9

his players through their paces on a snowswept training pitch down at Brighton, prior to the Sussex club meeting Liverpool in the FA Cup. In the kind of improbable circumstances that are so often the midweek condition for preparation by smaller clubs, the writer has an instant affinity with his subject. The motives and the emotions are little different whether you are lesser professionals facing a seemingly impossible task in the Cup or a collection of itinerant amateurs, too many of you the wrong side of 35, on tour and confronted by the intimidating muscle of Yorkshire pub teams. It is this identification with every level of the game that makes this book so readable. The magic of football can draw a direct line between famous international players and the kind of substitute upon whom John's park teams have tended to rely – bespectacled accountants in regulation shirt, cavalry twill trousers and gym shoes. John's reflections on the Heysel disaster are as relevant, indeed more so, when they come from a Merseyside pub rather than a Fleet Street desk. There is about his writing a classlessness which is perhaps to be expected from someone with his background, who has retained into middle age that clarity of the child's eye: conscious of people as much as of the events of which they are a part.

For some years I sat happily alongside John at Cup Finals at Wembley and was entertained by his dry, often half-audible humour. It is a pity that the *Sunday Telegraph* have tended not to give his unique style its head, requiring him to be more reporter than commentator; for in condensed form the kind of reflections which he gives us here would be so enlightening for the Sunday reader. He gives us the feel of what it was like to travel with that distinctive club Ipswich, from the county of Suffolk where his mother painted so illuminatingly, in the days when John Cobbold was chairman; of shopping and eating and playing cards and talking into the early hours in St Etienne; the many anecdotes such as Lady Blanche, Cobbold's mother, being asked at half-time whether she took sugar in her tea and replying that, actually, she would prefer a gin and tonic. He is sensitive to that special relationship between grateful supporters and their favourite players. 'Well done, sir, well done,' a jovial farmer says to Mick Mills.

We can feel the sweat running down our chest during an airless night in Barcelona as John sits in his Y-fronts typing out his story on Brazil during the 1982 World Cup Finals, the orange juice from the fridge slowly turning to yellow soup in the heat and humidity. The Sarria Stadium on the afternoon Rossi laid low that Brazilian team which knew not how to defend; a surging mass of Italian and South American fans was, John recalls, like some raging Arles landscape painted by Van Gogh.

Only Moynihan, during the World Cup of 1974, would be found somewhere in the middle of the West German countryside watching a match between Amazonian women noisily exhorted by their beer-drinking husbands and lovers. Only Moynihan would turn up in western Ireland to see the boys of Athlone take on the millionaires of AC Milan; and when he watches England's unforgettable encounter with Brazil at Guadalajara it is a typically idiosyncratic account in the company of 'Tranmere Harry'. The replay of the FA Cup Final in which his beloved Chelsea defeat Leeds is bizarrely recorded from the anonymous chaos of a friend's flat and the euphoric impressions from television. Occasionally, we are stopped short by the baseness of the game's more unfortunate friends: by Karen, abandoned at birth outside a telephone kiosk by her 16-year-old mother, and subsequently a disturbingly deranged follower of Leeds up and down the railway network, and here observed with a detached lack of criticism.

We go to watch Burnley, once First Division champions, play for their survival in the Fourth Division of the Football League and the drama is established by the random conversation of disparate reporters in a taxi ride from Preston. The necessity yet futility of so many press 'enquiries' is amusingly emphasised by an abortive hunt for a missing George Best, at the time of Manchester United's sacking of their manager O'Farrell.

At all times, John never strays from that essential affection for the game, a recognition that football is simultaneously a part of reality and a life of fantasy, as Priestley wrote: 'Away from clanking machinery and into a splendid kind of life, hurtling with Conflict yet passionate and beautiful in its Art'. Anyone who has played alongside John on those Sunday mornings at Tooting or Hackney and witnessed his vivid attempts to enter into the orbit of Lawton well understands what football has been in his life. This book confirms it.

David Miller
The Times

1
Chelsea's Cup

July 1970

One important lesson I soon got to know during 30 or so years of covering the game was that, out of playing hours, professional footballers have a poor respect for timekeeping and honouring appointments. Hanging around a northern car park for an hour or two in the rain waiting for the arrival of an elusive hero has nothing at all to commend it, especially when a grizzled stadium gatekeeper approaches bearing a message from the missing party.

'Hughie's sent a message to you via the office, young man. Says to tell you he's down in London today. Can't see you, like.'

'London, but I've come all the way up from London. Couldn't he have rung?'

'Can't say I know, like. Thought I saw him too this morning. It must have been someone like him, the same long hair, they all look the same to me, they need a good flash of lightning through their hair. I remember the days when "Wor" Jackie Milburn played – it was short back and sides then, but he was better than most, was "Wor" Jackie.'

On those frustrating occasions, such anecdotes made a welcome antidote to one's natural seething rage; the appointment had been duly made, but this said, Hughie had acted true to style, turning a blind eye to other people's feelings. Inevitably, once contacted later on the phone, there would be a stream of jolly regrets, followed by a spell of heavy breathing, a clipped: 'How much then is it worth?'

There have been exceptions to the rule, of course. Over the years Jimmy Greaves, John Hollins, Tony Currie and Charlie

Cooke respected their watches, which is why on a sunny lunch-hour afternoon in the spring of 1970, I had no reason to believe the latter would fail to keep our appointment, which was against the general trend because Cooke was due to play in an FA Cup Final the next afternoon.

Our meeting venue was a secluded, heavily upholstered cavern popular with portly businessmen and with furtive directors and their mistresses playing out their own emotional games before another domestic weekend would separate them from their wild nocturnal embraces, carried out in stray hotel bedrooms throughout the week. A lonesome pianist with slender, polished fingers was trailing a sleepy passage through 'These Foolish Things' – was it indeed foolish, one wondered, seated in a faraway corner of the bar, to be in such a state of tension about the outcome of a game at Wembley next day. It is fair to say that there was a legitimate excuse as far as I was concerned; after all those years of watching Chelsea from early adolescence, the talented Stamford Bridge team now was blessed with the chance of winning the FA Cup for the very first time, though barring their ambitions were Leeds United, Don Revie's team of many talents, and considered in many quarters to carry too many plusses for Chelsea to overcome.

Charlie Cooke had promised this old fan a ticket after a recent match, promised it to me almost as a sideline as we discussed the writing of F. Scott Fitzgerald, a writer Charlie very much admired. In the world of pop and showbiz, George Best and discos, which engulfed the game at that time, Cooke, in keeping with the delicacy of his own playing style, liked to steal away and discuss the merits of literature with his friend from *The Observer*, Hugh McIlvanney. My own position as an assistant literature editor also intrigued him – we, of course, found Cooke's mesmerising excursions on the pitch, in which he weaved and darted, feinted and sprinted, hovered and accelerated, the magic of a supreme entertainer; off the pitch, and away from the action, his quick, inquiring mind and almost boyish Scottish charm, always made him good company. True, in those glamorous days at Stamford Bridge, he could be something of a hellraiser in a team of noted hellraisers – but his posterior, which was distinctly Rubenesque when Tommy Docherty bought him from Dundee United, had now slimmed down under the direction of the new manager, Dave Sexton.

Charlie had yet to arrive. Yet I had only been in the bar for five minutes and our meeting time was five minutes hence. This anxiety on my part was generated through the fear of missing out on the Wembley ticket, an almost childish inner display of anxiety for one who had been trundling round Fleet Street as a journalist for a number of years. My Bloody Mary, deposited on a small, round table in front of me, was the colour of a bullfinch's chest – rich, iced and all-powerful. Sitting on a bar stool was an expansive, middle-aged man wearing a royal blue suit, his face the colour of medium-rare venison, his laughter, which was frequent and directed at a know-all barman, surged out of his lips with the shrill intensity of a corncrake's call. He spoke with a Yorkshire accent. 'Leeds,' he declared, 'will walk all over Chelsea. They don't stand chance, Chelsea. Once Allan Clarke and Mick Jones start going for goal, they'll be regretting they ever went to Wembley. Chelsea don't stand chance, see.'

Evidently, other punters with rather more awareness of the intricacies of the game, like Geoffrey Green of *The Times*, had other ideas. Geoffrey, in contrast to a strong Fleet Street lobby, declared a sneaking suspicion that our former clowns of the music hall would spring a surprise. As a masochist from the supporter's point of view, having watched Chelsea's fluctuating, often exasperating form over the years, I might well have disputed *The Times* man's forecast, yet Chelsea's form over recent weeks had been exceptional, with even Charlie Cooke showing he could clout the ball into the net as soundly as anyone in the country. Waiting for Charlie produced an action replay in the memory of his goal against Coventry, a goal that lifted a match from a goalless non-event. It came two minutes after half-time, and my in-built video caught the moment as I lit up a Gauloise, a fairly heavy smoker then. John Hollins lifted a centre into the box where Glazier, the Coventry goalkeeper, was waiting to punch the ball away with a tentative fist. The ball seemed to have spun to safety until Charlie, who had switched to the right wing, emerged to connect perfectly and send the ball hurtling into the roof of the net. . .

Waiting for a professional footballer induced not only memories of his own feats but also of the historic establishment I was in. The bar may have been modernised over recent years, but the Edwardian charm pervading the nearby grillroom and adjoining salons which, with their ornate chandeliers, brought home the awe that all those distinguished artists from Oscar Wilde to

Augustus John, Max Beerbohm to Cyril Connolly must have sensed as they examined their own hopes and frustrations while waiting for an expected wayward boy or sultry girl. Quite likely, all were stood up at some time or other despite their notoriety, joined later by other boisterous friends acting as bolsters to momentarily giant egos pricked in the bud. Charlie Cooke was now ten minutes late.

I began to get fidgety, lighting up yet another Gauloise, ordering another Bloody Mary. The Leeds fan was still downing the Pensioners from Stamford Bridge, unaware that a loyal fan was seated nearby. 'Chelsea will get lesson. Nowt's in their favour.'

Perhaps he was speaking the truth – Leeds had overcome Manchester United in a show of strength during a prolonged semi final duel. United had Bobby Charlton, Denis Law and George Best at their disposal. But then, Chelsea had beaten United 2–1 just before, with 61,749 breathless supporters bursting Stamford Bridge at the seams. Many had come to see the magic of United's feared threesome, but the skills of Cooke, Alan Hudson, Peter Osgood, John Hollins and Peter Houseman had made more impact on the day. Hudson, absent from the final because of injury, had shown astonishing flair for one so young; a potential which in later years regretfully only flickered in spasms for England. But his natural talents in midfield would surely have graced the Wembley pitch that muddy day in 1970. Charlie Cooke was now 15 minutes late, and my Leeds friend was picking up piles of nuts with chubby fingers, like a child building castles on Camber Sands.

Could Oscar Wilde have fretted for the arrival of a painted friend among all the chiffon and ballgowns of his generation, as I fretted now for Charlie's arrival bearing my precious ticket? I could not adopt Wilde's eminent disdain for some of his fellow mortals as they passed his table, a look that could make a third-rate artist feel like a tenth-rate one. But the Leeds fan's hectic laughter began to nag on the system – his 'Chelsea'll get their lesson' geared to his colossal assurance carried down from Yorkshire. 'It'll be a reet good do, Wembley, for Leeds, a reet good do.'

Chelsea had looked a team apart in the quarter final against Queen's Park Rangers at Loftus Road – they had played the game with such authority on a mud-pack pitch that Rangers, with Terry Venables and Rodney Marsh, were made to look distinctly second best. Of Chelsea's four goals to Rangers' two, Peter Osgood scored three, but the winners owed a great deal to the tight marking of the gifted Marsh by their captain, Ron 'Chopper' Harris. Chelsea's semi final against Watford at White Hart Lane had been a massacre by comparison, despite Watford scoring first. Memories: tomorrow would be another very different day against the all-whites of Leeds. I looked at my watch – and then Charlie walked in through the door.

He dribbled round the Leeds fan and came, nearly skipping, towards me, apologising all the way, his smile infectious. There was no need to apologise, he had bothered to turn up on the day before the Cup Final – the envelope, the magic envelope, was safely in the hand. Charlie, unlike many other finalists through the ages, had refused to sell it for a vast profit. The Leeds fan, his Hush Puppies solidly on the bar rail, failed to recognise the star. I asked Charlie if he felt tense. 'No, not really. We were there only three years ago when we lost to Spurs. The "Doc" had made us eat so much Chinese food down at Brighton that we felt like a bunch of walking chop sueys on the day. Tony Hateley couldn't jump for headers, he dribbled like Stan Matthews, which he doesn't normally – we were baffled. He ran like a dream, while Spurs were running all over us. It was a bad day. Incidentally, I've started *The Last Tycoon* – it's a marvel.'

In normal circumstances, Charlie would have enjoyed a Bacardi with his coke in such a social atmosphere – a drink he once admitted he enjoyed so much that it took his weight up to 12 stone when he first arrived at Chelsea. The mere fact, however, that he was sitting in a bar on Cup Final eve would now, in these more monetary, pressurised days have been leaked to the tabloid press. 'CHARLIE COOKE ON PRE-WEMBLEY RAMPAGE. SEXTON EXPLODES.' But on this occasion Charlie could at least enjoy his privacy, at least until the Leeds fan suddenly registered recognition. Now he was up on his Hush Puppies, grabbing a bar menu and a biro from his inside pocket. He sauntered over. 'It's Charlie Cooke, reet? I bring you the best of Yorkshire and the best of Leeds – and would you do me the honour and sign here?' The fan's hairstyle in a way resembled our Peter Pan of the wings, longish in the fashion of the time, but glued down against his cranium almost in the shape of a Prussian tin helmet. The subtle difference was that Charlie's was beautifully coiffured in keeping with a footballer who, next day, would be presented to Princess Margaret.

Charlie, all charm, duly signed. 'You'll get a licking, you know,' the Leeds fan said, almost coyly, stepping back half a yard like a King's Own Yorkshire Light Infantry private on pay-day.

'Go on,' Charlie replied mischievously. 'We've got it taped. We'll cash in on their mistakes, their bound to make one. We'll make them pay. Have a good game, sir.'

It was a friendly signal for the fan to get on his bike. He did so, eagerly showing the autograph to a withdrawn barman. No doubt, he was an angler, a hater of football. As the pianist tinkled through 'Give me the Simple Life', I pressed good luck messages on Charlie, from friends and colleagues holding affection for the Bridge. We would soon say farewell outside the swing doors, sunshine beating down as shoppers and fresh secretaries streamed by. 'Well, so long,' said Charlie, giving my arm a playful punch. 'Enjoy the game and give us a cheer.' With that, the ball magician leapt into a taxi to rejoin his team at headquarters, a ball juggler who had learnt some of his art watching conjurers at the circus while at school at Greenock.

My wallet primed by Charlie's ticket, I began to search out a cab along a bustling boulevard where, as a schoolboy, I had witnessed platoons of happy, drunken American servicemen celebrating VJ night in August, 1945. Anyone, male or female, who got in their way, tended to be kissed, to be rocked back frantically towards the pavement, younger girls on their footstool heels happily agreeing to a smoochy smack. Reminiscing in the warm sunshine, I suddenly felt a hand on my shoulder. It was the Leeds fan from the bar, heaving slightly from the sudden influx of oxygen, his face, losing the strength of venison pink and becoming noticeably blotchy, like a whore's powdered neck.

Half an hour later Basil, as he was called, had revealed most of his life history over another 'pick-me-up' in some raffish tavern off Leicester Square. As a travelling salesman, employed by a textile firm outside Leeds, he moved around the country a great deal, which allowed him to watch his favourite football team at away matches. Wembley was the big prize, although he admitted he had almost lost his ticket when he was fleeced by a hostess at the Crane Club a few hours from daybreak. 'She led me raaht up garden path, 100 smackers for champagne and a toy pink tiger. Then she just pissed off without a word. A fuckin' con! But I'm chuffed to shit – still got Wembley ticket.' He put a fat hand into his pocket – it was worth a wince to see if the magic slip was still his: it was.

'I should keep an eye on that if I was you,' I warned, giving my own wallet a gentle squeeze to make sure all was well. But would he? Would he survive another night around the depressing sex shops of Soho, another night of being conned and insulted, propositioned and humiliated, menaced by London fans loyal to Chelsea, bullied by night-club pimps? Would he keep hold of that ticket that would allow him a saintly passage into the stadium? Only 24 liquid hours would tell. His favourite watering hole, he toll me, was the bar of the hotel in Bayswater where he was staying. 'They're raaht hospitable – no closing there,' he said. 'I'll go and have a kip soon. I owe it to meeself.'

Basil, a bachelor, was thrilled that Charlie Cooke had signed an autograph for him. 'Chelsea's goin' to get a raaht lesson tomorrow – but we'll have to watch that Cookie, he's a bit of a conjurer when he gets ball. But Norman Hunter'll bite his ankles, you see.' The effects of unlimited jungle juice began to take their toll on this much-travelled fan – paranoia began to rage at the bar as he began to tell me what 'a raaht bastard' his boss was, up at the textile factory.

'He's a little führer, right up the arse of Harold Wilson as they all are up there. But when a Prime Minister supports Huddersfield, what do you expect? Harold'll lose next election, you see. He's got too complacent by half. My boss doesn't be-lieve in loyalty; he's just a little bighead who believes in using people, and then sacking 'em.'

It was a relief to know that our Sunday pages had gone away early – the subsequent afternoon could be used on return for pencil nibbling, and looking ahead to the next day's torments and challenges. Basil, engulfed by his feelings of hatred to-wards a squat garment–tyrant in the North, could now be left to occupy his own lonely hours on the road to Wembley, free to pin down a willing bar partner and cradle him in the nuances of Leeds United history.

My wife, Clare, had sensibly allowed me a private corral, where I could prepare my own homage to my favourite football club without domestic pressures over the breakfast cornflakes, or fears of dry rot in the basement of our Paddington house. She ignored the big occasion, not that there was very much evidence of a Cup final around our area, and to this day I cannot remember there being any passion involved in going to

Wembley that day. The Leeds fans with their blue, yellow and white scarves seemed to dominate Wembley Way.

The sun failed to shine as it had done the day before, and I wondered if Basil had managed to rouse himself to make the short journey from Bayswater to Wembley. The seat Charlie had given me was just to the left and below the Royal Box, the enclosure nearer the dressing-rooms, where eventually Don Revie of Leeds and Dave Sexton would lead their teams out for the presentation to Princess Margaret. The royal visitor – who once had a passion for dancing on small night-club floors with such chinny escorts as Billy Wallace – had prudently donned a pair of fashionable black boots to cross into the playing area for the handshakes. Charlie was down the Chelsea line, as the players warmed up, trying not to look nervous. Charlie's hair looked as beautifully coiffured as it had the day before at the Café Royal. It looked as if he had avoided sleeping on the groomed locks. Princess Margaret muttered something about 'winning' and moved regally on. Leeds, meanwhile, looked too masculine for words, primed and ready, like Tudor pikemen. Big Jack Charlton seemed to hover in the sky, his nickname 'Giraffe' aptly tuned to the extravagance of his height, in comparison with the arrival of a much smaller princess. Revie smiled benignly, almost smugly.

Sitting there on a wooden plank that Wembley called seats produced a brief flicker in the mind's Movietone news of why it was so intrinsically vital to be where one was at that precise moment as the players, free of football's establishment, and its often patronising grin, began to warm up in their own goal areas. The flicker began in 1945 with a window cleaner in Chelsea telling me about the famous Moscow Dynamos' match at the Bridge; Tommy Lawton's heading powers; the old, slug-shaped terraces beyond the bomb-sites; thousands and thousands and thousands of spectators who flocked to Chelsea after the war; great dramas – the man who threatened to put his head in a gas oven if Chelsea lost in a Cup semi final in 1950 (they did, after a replay); Roy 'Gently' Bentley, a much-loved hero leading Chelsea to their first and only League championship in 1955; the subsequent battles against relegation; Ted Drake's ducklings becoming Tommy Docherty's wonderkids; Jimmy Greaves, genius departed; Peter Osgood, was 'good'; goals easier to come by, and, with Sexton in command, the club began to resemble that wonderful steeplechase hurdler, Arkle;

the old decrepit mare, the sullen Shetland pony, the shy donkey, were banished to the past, at least, for this particular period of time before the club bankrupted themselves, the magic departed, and a new era of disillusionment and spectator violence began. But why rush history? Here was a man approaching middle age, sitting among strangers, awaiting a contest which in every section of the official team line-up offered tantalising comparisons.

Where was Basil? Vaguely I recalled that he had shown me the entrance area, his seat number. Perhaps, if Soho, or the Crane Club, or one of those seedy little Greek tavernas off the Bayswater Road had allowed him a free passage, he was up there, yelling and sniggering: 'Chelsea'll get raaht lesson.'

The pitch that afternoon was a remnant of some recent 'Horse of the Year' show, a disgrace to a stadium which once boasted of its billiard table turf, fit to grace the skills of Matthews, Puskas, Law, Altafini, Best, Bobby Charlton, Baxter, Di Stefano, Gento, Finney – to name some of the most eminent supremos who had played on it in their time, and our times. It was the dreadful, cloggy surface which allowed Leeds their early lead after 20 minutes. It was the type of goal to tuck away in some distant dustbin, although no doubt it delighted Basil, a dirty mac of a goal – unmemorable – except that it was scored in an FA Cup final.

Eddie Gray, already threatening in a display which would ultimately tantalise and virtually humiliate his loyal but mocked marker, Dave Webb, took a corner. No panic so far in Chelsea's defence, Ron Harris and Eddie McCreadie having taken up sensible positions on the goal-line; but now the 'Giraffe' came rampaging in to deflect the ball down on to the pudding surface. Again, there was no threat; McCreadie seemingly having masses of time to clear, but the surface won, the ball creeping insidiously under the Scot's poised foot over the line. A great ocean of white banners celebrated the goal; Chelsea's fans at the other end seemed almost mute, conscious of being the underdogs pinned against the wall. How Basil must have chuckled, if on parade. 'Chelsea'll get raaht lesson.' It was difficult to like Leeds in such a mood: cocky, arrogant, employing gamesmanship methods to bewitch their opponents, they had never quite emulated the feats of Manchester United and Liverpool during the recent years which marked their arrival from the Second Division. Revie's men now had the determination to win almost everything that was going, but their supreme effort before Wembley of trying to win the Grand Slam (League, FA Cup and the European Cup) had disappeared. Celtic, Jock Stein's European supremos, had made sure of that.

Now Leeds sensed Chelsea were for the taking, Billy Bremner and Johnny Giles driving forward through the mud of midfield to create chances. Charlie Cooke was not impressed by the heavy going and hung away from the central action. And yet, from my seat near pitch level, Chelsea still had a few tricks up their sleeve, despite Gray's magnetic dribbles down the left-hand touchline. Webb's tendency to sit on his backside was not followed by his team-mates who hacked the ball to safety time and time again. Half-time was approaching, but before Leeds could trudge arrogantly back to their dressing-room, they conceded the type of equaliser upon which boys' comics thrive. Chelsea's gangling striker, Ian Hutchinson, sideboards bristling, managed to glance the ball sideways to Peter Houseman stationed some way out, at an angle to the goal. Peering forward, I anticipated a wild attempt from the Chelsea man that would easily miss the target. But Houseman decided otherwise. He let loose a shot which though accurately struck did not contain a ball of fire hot enough to worry the Leeds goalkeeper, Gary Sprake. The Welsh International was renowned for his howler, however, and on this occasion, the howler was even mightier than most. He appeared to have the ball covered, but it suddenly spun away from him on the puckered surface, and with Tommy Baldwin celebrating on the far post, Chelsea were level.

The Chelsea fans had every right to cheer their team lustily to the dressing-rooms; games are often won on luck, and luck had definitely been on Chelsea's side on this occasion. The party round me, all looking like prosperous Edgware Road restaurateurs, confessed they were Queen's Park Rangers' fans. 'Lucky Chelsea. They'll get murdered in the second half.' In a sense, Chelsea were, as Eddie Gray continued to weave and dart and turn Webby round the clock face. How they did not establish an unbeatable lead still remains a mystery – yet Chelsea's teamwork kept them in the game, while Peter Bonetti was not in a mood to emulate Sprake's *faux pas* in goal. Those Chelsea fans with nails long enough to chew, busily chewed them. Cooke had by now extended his brief to keeping possession of the ball and dribbling confidently forward, thus taking the pressure off his toiling defence. Dempsey, McCreadie, Ron Harris, these were

Charlie Cooke, ubiquitous, elusive, masterminding Chelsea's Cup.

the Chelsea heroes now, as Leeds put in a late onslaught to win
the trophy before the end of normal time.

With seven minutes to go, they struck with the type of goal
to send the opposition scuttling into a loser's vole hole. Allan
Clarke showed why he was nicknamed 'Sniffer', striking a post
with a header before Mick Jones followed up to steer the ball
with precision away from Bonetti into the far corner. So, once
again, our Chelsea hopes and dreams had been shattered, as
Jones raced towards the team benches to be embraced by an
almost hysterical Revie before being shooed away by irate stewards. What would Princess Meg say? Frankly, when I glanced
up towards the Royal Box, ma'am looked nonplussed.

So it was over for another season and Charlie Cooke could
look forward to a trip to Mexico to watch the 1970 World
Cup finals. It would certainly raise his morale after the bitter
disappointment of going so far. But why complain? Leeds had
deserved their victory that afternoon. But suddenly, all was
sunny again down Chelsea's side of the street as we raised
hosannas to the roof. With the FA Cup on its way to Leeds,
and the joy of the occasion already occupying the minds of the
victors elect, John Hollins took a free kick not far from where
we were sitting, out on the left-hand touchline. It was a well-
rehearsed move, and as the Leeds defence relaxed, Hutchinson
emerged, using his considerable strength to head the ball down
and in by the near post. So it was extra time, an anti-climax as it
turned out, with both teams flagging on the heavy surface. Even
so, both teams might have edged out their opponents, Dempsey
narrowly missing with an explosive long shot, Clarke hitting the
crossbar for Leeds, and the harassed Webb redeeming the agony
of his afternoon by clearing an effort from Giles off the line. And
so a replay was ordained – at Old Trafford, Manchester. Basil, no
doubt, would be there; I would not.

The Replay

It was on the Monday before the replay that Valerie Jenkins, an
Evening Standard feature writer, rang asking for the names of
some well-known Chelsea fans connected with showbusiness
and the Arts. Although long associated with the club as a frustrated fan, the names she needed for her impending column did
not come readily to mind. It was much easier to look back to
one's boyhood days on the Stamford Bridge terraces and picture

some of the oddballs who rolled along every other Saturday to bawl out their frustrations at a sagging team, much easier to recall the anonymous thousands with post-war, under-nourished faces wearing khaki berets and bus conductors' caps, the thin wedges of greased hair that emerged from those greasy interiors resembling layers of intrusive weed growing out of a garden wall.

True, Stamford Bridge had become a haven for a number of distinguished Chelsea artists and poets, if only for a short spell, while the craze lasted. These included Laurie Lee, the late John Minton, Jeffrey Bernard, Lawrence Toynbee, David Sylvester, the art critic, who chose a major article he was writing about the painter, Francis Bacon, to discuss with my father while Chelsea kicked the ball three times off their goal-line in as many minutes, and Susan Benson, a young illustrator, who used my back to draw winter scenes of the old New Stand.

The fever caused by the Wembley draw had restricted itself, as far as I was concerned, to spying one or two streets near the 'World's End,' cheerfully painted in VE-style, blue and white, but the general hype that might have gone into the build up of a Superbowl game had failed to produce a shock of overall concern in the Royal Borough as a whole; so far, that is. I mentioned a name or two of stars I had seen in the Old Stand from time to time, including Tommy Steele and Dickie Attenborough, who was now a director of the club. Valerie, always noted in journalistic terms as a 'digger', took her brief on from there. So it was a surprise to read next day, the day before the two teams met again in Manchester, how many 'gilt-edged' fans had stepped forward to wave the Blues' flag. 'Whatever stars Leeds may have on the field they can't beat Chelsea's line-up on the terraces!' the introductory headline read, enticingly. Here they were, paraded by Valerie as glossy refugees from the days of Swinging London; some of them, like Michael Crawford, (18 years on, a star in Broadway's 'Phantom of the Opera') now established in the hall of fame. Others, who jumped on the Chelsea bandwagon for a time, simply faded away, both as personalities and as Chelsea supporters once the riverboat began to lose its paddles.

Crawford and his then wife, Gabrielle, were affluent examples of the Stamford Bridge fan club at the time – enjoying the privileges offered by £500 executive boxes, and for the replay,

Pullman seats on the official Chelsea train. Crawford was making a name for himself on television, and Chelsea's spectacular form fitted in well with his image as a loyal fan with cashmere sweater and a rattle, if needed for promotion photographs. And Terence Stamp and Vidal Sassoon were very much on the scene on Saturday afternoons, in those boxes where cigar smoke drifted against glass, dividing self-made wealth from the plebs. According to Valerie Jenkins, '(for Crawford) to be so privileged after just one season's support – since he moved to Chelsea – is a bit of a fluke. He started going because his manager has a £500 a year box: "It's great to watch this way in deep winter, but you miss the noise and you can't swear because there's children around." But Crawford is undeniably keen. He went out and bought badges and car stickers. "Trouble with stickers is when you go up North they smear jam all over your car."'

Such ballyhoo began to take over large sections of the national press with football reporters flowing north to Manchester to give graphic details of what was, after all, a novelty – a Cup final replay. With Book Page commitments anchoring me to Fleet Street, I willingly accepted an invitation to a party to watch the replay, in a girl publisher's flat, off the King's Road. A number of punters with Chelsea affiliations had also been invited – and the girl being Australian, a rowdy night was expected. There seemed little chance that Chelsea would survive another battering from the Leeds machine, despite their willingness to stand up and mix it when their sinews at Wembley had looked like turning into creamy jelly.

The fear again was that Eddie Gray would run rings round the unfortunate Webb again, giving Jones and Clarke ample opportunities to provide a comfortable win. I thought of Basil, no doubt scurrying over to Manchester on the pretext of selling items of ugly textile wear to some reluctant Lancastrian haberdashers. Basil perspiring at the thought of being late for the match at Old Trafford. Basil confined to a waiting room, looking at his watch, gently swearing beneath his breath; Basil pleading with a nubile secretary, with long legs and a strawberry smear of lipstick on ample lips, about the rapid movement of the hand on his wrist watch and the necessity for him to see the boss 'raaht now – I've got other appointment'. Basil, suddenly released, racing to his car, foot down on the accelerator, and hitting an almighty traffic jam, his fat fingers banging a drumbeat on the steering wheel, a large cheroot indulged in to soften panic, the BBC man announcing on the car radio that the replay commentary was due in two hours' time.

Basil's predicament was not mine. Fresh from subbing a long review by Dame Rebecca West – 'Don't alter a word, old boy – not even a comma' – I took a taxi to the Royal Borough, where those fans who had not travelled to Manchester were assembling in pubs, restaurants and bars along the King's and Fulham Roads; those, that is, who offered television facilities, and a willingness to allow a certain boisterousness, especially if Chelsea won. There were also quite a few flat owners, like our Aussie friend, Glenda, with nerves strong enough to allow their precious salons to be threatened by various outrages like crater cigarette burns in luxurious Persian carpets, beer cans stuffed down the backs of sofas leaving a snake-like grog stain on fabric, a pile of dirty crockery in the sink, a slumbering, happy marmalade cat abruptly turned into a neurotic, unfriendly feline, a mountain of broken glass rising treacherously amid stacks of discarded wine bottles in a waste bin, a discarded male sock mysteriously left under a study desk, a handkerchief smeared with lipstick abandoned on the owner's silk pillow. . .

Glenda opened her apartment door, showing no signs of apprehension . . . her abundant energies and flair for perpetual motion, linked to a promotions role, were enclosed inside what looked like a yellow boiler-suit. 'Hi,' she said. 'The lads are here, and on the beer.' There was no mistaking Fred, an East End trained actor, slouched on Glenda's prize Chesterfield, his stocky legs pushed forward, like two unattached drainpipes, towards the television which was still showing a soppy soap opera; or Paul, a fastidious intellectual, less inclined to totally possess Glenda's quarters with his presence; and Rita, a dominating party-hopper, with straight black hair and an over-flushed face, who paid her rent by acting as museum guide for visiting American evangelists. Her own legs, bursting from a fading red mini-skirt, leapt forward far more compellingly and fleshily than Fred's blockbusters. Fred raised a beercan of Aussie froth to his lips: 'Just in time for the kick-off, then. See Webby's been put into the centre of defence. He had a stinker at Wembley.'

'You had to feel sorry for Webb,' Paul answered cautiously. 'Gray had a marvellous match, truly wonderful.' Paul chose his words carefully, a faint Borders accent fanning softly over a salon crammed with bookshelves offering volumes on subjects from 'Aphrodisiacs' to 'Zebra Culture'.

'Oh, go away with you, with your Scottish bias,' Fred chortled. 'And you a Chelsea fan.' Rita chortled, tucking herself nearer to Fred on the sofa. There had been rumours of a Fred – Rita foxhole dug out in rural Kilburn. Glenda swept into the lounge again, bearing a tray of sandwiches piled in mounds. 'Half-time refreshments,' she barked. 'Leave some for the second half.'

The doorbell sounded for the last time as Old Trafford emerged on screen with Brian Moore, headphones at the alert, introducing the evening's fare as commentating master of ceremonies. James, whom we nicknamed 'Napoleon' on account of his compelling, circumnavigating presence, sauntered into the salon of action bearing a bottle of plonk and warming every sector with his usual captivating smile. With some experience of the theatre world himself, James, with his tall, muscular build, long, dark hair, and outstanding looks, did not suffer fools gladly, and Fred, with his rattlesnake sense of humour, tended to retreat when he sensed 'Napoleon' was tiring of his over-zealous utterances.

James settled amicably next to his old friend Paul, seated well away from the sofa-bound Fred and Rita, while I found space with a good view of the pitch on a vacant cushion. Glenda arrived from the kitchen with three bottles of particularly viperish South Australian plonk, gave James a passing kiss on the cheek, and handed me a corkscrew. 'You're mighty quiet for a football game,' she quipped. 'Back in Melbourne on Australian Rules final day, you can't speak without shouting – or swearing – that's more like it, swearing to make oneself heard above all the gassing in the bars. Right, Fred?' 'Come on you Blues!' Fred warbled, rather like a St Paul's choirboy with a mouth full of spare ribs. Glenda must have felt we Poms were a bit too laid back as the game got under way, relaxed to such an extent that our Anglo-Saxon instincts had so far refused to muscle in through a blast of loud-mouth observations. In fact, Paul, turning to James, suddenly enquired: 'Have you finished that thesis on Maurois yet?' 'Not yet. It's driving me up the wall. I was up all night struggling with it.' 'Let me see it as soon as you can.'

'Come on Chelsea, come on you bush whackers.' Glenda's roar of encouragement nearly shattered her window panes, the call for arms was in marked contrast to a serene view of trees leading away towards the Royal Hospital Grounds. It was a

sunny spring evening in Chelsea, and Glenda's tendency to
bellow as she sipped her wine from a free area in front of the fire-
place must have warned many an affluent neighbour that this
was not going to be a night for gentle dozing in front of the telly.
It was soon evident that Harvey, Leeds' substitute goalkeeper for
the butter-fingered, injured Sprake, was having a far easier time
than the beleaguered Bonetti at the other end. With Chelsea's
defence under pressure again, captain Ron Harris began felling
opponents like loose timber, but Leeds were getting stuck in as
well. Another crunching tackle by Hunter felled a blue shirt.
'My, my,' said Paul, sounding huffy. 'This is going to be an Adult
Only affair.' 'Norman, you're a big shite!' Fred bawled, his lean,
hungry face twitching. Rita gulped her wine. 'The big bully.'

Glenda, stretched out on her white carpet with a pink cushion brushing her petite chin, one arm outstretched clutching
on to her plonk glass for dear life, was inwardly summing up
our Pommish attitudes to the fray, her eyes darting from one
of us to the other, keenly spying for any threat of a complete
mental breakdown taking over the weaker-nerved as Chelsea
were pushed back by a rampant army of white shirts. 'That
sod Jones has done Bonetti, look at "The Cat" writhing on the
ground,' Fred gasped. 'What a bastard!' said James, searching
the television screen with penetrating eyes. 'That's typical of
Jones,' Paul added. 'He just goes in as if he wants to kill goalkeepers. Poor old Bonetti.'

Indeed, it was poor old Bonetti because with nine minutes
to go before half-time, he was left staring forlornly on one leg
as Jones swept a mighty shot into the roof of the Chelsea net.
'That's it,' I said, the senior fan on parade, the ace masochist,
the voice of doom. 'We'll never come back now.'

At half-time, Paul got up and walked gloomily to the window,
staring out with unabashed Celtic despair on the urban landscape below. His long cheroot trailed from his lips, a sullen
brogue used by him to pass on his own doctrine of doom:
'Charlie just can't get things moving in midfield. He's such
an elegant player, but Leeds are expressing their magnanimity
in all departments at the moment. I know how you feel,' he
said, looking over at me. 'I sense a feeling of suicide creeping
into your morale.'

'Oh, come on, you cobbers,' Glenda roared, handing round
the sandwiches. 'Get cracking on the wine. And Fred, sit up,
don't sprawl there like a cry-baby. Give us a laugh.'

Chelsea managed to survive some more heavy pressure from Leeds, with Webb timing his tackles to perfection in the heart of defence – Brian Moore's commentary, while not being entirely despondent from the London team's point of view, did register concern as Clarke and Jones continued to search for a second. We fretted and fidgeted as the minutes wore on towards the closing whistle. We smoked, and drained our wine, Rita tried to soothe the strain by making pointed, low-key remarks which did not work. 'Come on, you darling babies, get up the long ball,' Fred roared, his voice trained to reach beyond the orchestra pit sounding very loud indeed. But Chelsea failed to heed Fred's advice. They concentrated now on moving the ball forward stealthily from midfield; Osgood, Cooke and Hollins defying the Leeds trojans, who once more were made to wonder if they were going to catch a crab again.

It all happened quite suddenly, just about the time I was lighting up another Gauloise, with the clock ticking ominously towards full time. It happened because the player who had brought me a Cup final ticket produced that singular thrust of genius which divides great players from the plebs. Hollins, Hutchinson, Osgood and finally Cooke manoeuvred the ball forward towards Harvey's goal. Cooke quickly took stock of Leeds' sudden vulnerability at the back, swinging in an inviting chip which looked as if it might elude everybody and get cleanbz away out of our screen. But there was Peter Osgood, diving forward on the blindside, and, according to many Leeds witnesses, offside, before heading the ball with devastating force past Harvey.

The scenes of joy at Glenda's were fairly typical of what happened all around the Royal Borough. Glenda grabbed me by the hair, yelling 'GOOAAALLL!' while Rita fell simpering into Fred's arms. Paul's face had turned into the shape of a crow's, his cawing voice repeating over and over again: 'Oh, what a smashing delivery, Charlie.' Released by a cheering Glenda, I felt James's hand on my shoulder. 'We are back in business then.' On the screen, Moore was trying his best to keep his cool. 'And Chelsea have come from behind for the third time. What a marvellous fighting spirit they have shown.' Now it was extra time; massage for the Chelsea and Leeds players on the pitch, more South Australian vino for us. Paul lit up another cheroot – 'I don't think I can really stand this,' he said. 'I feel like going for a walk.' And he did, down into the street, striding out, trying to relax, by taking deep gulps of fresh air. But he was back before the extra time, first period whistle went, standing behind me, as I endeavoured to dampen my own emotions through constant muttering – much of it gibberish. James, never one to put himself in a situation where he might be considered to be on the verge of panic, nevertheless gave away a fragment or two of personal fear by biting his nails as Leeds tried to make up for their late error and win the match and the Cup.

Glenda now went out to make her presence felt with war-cries urging on the Chelsea Poms. Fred seemed to have lost his voice, his entreaties aimed at the tiring Blues hoarse and restricted. I felt two sweaty hands clutching the back of my neck; it was Paul. 'It is now more of a punishment to be here. Chelsea's destiny lies in their hands in the space of 20 ghastly minutes.' 'I feel sick,' Rita said. Nobody took any notice. Then came the moment when Poms turned into Latins, and the glory of victory became fact rather than romantic fiction. There were only seconds to go before the extra time interval period when Hutchinson swung over one of his powerful throw-ins from the touchline.

The television screen became a chasm of chaos and confusion as we peered idiotically at a pile of straining blue and white bodies near the Leeds goal. Hutchinson's throw-in had produced a favourable situation for Chelsea because in the subsequent panic, Charlton, who had strayed out of position and was under pressure from Osgood, misdirected his header across goal. And there was Webb, the dunce of Wembley, battling in to direct his own cranium delivery just under the bar from the very goal-line. Webb, apparently, was nearly strangled by his own rejoicing team-mates as they flung him to the ground, while the Leeds players barely suppressed their rage and frustration.

By this time, Glenda's flat had taken on its own chaotic state, the Aussie go-go girl jumping into a joint armlock provided by James and myself. 'Goddagoal!' she roared. But where was Paul, master of pom protocol and a debonair scholar with a background blessed through taking a first in medieval history at Oxford? While Fred and Rita simpered in their own embrace, Paul knelt on the carpet banging the fabric with two extended hands and making various monkey noises. This display of gross celebration brought the remainder of the party back to mild sanity. The sight of Paul in such an extraordinary

position aroused laughter and a great yell of pleasure from
Glenda.

'Come on, you Poms; show 'em, you Poms.'

'Up, you Blues, show us your medal, Webby,' Fred squeaked.

The second period of extra time was totally unbearable, with
Paul twitching behind the sofa as McCreadie twice kicked off
the Chelsea goal-line during a ten-man Leeds attack. The tension
had never been the same since another time, long before, when
I watched the Stanley Matthews Cup Final in a friend's house
in Hampstead. The draining of passion, the sudden uplift as
Matthews went out and dribbled Bolton out of the game, was
now being re-enacted with similar scenes of uproar, years later,
in Chelsea.

It seemed hours before Mr Jennings blew the final whistle and
Ron Harris held the Cup aloft to celebrate Chelsea's first winning grasp. A wine glass on Glenda's carpet had left its contents
as a souvenir, forming a red ox-bow lake alongside a stuffed ashtray. Somewhere off-screen, as Brian Moore tried to raise a voice
completely lost, the Leeds players were sulking, sulking so
much they refused to pick up their medals. Osgood and Webb,
the scorers, gave the FA Cup a joint kiss. And along the King's
Road down south, car horns began to blare and people rushed
out from their houses and flats to sink a celebration pint or two.

The fairy story was now in full swing, and it was lucky I
and my friends, rather than a suicidal Basil, who fell laughing
into the nearest pub which was already bulging with cheering
customers. Blue scarves were waved in the air as a kestrel-faced
dowager chirped: 'It's just like V.E. night.' It was nearly like
that – winning a Cup is not quite the same as winning the
war, but on that night of victory, we Chelsea fans felt as if
the Holy Grail had been captured. Maybe it was only about
winning a football match, and a bit of old silver, but in the
same way as American baseball fans celebrate the winning of
the World Series, or American Football fans celebrate winning
the Superbowl, and Italian fans celebrate winning the World
Cup, we added our own contribution as our landlord offered
free drinks amid bedlam.

A Chelsea Pensioner seated near our gregarious party, in
which Glenda conducted salvo after salvo of homage to the
Blues, pecked the froth off his Guinness and offered his own
post mortem. 'They're a good side, this Chelsea one. But they
ain't as good as our 1932 side. They ain't as good as the side

Jackson, Wilson and "wee" Hughie Gallacher played for. They got good players, but the players Chelsea had then were right better, they could play the game on the carpet, Scottish wizards, they were, they could knock the ball around and they were magic to watch. They should have won the Cup, but they lost in the semi to Newcastle. Newcastle went on to beat Arsenal in the final, but Chelsea should have been in the final, but they weren't because they lost, unlucky, like. Gallacher was real magic. He was better than Cooke and Osgood put together, and Jackson could run the balls off everyone. This lot did well, right, but they never did it as well as Chelsea did it in 1932. They knew a thing or two, they did. They played the game on the ground, pattern weaving, they called it, they had it all, they really did.'

His ode deserved another pint of Guinness, and another, as the merriment went on past closing time. And in Manchester, dawn would bring an outrageous Chelsea hangover as chairman Brian Mears, after sleeping with the Cup, prepared to bring his party home. I would have liked to have been there to see the winners depart, enjoy the rapturous merriment, savour the perfume of victory. This is what my sports writer friend, Frank Keating, then an ITV sports producer, told me happened later, after he joined the fun as the Pullman arrived at Euston and the players embarked on a special open-deck coach for the drive to Fulham Town Hall: 'ITV had put a fee into Eddie McCreadie's player pool to cover the triumphant coach-run exclusively. So we had a shock at Euston when the police refused to allow me and our cameraman on board. We pleaded with them, but they refused and the victory bus drove off without us. We decided to give chase, my colleague lugging his camera along with him. You could hear "Ossie" and the boys singing their heads off. Then the bus stopped at a traffic light and we caught up. Nobody stopped us getting on this time and we had a whale of a time for the rest of the journey.

'Ossie was "mein host", and I remember Dave Sexton sitting quietly in a corner downstairs saying nothing and hardly believing Chelsea had really won the Cup. Most of the boys were on the open deck upstairs and when we hit the Fulham Road, the crowds went barmy, waving and singing. The "welcome home" reception was held at Fulham Town Hall because Hammersmith Council had put in their claim before Kensington and Chelsea who wanted the show to go on in Chelsea. The players weren't worried – they could have held it in the buffet at Euston Station for all they cared – they were floating up in the blue, blue sky. Brian Mears, the chairman, had a permanent grin on his face. Honestly, mate, it was a lovely day to be at Stamford Bridge . . .'

For the rest of us, the laughing, hungover Glenda, the twitchy, inwardly rejoicing Paul, the long-striding, exuberant James, the red-eyed Fred, the long-legged Rita, and yours head-gonging truly, it was back to business on this celebratory day when Chelsea and Fulham rolled through hours of liquid triumph. Fred, rehearsing a lunch-time theatre production in a seedy riverside pub near Chiswick, constantly apologising for forgetting his lines. Basil, too, was in my thoughts, late on parade perhaps after drowning his sorrows in Manchester, his monster boss delivering a final warning through lips sucking squelchily on a prime Havana.

We all had our lives to live – but now Chelsea had won the Cup, and all those years of trying could be put in the attic. It was time, in fact, to get on with other matters. As Clare remarked at my reluctance to come down from that 'blue, blue sky' – 'You seem to forget we are having your book launch here next week. What on earth are we going to eat?'

2
Sans Blanchflower: a Rout in Barfleur

The population of the charming, gusty Normandy fishing hamlet of Barfleur, near Cherbourg, were convinced they had a famous Irish footballer in their midst. Every shop window round the pretty port blazed with posters declaring Danny Blanchflower would be playing for a less famous football team, Battersea Park de Londres, in a football tournament at the Stade Louis-Debrix.

Veteran, storm-gnarled fishermen hovered over their fourth glass of Calvados and inquired where 'Denny Blunchfleur' was to be found in Barfleur. 'No, sorry,' the English squad members sadly admitted – it had all been a tragic mistake.

The official club handout, sent from a Notting Hill basement with facts about this ubiquitous and decidedly bohemian Sunday club, had mentioned that Danny Blanchflower had turned out once for them in 1966 but had said nothing about him coming to Barfleur. 'He's an awfully busy man, you know. He loves his golf, too.'

The proud Normans wouldn't believe it. 'Monsieur Blunchfleur' was surely limbering up somewhere as Battersea's secret weapon. He was known to the actual squad members on beery duty as 'Danny Baking Powder'. He was certainly going to play for the English team who, according to the locals, would hammer their lads that very afternoon.

It was one of the many charming misunderstandings which tend to happen on these zealous little football tours across the Channel. This was Battersea's third French tour, and, like the previous ones, they didn't win a match; on this occasion they did not score a goal either.

In the first match against Barfleur, which they lost 7–0, the locals put out a long-haired winger nicknamed 'Aztec'. He dribbled round the Battersea players in turn and then came rushing back to do it again. Battersea could have done with Danny Blanchflower. As it was, the Barfleur crowd were expecting the former Spurs captain to emerge from the dressing-room as substitute. 'Denny Blunchfleur, Denny Blunchfleur!' they chanted excitedly. The Union Jack, raised at one corner of the ground, was suffering decidedly from brewer's droop. A far-off foghorn provided a tearful lament for the rout confronting the confused visitors.

When Battersea did call on their only substitute, a bespectacled economist, the crowd howled with disbelief. He was wearing the correct number 12 shirt but why on earth was he wearing cavalry twill trousers and white gym shoes? And those steel glasses perched on the end of his florid nose – 'Ooo la la!' groaned the crowd. It was not surprising that the légume factory manager who had arranged the tournament faced the action with an angry complexion the colour of beetroot.

The economist rushed forward at Aztec, dallied a second, looked heavenward, squinted in a shrewish manner, and then fell flat on his face. A huge cheer burst forth from the Normans. 'Non, that is not Denny Blunchfleur!'

'Why do you play like a dancer from the Moulin Rouge,' Battersea's player-manager asked the resident centre half in the early hours at the port's only discotheque. 'Because, monsieur, your team was so bad I could afford to play like a dancer from the Moulin Rouge.'

Misunderstanding continued to haunt the jolly tour which had started early on Saturday at Southampton with a garrulous defender losing most of his francs at poker.

Later, at a dinner party in Barfleur at the local sporting café, the visiting player-manager rose above the flagons of Muscadet and in atrocious French welcomed the local committee to their country. This bemused the vegetable exporter who had done all the organising spadework that end. Mr Aubergine was not amused. About this time, Battersea's young goalkeeper began to show signs of complete intoxication, his legless platitudes delivered from a wavering standing position booming into Monsieur Aubergine's slightly cauliflowerish left ear. 'And here's to Daniel Baking Powder, the apple of our hearts, the stuff that Irish butter feeds. Nice one Danny, nice one son, nice one Danny, let's have a nuvver one.' The consternation on Monsieur's face was now far more pronounced because Battersea's proud custodian had slid down beside him and under the table.

There were cheers all round – but somehow the worthy légume factory manager never really smiled the smile of Welcome he had revealed on the quayside at Cherbourg when he had gone in eager search of Denny Blunchfleur. His mood in the declining hours of Battersea's tour became decidedly frosty, Norman style. I'm sure he felt he had been completely fooled by the upstart Battersea player-manager who had visited Barfleur a year before, on the pretence of suffering from writer's block, and persuaded Monsieur Aubergine to arrange the tour on the pretext that the great Danny Blanchflower had once turned out for this glorious urban team who were one year away from winning their own motley League championship.

The local Press tried to be kind about Battersea's performances, which certainly improved next afternoon when they lost by only two goals to A S Montebourg – a town with strong associations with the Battle of Normandy and the American capture of Cherbourg. The Calvados-swigging scribes called the visitors 'prestigious – on paper. . .' And nobody present in Barfleur that weekend could have denied this succinct observation, in view of all those glorious red posters proclaiming that the former captain of Spurs had ridden into the little fishing port with all the gum-chewing charm of a Yank in armour. The newspapers disloyally criticised their own footballers for not allowing Battersea the courtesy of at least one goal. Actually, a Battersea shot nearly did find the Norman net once but the ball got stuck inconveniently against a molehill.

The Mayor of Barfleur was highly sympathetic, hoping that Battersea's defeats would not make the visiting team feel 'too ulcerated' – choosing his English with almost clinical zeal. He then produced an excellent selection of local vin blanc with such speed that Battersea's young goalkeeper was soon in chirpy form again: 'Blue is the colour, Battersea is our name . . .' Muscadet, Bordeaux, Muscadet, Bordeaux.

The Londoners introduced themselves to the local teams and their conquerors. The Battersea team included a publisher, two schoolteachers, one inflation expert at the Treasury, two writers, two artists, two undergraduates and two actors. They had, unlike numerous other British teams on the Continent at Easter, invited along wives and girlfriends, while one player brought his three young boys. They showed an outstanding appetite for the local oysters.

On the last night, following the Mayor's reception, Battersea's player-manager was the victim of another misunderstanding. Leaving the discotheque, he was waylaid by four French hooligans from Cherbourg who mistook him for a member of the Barfleur squad. The English player-manager was victim of three tremendous kicks to the groin before members of his own side came to the rescue, the wounded party, by now curled up against a stone wall making strange gibbering noises. The assailants escaped back to Cherbourg by car, nearly driving off the quay into the sea in their desperation to escape what looked like being an act of Anglo-Saxon revenge for the beating of a peace-keeping man who liked being called 'Boss' on Sunday mornings at Hackney Marshes.

The player-manager said he was determined to carry on arranging these foreign tours despite his painful bruises. He was even well enough next morning to devour a huge platter of crab, lobster and oysters at a beach café.

Barfleur, a hamlet often frequented by artists, including Paul Signac, was where William the Conqueror sailed from to fight the Battle of Hastings in 1066. There is a plaque marking the event on a rock at the harbour entrance. There were only nine men in his boat, including himself, but they did better on the other side than Battersea's 12 soccer players did in Normandy.

On the car-ferry home from Cherbourg to Southampton, Battersea joined forces with two other returning tour teams – an Honorary Artillery Company rugby side and members of the Welsh amateur team, Aberystwyth. The part-time soldiers were wearing smart felt hats with tiny tricolours stuck in the brims. 'Yes, old chap,' they said, 'we won.' The Welsh lads sat drinking pints of beer. 'Yes,' they said, 'we won, boyo.'

The Battersea lads were not too displeased by their performances either, having had a splendid time. 'But I don't think I'll go back to Barfleur,' the player-manager reflected. 'Did you see old Légume before we left. His eyes were like daggers. All to do with us not bringing along Danny Baking Powder.'

3
Pele versus Banks

'Mexico. . . a land of great wealth and greater poverty, a land
with a violent past and an uncertain future. . .'
(Michiko Kakutani, *International Herald Tribune*)

For the great majority of England supporters, this was their first
visit to Mexico's strange and often alien land. It was true to say,
however, that those feelings of desperation felt by a coach-load
of these fans en route to Tequila one bluish-tinged morning in
June 1970 was not the fault of all the bloated cactus menacing
each side of our puffing coach, rather the recent shock of
sudden defeat observed in the heat of Leon, where the reigning
World Cup holders had blown their quarter final against West
Germany. Scapegoats, there was a'plenty.

As the coach twisted and turned down narrow lanes amidst
those towering, fleshy xerophytes grappling for superiority like
so many prickly Henry Moores engaged in a muscular image
contest, my ears throbbed to the continuous Anglo-Saxon wails
of ill-humour.

'That fuckin' Ramsey should be shot! Bringing off Bobby
Charlton was a diabolical disgrace.'

'That Bonetti should be shot! Just standing there like a
prickless pansy watching the Krauts potting peas past him.'

'We should have beaten Brazil but that bugger Astle missed a
sitter. We should have beaten the Germans, we had'em going –
2–0 up and doing nicely, and then that Bonetti throws in a goal
from Beckenbauer – and that's our lot for the semi finals.'

'It's a reet shame, lad. Thought we'd reach final, I did meeself.
Thought we'd meet Brazil in the final. It was a wonderful game

in Guadalajara. All the reet techniques were there. Thought meeself, Brazil were a little lucky to win, like. But we should have beaten the Germans, for sure, lad. We had 'em going, like.'

'That's for fuckin' sure, Geordie. Geoff Hurst had a chance later. If that had gone in, we would have been home and cocky dry, mate.'

The Mexican party guide interrupted the sometimes lewd post mortems by offering an unwanted geographical guide to the forthcoming tour. 'We are now approaching the headquarters of the famous drink, Tequila, señors. You will be able to sample some Tequila at the production factory. I do not advise too much indulgence or inhaling, señors – it can be very intoxicating.'

'Only piss water,' muttered Tranmere Harry. 'Tried some the other night. It's not as strong as a Crosby toilet flush.'

'We are very happy to have you with us today, señors, especially as you must be very disappointed about the sad result for England. We all wanted England to win the World Cup, if Mexico couldn't, of course.'

'Go on,' a Brum voice shouted. 'You're just saying that to be polite. You lot made it hell for Alf's team, shouting and writing shitty things in your newspapers. You never wanted us to win, that's for roit certain.'

'Calm down, lads,' big Ted from Northampton barked from the middle of the coach in his matter of fact, warrant officer manner. 'We're visitors today – be proud of your Union Jacks.'

'What's this – a bleeding working parade?' Ernie from Poplar grumbled. Big Ted had been observed before breakfast at our Guadalajara motel walking around the kidney-shaped pool picking up bits of offending litter and returning to reception in step with himself but not with a host of scoffing fans leaning out of their bedroom windows.

I, for one, as a reporter on a working holiday, had been with this party of fans from the start of the finals, and had observed their emotions; first escalating with wild hope as England made it safely to the quarter finals and then crumbling like mouldy pancakes as West Germany came through at Leon, more by England's mistakes than their own skills. Many of these supporters, who included a Dorset farmworker, a Huddersfield lawyer, an East End barman, a West End policeman, a retired publican, a Suffolk sanitary engineer, a Birmingham electrician and a

Sir Alf Ramsey, Mexican victim of controversial substitution.

Liverpool machine worker, allowed their frustrations to flow into their cups as vigorously as did the beaten team brooding by a lamplit pool not far away from a noisy chicken run. It was now, on a day trip into remoter Mexico, that the twinges and remorseful bowel stabs caused by heavy drinking began to blur the thoughts of many of those present and there was much relief when the coach pulled up in the attractive, highly Mexican Zapata setting which looked more like a mustang ranch than a booze factory.

No sooner had we alighted from the coach than I was whipped away by Alf, a greenhouse expert from the Norfolk Broads, and an ardent Norwich City supporter, to inspect the colourful flora and fauna growing up the walls of the colonial building alongside the steaming factory. Alf ran a delicate hand over a smouldering pink clematis and purred with appreciation. 'Didn't you know it was the Mexicans who invented the clematis? The Spaniards took cuttings over to Madrid with them after they came to this heathen land. They did the flower world a favour, mark my words.'

An Evertonian who had been nicknamed 'Jack the Jump' because of his way of pulling local Mexican birds, wandered over aglow in a black leather jacket and a white straw cowboy hat. 'Admirin' the local scenery then, wack. Where's the booze then? I could do with a pint or two after that rave-up last night.'

We wandered back over a resplendent, green, clipped lawn to join the main party, lying about in idle lassitude in a range of bizarre costumes, including outlandish sombreros, Blackpool beach slacks, Woolworth's T-shirts, Union Jack embossed sports vests, tight-fitting jeans, sandals, and many a shoulder clinging to an inevitable camera case.

The guide was addressing the party which numbered a hundred or two debussing from a flotilla of fairly ancient coaches.

'It was in this place, señors, that the Indians discovered after a thunderstorm that there was booze in a burnt cactus. They became what we now call blind drunk – but that didn't stop those who had it about them from going on burning cactus and making a drink which we now call Tequila.'

'Christ, do I need a pint!' whispered Jack the Jump.

The guide led the supporters off to the factory where in a steaming work interior, Cockneys, Geordies and Scouses were invited to file past tanks of brown, embryonic Tequila. There was something invigorating about inhaling the fumes, like, as one former expert reared near Scotland Road bomb sites observed, 'sniffin' glue'.

Outside the factory, Mexican labourers dressed like members of Zapata's peasant Army were hacking up droves of cactus – the liquid squelching into handy vats. 'Take a cup if you dare!' our guide called out, pointing to a table filled with glasses and jugs of the lethal drink. The guide had meant to say 'like' but 'dare' seemed far more appropriate. Barman Bill from Poplar tossed his sample back and declared the liquid was no more potent than lemonade on Southend pier. And his companion, nicknamed 'Mr Tetley's Teabags', looked desperately around for a cuppa.

Some of the older supporters went back to the lawn, sprawled down and began to doze while Jack the Jump led another raid of available liquor, the guide imploring that the samples should be drunk with touches of salt and a squeeze of lemon. 'They're pouring it down like water,' Big Ted grumbled, as he was always wont to do. 'Just because it's free.'

'Come on, Ted, you have one,' Barman Bill from Poplar yodelled. 'It won't do you no harm.'

'Well, just one then.'

The revelry went on – but with a calm and politeness far from the beery cursing which had followed England's sad end at Leon. Grown men tipped their Tequila back, giggled, and sauntered with some difficulty towards the lawn which might have been prepared for a croquet game.

Now that so many years have gone by, the thought of what might have happened if the infamous hooligan brigade, who condemned many European cities to constant harassment on their trips with our national team in subsequent years, had been present on that occasion, defies thought. No doubt the factory would have been burnt down and the lawn ripped up and the residents and workers abused and assaulted, the coach drivers threatened, and the café on the way back to Guadalajara turned over for cash. That might well have happened, though so terri-fied were the England fans of the Mexican police at the more recent World Cup in 1986 that there was little to report from a violence point of view.

Yet some of the gentle people present that high noon day at Tequila in 1970 would quickly evaporate from the scene as travelling England supporters – they felt it was safer to stay behind, play bowls, watch their beloved sea views, and tend their greenhouses. It was a time before another time, when patriotic enthusiasm and a sheer love of the game were superseded by mindless, cretinous attitudes geared to smashing up little places like Luxembourg with a Union Jack in one hand and the other a blazing bunch of fives.

When our coaches eventually departed the prickly landscape of Tequila, I allowed the liquor fumes and free samples to sweep me back into my seat with an almost hypnotic intensity. This was the country D.H. Lawrence had written about in 'The Serpent', the passing cactus engulfing the senses with the images he so powerfully conveyed of his time in Mexico, years before. But now I was dreaming of something more contemporary – a certain save by Gordon Banks from Pele which is still talked about as the save of the century, and one which happened not long before our visit to Tequila.

Even today, the images and splendours of that noon match at the Jalisco Stadium, Guadalajara, seem bright and powerful; England's all-white strip matching the yellow and green of Brazil's on that bowling green of a carpet, below a blazing sun. The dramas of that match were still not totally possible to comprehend so soon after they had happened, but, over the years, through numerous television and video screenings, it has been an honour to tell younger audiences that this match was not only a stage for a goalkeeping save which defied reality, but a great tactical battle, played for real by two superbly equipped teams.

But then, in a desert of cactus, I could only mull on the blurred vision of Banks, suspended under his crossbar and so close to all of us, sitting behind the goal, that we could have thrown a quoit at his head as it dangled towards the grass in his perambulating frenzy to reach Pele's downward header. My version of what happened was quickly put down on paper at the time – and as a record stands today, as it did then, to Gordon Banks, and the match which enthralled the world. The morning of the match was strictly the morning after the night before, because some of us were at the Hilton Hotel in downtown Guadalajara, where Alf Ramsey and his team were staying. The Mexican and Brazilian throngs had gone out of their way to make as much racket to disturb the England squad as could be banged out by dustbin lids, drums, trumpets, human voice, siren, whistle, bongo, transistor, and the odd barking dog. The same racket would be with us on the road next day as we drove through the poorer quarters, surrounded by dust and mangy hounds. Every street corner seemed to contain a crowd of mockers, making rude gestures at the wearers of the Union Jack T-shirts. The noise, if anything, was louder than the night before: 'Brazil – Mexico – Mexico – Brazil.' Who were we, a party of white-skinned mongrels looking absurd in our straw hats and dark glasses?

'The mockers,' I recalled afterwards, 'were so near our coach you could look down the throats of the younger ones and see the colour of their tongues dragging forth abuse. The odd trace of spit splashed against our coach windows; the odd plastic water bag thrown harshly at our belching rear...'

I remember the coach wandering wearily to a parking lot on wasteland outside the huge, circular-roofed Jalisco bowl and walking towards a maze of turnstiles with Tranmere Harry.

'This is something we'll tell our kids,' he murmured. 'It's not like a rainy night at Tranmere with the wind blowing against yer face and the water dripping down yer neck and the puddles below yer feet and the flickering lights and yer team three down and pissin' awful.'

'No, Harry, you've got a point there. We'll do well not to get sunstroke – even with a roof over us.'

'Yer right. . . it's God-awful hot already.'

People were moving very fast in all directions outside, and we did well not to collide with some of the throng, jostling and shouting and baying, laughing and shoving and in some cases just being bloody-minded. There were still two hours to go before the match of matches and pedlars were hovering in the shade of every straggly tree. The sun's heat would have cheerfully fried an egg in a spare pan. There was the atmos-phere of a duel; one team would win, one would lose, it was impossible to imagine a draw. We joined the mobs walking towards the high steps leading to the high-tier boxes; a long procession of Brazilian supporters followed behind a band, striding and thumping along: BRAZIL – MEXICO – BRAZIL – MEXICO – thump, thump, thump! The band marched round and round the stadium and the Brazilian crowds massed behind, chanting Pele's name and we marched with them, pushed along by hundreds of small Mexican boys with their hands out begging for a spare ticket.

We sat down to wait the long hours before going into the stadium for a last half hour's wait for the match to begin at high noon. Tranmere Harry, Poplar Bill, Ted and many more English lads you might have seen drinking happily outside an English pub during a heatwave were soon hovering over their oily glasses of heavy brew. 'Cevesa!' roared a barman. 'Engleesh drink before you get killed.' He slid a finger wickedly across his pumping Adam's apple. The soul of the party was a tall, reedy Brazilian negro, wearing a green boiler-suit with the name of his country glaring from his chest. On his head was an enormous sombrero, and a gargantuan smile never left his face, sometimes toothily expanding as he taunted the England supporters in red, white and blue with frenzied gestures of his arms. A resident drummer joined him and thumped out a beat as the Brazilian bellowed: 'BRAZIL, BRAZIL.' A blonde, pony-tailed man walked by, revealing a newborn baby clinging inside a canvas bag tied to his back. His pretty girl companion was dressed as a squaw in a leather mini-skirt and barefooted, despite the furnace heat coming from the ground.

They joined us for a time. We were curious about the infant making sucking noises on the hippie's back. 'We've walked tall all the way from California,' father drawled. His girl's feet looked red but hardened to the task. 'Jimmy was in Vietnam. He knows a thing or two about walkin', and those boots were made for walkin'.' She turned abstractedly towards her baby. 'You wait for milkies until we in the stadium, Tippy. You can have your lunchies there.' Such bizarre meetings were two a penny in Mexico but the keenness shown by this American couple to watch the World Cup matches seemed quite extraordinary in view of the lack of regard their fellow countrymen had shown for the round soccer ball.

And now we were looking for our seats behind one of the goals and hearing on all sides a murmur of expectancy, willing a great defeat for the present World Champions, England – a murmur which would soon build into a stunning howl of welcome for Brazil. Above the stadium whirled an hysterical pigeon carrying a green and yellow banner. It flew on and on and round and round until exhaustion hurled the bird to the ground.

There was a hushed silence as the bird lay in a bundle of feathers near the centre circle, a grey speck on a vivid green sea before rising again released from its patriotic burden. The cheers and chants rose again, and the marvel of this display of patriotism for what was after all only a football match, a game of footer played with a round ball by 22 men, was projected through a great hazy spread of colour in which the pitch itself almost burnt the eyes, so opulent was the turf under the noonday sun. Some of the wives of the England players were also sitting behind our goal and Tina Moore gripped her bead necklace nervously, like a heavyweight boxer's spouse sitting tense at the ringside during a championship fight.

Now here was her husband leading the England team out into the arena, stoic in crisp white strip, and lining up with the nimble Brazilians and the Israeli referee and linesmen for the national anthems – the Brazilian anthem romping on and on, always about to end but never quite doing so. Now the England players were rumbling gently down towards our goal for a kick-about. Tranmere Harry, with his cow-puncher's hat, was on his feet shouting: 'Save your breath, Bobby.'

Charlton trotted amicably around as if preparing for a Wednesday night charity match at Bolton. The crown of his balding head was bare against the ravenous sun, like a new-laid egg, and soon a thin layer of moisture would form round the frontiers of the egg into the receding yellow hair of the hero from Manchester United, and he would make a quick movement with the sweat-band on his wrist to mop it away from his eyes.

Ceremonies over, Mr Klein waved the match away, the crowd roaring for the extermination of England. But it takes a professional executioner to chop off a·man's head with one slice, and the England team were most reluctant to put their heads on the block. For the first ten minutes, their possession football held the Brazilians back as they played the ball calmly to each other, intent on holding on to the blessed ball for ever and ever if necessary. Sitting there on our brick-sized green cushions covering solid layers of concrete, only a few yards from Banks's net, the sun beating down above the scoreboard, high up over the Brazil goal at the other end, we became absorbed as comrades in the ghastly responsibilities of an English goalkeeper facing the combined striking talents of Jairzinho, Pele and Tostao. Banks had become our friend, a lonely figure pacing his line, almost within touching distance. As he turned to gather the ball for a goalkick, he looked so calm, he might have been watering his roses.

Although Banks had Pele on his mind now, what a great defence he had in front of him. Bobby Moore marshalling his forces with no hint whatsoever of his recent ordeal in Bogota when he had been wrongly accused of stealing a bracelet. One tackle on Pele, as the hero of Santos swept in on England's goal, would have stopped a rhinoceros. The sound of jarring legs making contact crunched all over the stadium.

Banks, with one long blue arm dangling forth lightly, signalled his approval. If his sinews screamed with tension, and his fingers tingled for want of a save, no real tension showed. What Banks wanted was a save, to get the adrenalin working, and he would soon get the opportunity with a vengeance. The Brazilian crowd seated around us mocked and taunted their Anglo-Saxon rivals as they had done for the past 24 hours – one of the longest in the annals of international football. We had been waiting for this match for months, the meeting in Group Three of the World Champions of 1966 and the World Champions of 1958 and 1962. The save to come would be the point when the tension burst its dam. This was my description at the time:

'It arrived after ten minutes, when Jairzinho was sent down the right by Carlos Alberto. Jairzinho's strength took him past Terry Cooper to the byeline and he swept the polka dot ball with the ferocity of a trench mortar, over to the far post, way beyond where Labone, Moore and Banks were stationed. Towards the blurred object now hurtled Pele, leaping over Mullery and heading the ball down towards a layer of black netting and all for one were shouting 'GOAL' and rising to acclaim the KING. What happened next remains indistinct in the memory, a blurred and outrageous flash of movement, a combination of sprawling arms and legs. Banks was suddenly over on the right side of goal, lying sideways with his left leg thrust out straight, his right leg bent at right angles and his groping right hand scooping the ball up and over the crossbar.

'The ball seemed to tumble over the goal and roll down slowly on the other side of the net with the sudden abatement of an ocean wave breaking on a rock. One wondered, amid all the confusion, the commotion, the shouting and screaming, whether Banks had broken his arm and suffered grievous damage. He lay on his back with his shoulders on the grass, his colleagues standing around, too nonplussed to yell their praises. The Brazilians took a very quick corner. It was all over before it had begun, like a short Disney cartoon. So let us once again, video-style, drag Banks back by his ankles and give him a rerun for the umpteenth time. Jairzinho's rushing centre; Pele, on top of Alan Mullery, heading fiercely down towards the gaping hole left by Banks guarding the near post; Banks, in the attitude of a preying mantis, after spinning on to a new twig, playing the ball up and away with an extended arm into oblivion.

'Did you see that!?' roared Tranmere Harry, turning round at us, his cowboy hat tilted back on his head, his yellow nicotined fingers trembling with tension. 'By Christ, did you see that?'

It was a fatuous remark, but he had to say something to relieve his windpipe. He wanted so much to convince his mates that he really had spied a miracle and to make sure that his normally placid mind had not fallen victim of some strange figment of the imagination, a confidence trick, a sudden mirage brought on by the unrelenting rays of the sun. To this day, I cannot recall how Banks managed to get across the goal and touch the ball as it rose off the turf and towards the roof of the net, first bounce. Nor could Pele, or Banks's mates. Francis Lee, based downfield as one of England's strikers, commented later that 'Gordon made a save that defied description, when he somehow juggled a Pele header up and over the bar, while on his knees going for a cross. It was an effort which had all Brazil shouting GOAL. . .'

So the match went on with England alive and breathing after near disaster, Moore commanding his defence without a trace of anxiety, Mullery sticking to Pele with the fixation of a Latin pursuing an earthy blonde, Ball and Charlton funnelling through from midfield and Lee and Geoff Hurst crying out for a goal down at the other end. It might have come England's way when Lee squandered a good chance after Wright crossed the ball beyond Felix, a goalkeeper in a very different class from Banks. But Lee missed the opening, and the thought of it still niggles him, a decade later. 'I was shaping to volley the ball home, but my studs caught in the grass and I had quickly to change to a diving header. Even then the ball hit the body of Felix, rather than him making a good save. But he still deserves credit for diving in the right place. That goal could have made all the difference to me, because any striker is given added confidence by a goal. I left Mexico not only disappointed that we had lost, but that I had not made more impact with my shooting.'

Lee's important miss, which turned out to be not half as bad as another England one, prompted a small rumpus after he had been warned by Mr Klein for fouling Felix. There was a whirr of yellow and green as the Manchester City player was surrounded by gesticulating Brazilians which was another of those less than diplomatic upheavals in which foreign teams have been incensed by the Anglo-Saxon treatment of their sacrosanct goalkeepers.

It was all over very quickly – and with the scores level at half-time, England should have been well satisfied with their efforts, in particular the modest Banks. Brazil missed their injured midfield genius, the chain-smoking Gerson, and had been unable to pierce a tremendous England defence but, after time, this extraordinary battle of wits began to change in South America's favour as Tostao and Pele began teasing the fringes of England's defence. And then came the goal and the insufferable noise which went with it, requiring Tranmere Harry to lean forward and hide his ears with a thick pair of hands.

From our end, the preceding moments leading up to the goal seemed innocuous – a flurry of activity beyond the halfway line on the left between Tostao and Moore which normally might have ended with a throw-in or a jumbled clearance. But suddenly Tostao turned inwards beyond Moore's challenge, with the regimentation of a clockwork soldier. A leaden ball passed square to Pele was delivered with that marvellous sense of the unexpected which Pele's genius instantly capitalised upon. As Labone struggled to make contact, Pele slid the ball into an open gap on the right, out of Peters's reach but within reach of Jairzinho pounding in with all sails blowing.

Banks came out to narrow the angle, but in vain. The force of the shot that whizzed past him seemed to drive his hair up into a frenzied frieze of black, his arms hung up as if forcing themselves towards the ball. But the deed was done and we nearly cringed as Jairzinho danced away, howling and hollering, towards the touchline on the right. His beefy legs forced him over the pitch until finally he crashed into the edge of the barrier where his team-mates mobbed him. Fireworks, supplications, hideous noises, this was a Brazilian fiesta going mad: we froze, sitting horribly still. The deed was certainly done.

England were thus a goal down and the atrocious racket and boiling heat were telling on the Anglo-Saxons. It was hard enough sitting, let alone running; Bobby Charlton had given everything, and Sir Alf decided he must give way for Colin Bell, a substitution which would prove so costly when England played West Germany later in the quarter finals.

Jeff Astle also loped on in place of little Lee in the hope of giving the England attack more thrust in the air where the Brazilian defence had been notably suspect. Astle at once started heading balls down to his fellow attackers, and nobody strained more for an equaliser than Alan Ball, his red hair whisking all over the pitch with the fever of a flying squirrel leaping from branch to branch. Ball was everywhere – coaxing, demanding, leaping over tackles, urging on his colleagues, drenched with sweat. And then came a chance that Astle must forever live with. If this classic match has become celebrated for Banks's save, it has also acquired notoriety for Jeff Astle's miss.

The action was back again at our end but there seemed little danger when Everaldo took possession of the ball, yet some freak lapse of concentration which the Brazilian would reveal more than once in future World Cup games, almost to their ultimate cost, prevailed him to pass the ball gently over the grass to Astle standing alone and unmarked near the penalty spot.

I can still see Astle gathering the ball in front of Felix, the quivering goalkeeper, growing smaller and smaller, the net growing wider and wider, the ball itself swelling and inflating into the size of a medicine ball. Astle, the big West Bromwich lad, so big now in front of the net itself that his head with the Beatle fringe on top almost soared out of the stadium.

We stood up, bowing in allegiance to the hero who was about to score and save England's honour. Here was the striker who, while playing in the FA Cup final two years before against Everton, had struck the winning goal with a mighty thump in extra time. Felix had now achieved the size of a mere ant; he bent low, he waited for the moment when Astle would unleash his decisive shot which would cause lamentation all over Brazil, not to mention Mexico, and make us Anglo-Saxons praise Astle as our Brum saviour for ever more. The players stood still, there was a hush, the game virtually stopped in Astle's favour, the whistle could have gone for half-time in a park match. All Astle had to do was SCORE. But he didn't – he MISSED.

Astle missed because he tried to hurry things, instead of selecting his target. He chose to shoot at the left foot at the near post corner and Felix bounded gratefully round the post to gather the ball as it sped past the photographers. The goalkeeper almost danced with relief. Astle stood there, his shoulders sagging. 'By Christ, did you see that,' Tranmere Harry blurted out, turning round again. His ruddy face was blanched with rage. 'He could have blown the bugger in. My old grannie could have stuck that one in.'

The Brazilian spectators howled with laughter and their own considerable relief, their titters and splutters of amazement sounding almost squelchy in the heat. I couldn't stand looking at Astle any more. He lumbered away out of our lives for the duration. One more chance came to England, 12 minutes from the end when Astle, trying desperately to redeem himself, headed down a centre from Moore to Ball, and the little fellow, taking aim, shot out of Felix's reach from a difficult angle, but the ball smacked against the top of the crossbar and over. And now it was time to end it all as the players exchanged shirts – Moore, the defensive master, swapping his with Pele, his black torso dripping with sweat. Fireworks exploded all over the stadium. We walked out of the Jalisco bowl to the bus.

Tranmere Harry was visibly shaken by it all on our way back to the motel. He kept overlapping choice phrases about 'diabolical Astle' with juicy eulogies about Banks's 'fantastic save'. In retrospect, it was the save rather than the miss we discussed in the days following, but that was all over now, with England eliminated and our coach almost out of the cactus jungle – my mind zigzagging with memories such as this and Tranmere Harry dozing benevolently somewhere further down the aisle. England's subsequent defeat at Leon had been an agony to endure, and more so for the players who, in the words of Franny Lee, allowed their dressing-room to become 'a right morgue'.

If England had beaten West Germany and beaten Italy in the semi final at Mexico City, they might well have worried Brazil in the final. But there was no question of what might have been. The dreaded Mexican bug which many of us had suffered from on lavatory seats, with our minds creaking with nausea and our tummies scolding like so many tiny crabs gnawing into our guts, caught Gordon Banks before he went out to keep goal at Leon. A worried, harassed deputy went on to have a stinker.

Poor Astle, poor Bonetti. History will record their failures while hard men like Tranmere Harry splutter into old age about the way 'they fooked things up!' As for Banks, Tranmere Harry called his second son Gordon – ''cause I was there to see the save.'

4
The Monkey-hangers

Hartlepool United used to have a nickname back in their Victorian days – namely the 'Monkey-hangers'. This followed an incident much earlier in the century when there was a ceremonial hanging of a monkey found washed up on a beach during the Napoleonic wars and mistaken by some local residents as being the corpse of a French spy.

In more recent times, the more avid of the local football team's supporters have often had to stand by praying for mercy as once again their beloved club has been threatened by the noose of extinction from the Football League. That Hartlepool have survived all these years has been a tribute not only to the loyalty of these fans, who number about 2000 in bad times and 4000 in good, but also to the never-say-die Teesside attitude shown at the Victoria Ground butting on to the North Sea.

What draws this reporter to Hartlepool, in the backwoods of County Durham, is that tremendous spirit, that feeling that despite all the pressures of constant defeat and no money in the bank, the show must go on whatever the state of the rustic steel supports. Hartlepool United is not Liverpool, neither is it Arsenal or Tottenham; it is a club living almost permanently on the breadline, but there is still life in the old monkey.

One damp and sombre winter, I took the rattler from Darlington along the coast to Hartlepool to visit the patient who, from what I could gather from the local press, was very poorly indeed and considered a fitting contender for a spell in intensive care. From the train window, a landscape of mottled, derelict bypassed industry met the eye and beyond, the creamy waves introducing the sulky backcloth of the North Sea, gave notice of better times in this industrial part of the world, before the last shipyard closed down in 1962. The town I was approaching had certainly seen better times, and in its capacity as a thriving port, it had caught the attention of the Kaiser's fleet in 1914, killing 128 people, a death rate which in peacetime would be classed as a major disaster.

My own concern then, as I made my way into what once must have been a sumptuous honeymoon hotel suite before the First World War, but now was a travelling salesman's boudoir, based conveniently in the centre of Hartlepool which bore the eternal smell of boot polish, brandy, fag smoke, damp linen and detergent, was to seek out those who felt the local team was worth saving and those who felt it should be snuffed out in favour of Rugby League which happens to be very popular in and around that part of the world.

On lonely occasions like this, when a reporter lies down on his hotel bed and goes obediently through his contact book, the sound of a faraway foghorn can sound like a muffled invitation to blow one's brains out. Two or three calls tracked down our stringer who cordially accepted an invitation to meet in the bar in an hour's time. 'I'll bring the hearse along as well.' Hartlepool United, to be precise, were again struggling to keep their League status with brash outsiders like Hereford yearning to get elected after some gigantic acts of Cup giant-killing. In the event, Hereford did make it into the Football League, while Hartlepool survived, and continue to survive, the dreaded drop. But in those grey mists of wintertime, Hartlepool were in a desperate state, £42,000 in debt and barely able to pay the wages.

'Everyone is very worried about Hartlepool's chances,' the gaunt man said, sipping his whisky in an empty corner of a well-used pint-pot bar. 'It would be a bad thing for us if there was no League football here. Especially as there is a general decline of football in the North East.'

To add discomfort to his words, the lights suddenly went out and we sat in total darkness for a minute until a barman emerged with a candle.

'Another of those bloody power cuts!' the stringer said. 'Hartlepool is no place to be when they're on. You're likely to walk into a disused crane.'

Once the candle was flickering, and the barman had replenished his whisky glass, the stringer continued with his sad story about the ailing soccer club. His tone tended to border on the morose because the extinction of Hartlepool would mean a major loss of income to him. 'We were unlucky at the beginning of the season. If we had beaten Barnsley in the League Cup replay, that would have given us a match against Arsenal at Highbury. Football's a cruel game. And if we hadn't lost to Boston in the FA Cup, we would have had a draw against Portsmouth. All this would have helped Hartlepool's finances considerably.' The stringer, who had been watching football in this area since before the war, had put the club's plight in a nutshell, and before leaving, he gave me the home number of the present incumbent of the beleaguered Hartlepool manager's chair, as well as being on the playing staff himself – craggy Len Ashurst, a former defender at Sunderland.

Hartlepool at night is hardly Montparnasse, despite the presence of a thriving art school – but the occupants of a nearby saloon seemed determined to drown sorrows by drinking straight glass after straight glass of Newcastle Brown Ale. It was towards closing time that I ventured to cross-examine a party of young men, glowing pink at the jowls, about the state of their local team. This inspired such cackles of laughter and derisive grunts that I almost made a beeline for the public-bar door which stood between us and a miserable, damp, black, northern night.

'Hartlepool, you must be joking, what a load of rubbish!'

'Shit on 'em!'

'Never heard of 'em. I'm a Sunderland supporter, always have been. Away the lads!'

'They oughta close 'em down, the rubbish they play. I gave up watching 'em play five years ago.'

The tone seemed very much on an equal footing with the flak firmly directed towards the Victoria Ground. But progress was made, as far as my enquiry was concerned, by a chubby, robust young man advancing from the frothy throng and disclosing that he was a former Hartlepool player. 'They're a load of rubbish,' he said, without a cringe of remorse about his marked disloyalty. 'When I was there, they never allowed us to hold the ball. What would George Best say about that? They didn't encourage individual play at all when I was there. It was a bloody shame. "Get rid of it." "Get rid of it." It was like that all the time. I'm 27 and don't play any more. Top heavy!'

The young man's Pickwickian paunch revealed that kicking a football was no longer part of his week's curriculum, in marked contrast to his love of drinking in which he excelled, doing his best to imitate a wild buffalo enjoying his first watering-hole cocktail after a long plod in open country.

I left the revellers to their happy session; they having abandoned all thought of poor old Hartlepool United to concentrate on more earthy matters, like the sex life of one of their more rampant rams. Unemployment in Hartlepool was high, but there were enough people going to work next morning as I made my way by taxi to the team's practice ground, to verify my Shell Guide's disclosure that 'Hartlepool since the last shipyard closed down has concentrated on diversified industry, and among its products are telecommunications equipment, vacuum flasks, knitwear, crankshafts, anchor chains and marine engine controls . . .'

United's practice pitch turned out to be the local council recreation ground, and the facilities for Ashurst and his squad turned out to be predictably primitive. The team were already taking part in a practice game when I arrived with Ashurst, the trainer and groundsmen making up the numbers.

'If you'd had brought boots, you could have played, man,' the only spectator, a shaggy old man accompanied by an obedient mongrel, said on the touchline. The young man's baying call of 'Get rid of it' the night before still bayed in my ears, giving bitter fact to what was now being revealed before my eyes. For the Hartlepool players were doing just that. 'Get fuckin' rid of it!' The tackling was keen, and Ashurst showed he had lost none of the commitment he used to show down at Craven Cottage in the days of Johnny Haynes. I had been told that Ron Young, Hartlepool's leading scorer with 13 goals, and blessed with a droopy moustache, could hit a ball, and this he showed by stinging the knuckles of his first team goalkeeper. 'Take it easy, Ron,' Ashurst called out. 'I don't want to play goal at Aldershot.'

Later, Ashurst, wearing a tracksuit, gave me a lift back to the Victoria Ground giving a hint of the pressures on his team at the moment. 'We beat Chester last week, and a point at Aldershot would be fine. You don't change a winning team, so I won't be playing Saturday.'

The famous Main Stand with its peeling decadence was now revealed to me for the first time, a headquarters, I had been told in the town, for Saturday night shagging out of a nearby skating rink. As the team moved off to wash the mud from their knees,

Ashurst led me to his office. 'Afraid there's only room for me. I've got to make up the team-sheet, so if you could just wait a moment, and then I'll talk to you.' Ashurst's office was about the size of a small trunk, and he just about had elbow room enough to write on paper.

'We've got goalkeeping problems at moment,' Ashurst said, glancing up at the reporter bod filling the door. 'Mick Gadsby, our first team keeper, has been fumbling low shots recently. So we've been playing Ron Hillyard who's on a month's loan from York. The lad hasn't been doing too badly. Have you heard of any spare keepers?'

'I know of a balding, bowlegged, one-eared, two-fingered custodian who plays on Hackney Marshes – and regularly lets in six goals a week. But the average has risen to ten recently because his wife has run off with a fishmonger.' 'He'll do.'

The manager debated for a moment whether to add the name of Gus Strain, my suggestion, to the team-sheet, but then refrained. 'I think we'll stick with Ron. As for the sub, I'll put my name down, unless you want a run out?'

'I think you're more entitled to sit on the bench at Aldershot, Len.'

'Well, we are a bit short of players here, you know. My job really is to mould the players we have available into a winning combination. We have taken nine points from the last eight games which ain't all that bad. And scored 13 goals which isn't bad either. I know what you're thinking – Hartlepool are on the skids because everyone wants Hereford elected to the League next June and everyone wants poor little Hartlepool out. Naturally, I'm concerned – but I'm putting that at the back of my mind – and concentrating on picking up points on Saturday afternoons.'

The sound of a merciless drill came through a wooden panel as Ashurst struggled to extricate himself from his small cell.

'Are those the Zeppelins coming back?' I enquired.

'Zeppelins?'

'Yes, the Victoria Ground was bombed by two of them in 1916, and one woman died of shock.'

'Crikey, you've got a long memory. We don't have any zeppelins here any more, just the odd bod asking for money.'

An inspection of the ground later revealed a marvellously trim, green pitch. 'It's the sea air,' Ashurst reflected proudly. 'It gets the grass growing springy and lush.'

While the old place did look decidedly run down, and in need of a splash of paint, the floodlight pylons looked remarkably new – as they were.

'That was Brian Clough's work,' Ashurst said, referring to an illustrious predecessor. 'When he came here in 1965, all brash and young, he insisted they put on the lights.'

'Didn't he drive the team bus, and feed his players on fish and chips?'

'The first is certainly true, I don't know about the second. I don't, anyway.'

My next appointment was with the then chairman, who was literally staring down into a goldfish pond outside his bungalow in a smarter part of West Hartlepool. It was very much a residential area, reminding the visitor more of Hove. The chairman seemed very proud of his goldfish, and when the subject came up, very proud of Hartlepool United.

'United have been in this position before,' the chairman said, ushering me inside his home, generating a 'never-say-die' policy under the thin rays of winter sunshine beaming into his lounge. 'We have been in this position before, and it has become a way of life – but we have got a stronger team now. As a member of the League Management Committee told me once: "You only get kicked out of the League when you do something silly." And we haven't done anything silly.'

The chairman looked out of the window at his beloved goldfish pool, which had been slightly mangled in a recent storm. 'Some of my goldfish simply disappeared,' he mused, then added: 'When you come down to the hard facts of life, you come down to earth with a bang. Look at Peterborough. They're back at square one. The biggest problem is finance. But other clubs have far worse balance sheets than ours. Some of these non-League clubs don't know what they're in for when they apply for election. One applicant asked, "Do we have to pay the players' wages in the summer?"' The chairman laughed a sardonic laugh.

When I mentioned that there were rumours of the players not being paid, and being fed fish and chips on match days, he looked peeved, a slight flush appearing on his drawn cheeks. 'That's untrue. The players get their wages – and we stay in first class hotels and eat proper food at away matches. What we do need though is more financial support. Barrow have their shipyard to give support.'

I left the chairman gazing into his goldfish pond again – and took a walk back into the bleaker landscape of Hartlepool, the early dusk of winter already creeping over a jumble of bricked buildings, old warehouses, allotments, backyards stuffed with prams. I almost slid into the encroaching darkness, tracking down a local Catholic club in search of a Hartlepool hero.

It needed the help of an informed taxi driver, later on, to track the club down, hidden away as it was near a local housing estate. Nor was the subject of my enquiry, Tommy McGuigan, available, or on the premises, when I breached the point to a couple of club members standing by a well-stocked bar. 'But he's next door, like, Tommy,' one of them said affably, in his working overalls enjoying his first pint of the night.

McGuigan, a former Hartlepool player, was a hero in the area because he had taken part in Hartlepool's finest match against the 'Busby Babes', Manchester United, in the third round of the FA Cup on January 5, 1957. I knocked on his door in the semi-darkness, which prompted a chain of dogs barking from other abodes along the narrow corridor of this part of the estate. The hero came to the door, a trifle wary of my presence, perhaps expecting me to force an offensive piece of paper demanding money into his hand, or declare myself a Bible preacher with a mission.

Wearing a maroon jersey and a pair of bedroom slippers, Tommy cheered rapidly at the reasons for my unexpected call, and agreed with alacrity to come round to the club 'for a quick pint, like'.

So what was it like being a member of that illustrious side, all those years ago, when Hartlepool had come back from 0–3 behind to make the score 3–3, only to lose 4–3 at the last gasp with a record gate of 17,426 cheering themselves hoarse at the Victoria Ground, and McGuigan assuming the mantle of hero number one for his performance against the illustrious Duncan Edwards? A quiet corner of the Catholic club bar sufficed to unlock the magic from this almost humble former professional footballer with an amiable disposition geared to the close-knit fraternity in which he lived.

'You were proud to be a Hartlepool player in those days, like. We had a fair team, but when we heard we had been drawn against Matt Busby's team, we thought we were in for a real licking, like. It stood to reason, like. They were on their way to winning the League Championship that year. The football world was crazy about them, like. They were the mighty "Babes". They had players like Byrne, Edwards, Colman, Whelan, Tommy Taylor, Berry in the team, like. What we had was our fans, they were fantastic on the afternoon, like. They cheered us on, you couldn't hear yerselves shout to each other on the pitch, like. The old Main Stand was rocking like a concertina. Before the game, we had a glance at the "Babes" undressing. You couldn't miss 'em really because the dressing-room area was so small. Duncan Edwards came out, so big, so dominating, like. I thought crikey, is this the fellow I'll be facing, like?

'We went out there and they hit us with everything – it was dazzling, like. We were three goals down, and they were playing this high-class football we had never seen before. The crowd sounded as if they were sorry for us, like. But they kept roaring us on. It must have scared the seagulls over the sea.' McGuigan's face, well-seasoned by North Sea breezes, opened his mouth a little wider revealing two rows of rather wayward teeth. 'Then something happened, like. We scored three goals ourselves. It was quite unbelievable, like. But these things happen, like in David and Goliath matches. The crowd made us raise our game. The "Babes" weren't having any, of course, they were on their way to Wembley anyways. They got another goal, I think it was Billy Whelan. I can see him ploughing through the heavy mud, all determination, and planting the ball into our net. The crowd were shattered, like – we had them really goin' at one stage. It was magic. Afterwards, the "Babes" were very sporting, shaking our hands, and telling us what a good lot we were. I was shattered when I heard about them in the crash a year later. It was unbelievable, they being so fit and great. I cried, I have to tell you. What a brilliant player, that Duncan was. I didn't have a bad game meself that day, I have to admit, but you could tell what a great player the lad was. The authority was there – when we had them rocking in the second half, he stuck out his chest and you felt he was saying "You dare".'

And Hartlepool now?

'It's a wee bit sad. The old place has got a wee bit run down, and some of their teams don't offer much. The old team spirit is missing. But there are still a lot of people in the town who are very proud of Hartlepool. People stop me in the street and say: "Tommy, do you remember that game against the 'Babes'?" And the magic comes back again, like. Frankly, I hope Hartlepool survives, they deserve to, it's a wonderful little spot, this Teeside part of the world. So friendly, like. It's a shame there's so much unemployment, but people are not downhearted.'

One of the men at the bar came over and offered us a drink. 'This Tommy 'ere's a wonder,' he said. 'Everyone remembers the day he ran round the mighty Edwards.'

'Go on, Harry. Flattery will get you nowhere. Come on then, buy us that pint.'

The next morning I walked to the Victoria Ground to see the team off on the rotten, misty, dirty, weathered road to Aldershot. Who on earth but soldiers and professional footballers would bother to take a trip so far to the famous bullshit garrison town? But the Fourth Division clash between Aldershot and Hartlepool United was included on the Pools coupons, and a small knot of playing staff standing obediently by a rather amorphous, dingy coach explained the reason why there was so much urgency to get out of town and move fast down the motorway. 'Grab yer jackets, lads.' 'Whadya mean, Heaney, blowin' in the sea wind, you big fart arse, you left *Playboy* behind.'

An icy wind stretched needles and spikes into our cheeks as we hung around the car park area, waiting for the manager and his back-up team of two men and the resident rat-catching tabby to emerge from the dressing rooms. 'Well, this is another one, and on our present form, we'll get a goal or two down with the Tank Corps,' Ron Young said, his moustache near clinging to North Sea icicles. 'Hereford gave us a shock. We want to stay put. Never say die, I say.' Young jumped on the coach, and the lads followed their leading striker, like Tommies going up the line. Ashurst waved a cheery goodbye. 'Come and see us again sometime.' The coach rolled away, all exhaust and fumes and hopes and thoughts about the coming match which Hartlepool would lose. But it did not really matter – they survived, and still survive, drawn ever back by their own financial insecurities and failure on their own lush pitch.

I may go and see them again soon. Bobby Moncur has been appointed their new manager, with Pop Robson second in command. They can't fail to get promoted this term – although I note that only recently they lost five League games in succession, and fell below halfway in the table.

Time to get on my bike to Darlington again.

5
George Best – Decline and Fall

'I bear George Best no grudges. It was a privilege to play with him and marvel at his skills.'

Bobby Charlton

YOU GOTTA GO TO OLD TRAFFORD – YOU GOTTA GO TO OLD TRAFFORD – YOU GOTTA GO TO OLD TRAFFORD. The wheels of the dawn train to Manchester pounded out a rhythmic, urgent message of the necessity of getting to Sir Matt Busby's morning press conference on time.

My colleague, Malcolm Williams, lay in a huddle fast asleep as we approached Wilmslow and the smarter environs of Greater Manchester. There were four days to go until Christmas. Both of us, directed a few hours before to get on our 'bikes' and confront Old Trafford in flames, were not, in our unshaven states, part of civilised man. Malcolm had contacted me at a Cheyne Walk party given by a rich American and above the bellow of carol singers burbling 'Comfort and Joy' he shouted down the phone: 'Thack wants us to do a major piece on the Old Trafford crisis. We'll have to take the 5.45 am from Euston. I'll pick you up at five at your place.'

Much to my wife Clare's surprise, Malcolm did ring the doorbell at that unearthly hour. So I tottered forth, bristle-chinned, into the cold, dark dawn to enter his taxi.

What had instigated this mission at the end of 1972 was what the newspaper headlines called an 'explosive week at Old Trafford . . .' Explosive in the sense that England's favourite club had suddenly struck rock bottom after the glorious era under Sir Matt, struck rock bottom so badly that George Best had done another of his bunks, the manager – Frank O'Farrell

63

George Best – absent without leave again, at Old Trafford.

– had been bluntly sacked, and the respected international reputation of the Old Trafford club had been gravely harmed. It was, of course, a major story and required three of us to evaluate Sir Matt's crisis. (The third member of the party, David Miller, was dashing up the M1.)

After a quick shave and brush up at our Manchester hotel, and a romp through old Mancunian Malcolm's contacts book, we hit the Old Trafford training ground trail to find the car park crowded with press men and photographers. Without a manager to guide them, or Best to use his electric hare influence on either wing, United had held a practice match. Both Denis Law, tight-lipped and uncommunicative in contrast to his retirement days as a BBC sportscaster, and Bobby Charlton, solemn and bishop regal, departed in their cars. So we made for the club offices where Sir Matt was to hold forth. On the stairs of the training ground headquarters, we suddenly confronted the great man, who had opened his office door to let out three sheepish youth players he must have given a good wigging to. 'Come on, laddies,' Sir Matt said, with a matter-of-fact tone disguising the crisis of the hour. 'There's coffee in the canteen.'

Major sporting upheavals like this one can bring out everything – bar the last earwig hiding in the kitchen sink – and it was obvious that some of the tabloid boys were after a juicy scandal. But Sir Matt reacted as if this were a normal council meeting to reveal plans for a summer tour.

Outside the canteen, a grey December mist hovered over the pitch. 'Is George hiding out there,' a photographer quipped, 'looking for another double vodka and tonic?'

It was time for Sir Matt to face the Press, many of whom had savaged him in print. Now aged 63, he was undergoing an unaccustomed and gruelling morning after so many years of adoration. As David Miller was to write: 'George Best was not the worst of Manchester United's unhappy story in recent months. Disenchantment had set in long ago. Now it becomes possible to see what lay behind it. To put it bluntly, the point had been reached at which O'Farrell had to go, whether or not he was accompanied by George Best. When Busby was building United up he always tried to maintain dignity in personal relationships. It is this reluctance publicly to discuss the club's private affairs which fostered the conspiracy of silence that largely disguised from the public O'Farrell's continuing failure to master the problems within the club which had troubled him from the start.'

O'Farrell had cleared the desk, leaving his minder, Sir Matt, to sweat out the storm. The errant wizard, Best, had been put on the transfer list and it was announced he would never again be selected to play for United. On that morning at the Old Trafford training ground, as United awaited the announcement of their new manager, their pathetic record under O'Farrell was there for all to peruse, like the remnants of a rotten plum. A club which only four years before had won the European Cup against Benfica, had gone through 42 League matches and only won ten of them – and this with Charlton, Law and Best on the playing staff.

'It was a depressing record,' Denis Law wrote later, 'and whoever was to blame, the next manager faced an uphill struggle to get us out of the relegation zone. It appeared too he was going to have to do it without George Best. George had himself written to the club apologising yet again for his conduct and saying that he did really feel the time had now come for him to quit . . .'

Despite Sir Matt's cheerful front at the subsequent Press conference, the greyness seeped in. Flanked by his chairman, the Manchester butcher, Louis Edwards, and the rest of the board, Sir Matt made the most of his pep talk, which had followed an earlier one to the players. In a sense, it worked. Sir Matt's optimism was given a good showing in the next morning's newspapers, though he was still criticised for his part in the rift with the outgoing manager which had fermented since the previous January. Controversy raged over O'Farrell's match tactics. He had been obliged to use creativity, instinctively attacking players for too great a proportion of any game in cautious defensive patterns. This was because his defence was so bad. Busby had taken against these tactics, which led to the major showdown.

After Sir Matt's optimistic talk, we joined Pat Crerand for a cup of coffee. Pat was United's cultural hard man when they won the FA Cup in 1963 and the European Cup in 1968. He spoke benevolently, unheated by the smoke of battle at his beloved club. As manager of the club's juniors under O'Farrell and coach Malcolm Musgrove, who also had been sacked, he had seen the rot set in. 'Frank just couldn't raise the players,' Pat said, looking out at a centre circle shrouded in mist. 'A team has to be treated as a family. If you have three children it is likely that two may be perfectly mannered and the third a tearaway. You take whatever course you need to get the best out of each. And it's likely to be different in each case. But they've all got to submit to family discipline in the end.'

Crerand, who had done so much to encourage a homesick George Best during his early days in digs, assumed the mantle of a hurt Scottish father when he reflected on George's boozing lapses and continual absences from Old Trafford. 'There is the touch of the Walter Mitty about George,' Crerand explained. 'I'm afraid the kid-glove treatment he got here did rankle within the team. He might have done better if he had come to live at my place, instead of moving into that flash house of his.'

Crerand spoke in the same avuncular tone as Sir Matt when it came to discussing the welfare of the United players and the tragedy which had brought Best to the brink of quitting football altogether. From Malcolm's and my own point of view as travelling scribes, there was not time to feel much sympathy in our quest for the errant genius hiding somewhere in Greater Manchester.

While David Miller continued his overall investigation into various ailments which had fallen like Job on Old Trafford, we would make our way by taxi from a depressed training ground to confront the wayward star and entice from his lips a prodigious statement into the reasons which had once again brought about another disappearance, and his feelings about being dumped by his club. The challenge was irresistible, the rewards being surely major headlines and a pat on the back from our normally crusty editor.

'I've got the names of a few places where he might be crying in his cups,' said Malcolm bravely. 'Joe told me George had been spotted last night in one. Fasten your seat belts.'

So here we were like bloodhounds sniffing the Best trail as Noël-tinselled Manchester rolled into view with winking lights and Christmas trees galore, and jaunty, sexy secretaries carrying parcels, jostled the pavements on high stiletto heels. The enigma we searched for had been the same 'El Beatle' who had astounded the Benfica fans with his murderous runs and lethal shooting in one European Cup match in Lisbon in 1966; the same electric hare who scored a wonderful solo goal for United in the 1968 final against the same Portuguese club; the same Northern Ireland boy with magic in his feet, who, in the words of his colleague, Bobby Charlton, 'was about as reliable as a rusty watch'; the same weaving, darting, incredibly balanced goader of fullbacks whose praises had been sung long into convivial vino time by such admirers as Michael Parkinson and Arthur Hopcraft, and of whom Geoffrey Green wrote: 'He was a Leonardo da Vinci who wantonly threw away his paintbrushes and his genius. Yet he was generous, a lost child who loved to do tricks. One of these was to drop a penny piece on the top of his shoe, then flick it up into the top breast pocket. He never failed.'

Two upmarket pubs failed to reveal the lone figure of little boy lost, although one customer over a frothy pint announced that Georgie had been around the night before with a bird. 'She had her skirt up round her navel. It's a crying shame what's happened to that lad. He's got so much going for him, and he lets the booze eat him up. All that shagging does no good at all, let alone the drinking.'

The pub had filled up with lunchtime revellers, galvanised by the first sip of Worthington to relieve the heady pressures from office parties the night before. It was extremely doubtful whether our missing footballer would dare to enter this world of verbal diarrhoea, so we moved on to seek him out at his own prize boutique. There were no pressmen waiting outside when we arrived, and the joint looked locked up, a single pair of trendy slacks decorating the window, the bum width suitable for a boy with a six-inch waist. But the door opened and we slouched in, looking like two bootleg mobsters. A smooth youth wearing a bright yellow shirt and tight trousers emerged from behind a curtain and began an innocent survey of George Best's trendy menswear. There was just time for me to catch a flash of George moving back into the bowels of the boutique, the familiar Beatle hair looking as if a comb had not gone through it that morning. Just a flash – but George was there all right.

'We're just looking around,' Malcolm said.

'Our pleasure, I'm sure,' the youth replied.

'He's here,' I whispered to Malcolm. 'Did you see him?'

'Thought it was him.'

It was time to take the initiative. 'We're from the *Sunday Telegraph*,' I said. 'Is the owner by any chance in?'

The youth made some disturbing movements of his body as if he was about to take part in a body-building contest, flexing his arms and flashing a long look at the ceiling with a pair of perfect blue eyes. 'No, he's not in. And won't be. You can

Bobby Charlton, England's and Manchester United's favourite football hero, still relishing 'the joy of playing' in the limelight of an illustrious career at Granford Bridge.

always ring his agent. I think George has gone away. But I don't
know where.'

'I think you'll find he's here because we've just seen him.'

'Where have you just seen him then?'

Malcolm spoke calmly but formidably. 'We saw him through
the curtain when you came out. George is in there. Will he see
us? Can you ask him?'

The youth sucked a hiss through his lips. 'Well, I might try
and ask him, but I doubt if he'll see you. He's not talking to the
Press, you know. You'd better ring his agent.'

'Can't you just try and ask him? We want to clarify one or two
matters regarding Manchester United.'

The youth put his left thumbnail a fraction inside his mouth.
The sphinxy mouth closed on the nail, biting it in earnest until
there was a sudden eruption at the door which opened to reveal
a group of giggling supermarket checkout girls intent on finding
Georgie. The youth viewed them with distaste, as they started
whisking their way through a parade of sartorial splendours
hanging in clusters of fiery colour. We stood our ground and
waited for some kind of response from the youth, trying not
to be distracted by the huge bust boldly exhibited from behind
her pink sweater by one of the girls. The youth abruptly turned
round and swept lazily away through the curtain. We stood our
ground.

After three minutes, the youth returned and motioned us to
come outside into the street where the cold, damp Mancunian
conditions made our breaths billow into puffs of smoke.

'George will see you – but you'll have to pay a fee,' the youth
said guardedly.

'How much?' Malcolm asked.

'£200.'

'Well, we don't normally do this,' Malcolm replied.

'Suit yourselves then. Take it or leave it. That's the only way
you're going to see George.'

Malcolm turned to me. 'I'll check with the office. Get a
decision.'

The youth went back into the boutique while Malcolm made
for a convenient phone box across the road. I stood guard
outside just in case Best made a dash for it. He had a knack
of dashing into the back of a suddenly arriving Rolls Royce, as
I discovered some time later when I came across him waiting at
a bus stop in the rain. There was just time to introduce him to my

eight-year-old son before the inevitable Rolls appeared to scoop the former twinkling star back to Oakley Street in Chelsea.

Malcolm seemed to take ages on the phone, hanging on to the receiver with a glum look on his face. He eventually opened the kiosk door and bawled out: 'Thack's up in the proprietor's Christmas party. They've gone to get him. He's taking his time.'

Then I saw him talking and he looked thoughtful, a gradual frown flooding his expression. He slammed down the receiver. 'Bollocks!' he barked, coming out of the kiosk. 'Thack's in a seasonal mood. He says we definitely must not pay George anything. So the interview's off. And he wants us to come back and tie things up as soon as possible. So let's go off and have a good meal. After all, it is Christmas.'

Soon after getting back to London, we heard that Tommy Docherty had been appointed manager of Manchester United.

6

The Messiah Cometh

One of the first occasions I set eyes on Bob Stokoe on a football field was on January 28, 1956, when he played centre half for Newcastle United in a fourth round FA Cup tie against Fulham at Craven Cottage.

It was a dampish, grey winter's day by the Thames that afternoon, but the tie in which the lanky Stokoe played and scored, catching a deflection off a Fulham player, became one of those legends which older Fulham fans are only too eager to declare was the finest game ever to have been played at this scenic ground.

I would go along with this as far as to say it was one of those dazzling fluctuations in which Fulham came back through a Tosh Chamberlain hat trick in his first ever cup tie to lead 4–3 (Jimmy Hill scoring the other); but two late goals by the then FA Cup holders deprived the West London side of a fifth round ticket. It was 'Phew!' and 'Golly!' and 'Crikey!' all the way, with Stokoe taking an active part in the hectic rapid musketry, his patrols upfield giving the impression that he was running on tracks, his elbows pumping like locomotive pistons alongside his broad thighs. His massive smile exuded from below his black tousled hair after his shot hit the Fulham right back, Wilson, to give Newcastle a two-goal lead. This was to be repeated often enough on the football pitches of England, now that Stokoe had taken over Frank Brennan's spot at centre half. But the smile was never more apparent than after he became Sunderland's manager, an appointment the fraternity on Wearside believed was venerable, mystical and almost holy.

One of the last times I saw Stokoe was at Wembley in May, 1973, at the end of my first FA Cup final as a working sports journalist. It was the famous afternoon when Stokoe, wearing a skull-tight, brown trilby ran on to the pitch to embrace his goalkeeper, Jim Montgomery, whose fantastic goalkeeping had so ably and at times thrillingly given the Second Division side a 1–0 victory over the gladiator favourites from Yorkshire, Leeds United.

How had this extraordinary result come about, this adventure which Stokoe inspired in his role as Messiah at Roker Park? It really needs some analysing, especially when you consider that when Stokoe took over, even the pigeons were showing signs of retreating from this once hallowed ground.

Although warmly welcomed by many older members of Wearside Working Men's clubs who remembered his playing days with the mighty Newcastle cup-winning team, Stokoe's task at Roker Park when he arrived in December 1972 was primarily to alleviate the panic whipping in from the cold North Sea, as a once great club with great cup-fighting traditions was slipping seemingly irrevocably towards the obscurities of the Third Division.

'Well, we couldna do worse than have Bob Stokoe here,' the average, jaded Roker fan would say on waking and reading their *Sun* or *Mirror*. 'He's got the reet outlook, he knows the game, having played with "Wor" Jack Milburn, Bobby Mitchell and the Magpie lads, like.'

The appointment may have been news in the North East, but Stokoe's arrival that festive season was overshadowed by the news that Tommy Docherty had replaced Frank O'Farrell as manager at Manchester United and the wizardry of George Best at Old Trafford had been extinguished by the imperial announcement from the maestro that he had decided (temporarily) to hang up his boots.

No sooner had Stokoe put away the family Christmas tree than his new club began to revive like a recuperating stag, the once docile antlers suddenly burning hot on the verge of a new challenge in mating time. It did not take long for all those profusely filled beer mugs adorning the many supporters' club watering-holes round this once thriving shipbuilding town to toast Stokoe as indeed the new 'Messiah'.

Under Stokoe's shrewd guidance and Billy Kerr's captaincy, the Roker Park club soon put their house in order. They were to finish the season in sixth place in the Second Division. But there was something far more romantic afoot, which almost drowned the euphoria Stokoe must have felt at achieving his main task in keeping the club away from the Third Division.

A long FA Cup run had been promised once the club had come uneasily through replays against Notts County and Reading to reach the fifth round. It was after Sunderland had beaten Manchester City, the 1969 FA Cup winners, in a fifth-round replay at a jubilant Roker Park that Sunderland began to shape up as possible cheeky outsiders to win the trophy. Stokoe simply smiled an unabashed smile for his adoring Wearside following and played down the idea. After all, there was still work to be done in the anti-relegation field.

Even so, Stokoe could barely venture from his front door without hearing the joyful chants of 'HAWAY THE ROKERITES! HAWAY THE MESSIAH!' scorching through all the mazy brickwork of old Sunderland, now totally in the grip of cup fever. The local feeling was secure in joint belief that Stokoe really could lead Sunderland safely through to becoming the first Second Division club to win the FA Cup in 42 years.

Goals by Dave Watson – later to become possibly England's finest centre back in the white international shirt – and Ron Guthrie eliminated Luton in the sixth round at Roker Park; and so the historic scene was set, amid the froth of Newcastle Brown Ale, for a confrontation with Arsenal, the 1971 double winners, at Hillsborough in the semi final. Arsenal were expected to reach their third final in successive years, so the challenge which awaited Stokoe's team could not have been more formidable. By now, mother's laundry basket on Wearside was stacked with red and white favours and scarves soiled by sweaty hands clinging for support during the glaring tensions astride Stokoe's princely gallop. While there was euphoria in abundance in the North East, ominous progress was being made in Yorkshire by Don Revie's Leeds United, the team they said you had to beat to win anything. Leeds, that year, were intent on claiming the grand slam of three trophies – the First Division championship, the FA Cup, of which they were current holders, and the European Cup-winners' Cup.

In the event, Leeds came through safely in their semi final, beating Wolves through a lone goal by Billy Bremner. The sensation was at gusty Hillsborough, where Stokoe's glass of champagne was swamped time and time again after Sunderland had beaten Arsenal 2–1, through goals by Vic Halom and

Billy Hughes. Sunderland had fully warranted their first excursion since 1937 to an FA Cup final with a circumnavigating team performance against an Arsenal team packed with internationals. Hughes and Halom both looked sharp in front of goal and telling efforts by these two before and after half-time were the downfall of Arsenal, whose reply from Charlie George was far too late. The euphoria of reaching Wembley now produced a display of pre-final hype comparable to an American Superbowl game – suddenly players with names like Malone, Horswill, Pitt, Kerr and Porterfield were celebrities in their own right and talked about all over the country, instead of being modest members of a club which had been struggling in the Second Division before Christmas.

Stokoe did have the service of players who would run marathons for him, if necessary: players like the sturdy, unflappable Watson; Horswill, the terrier tackler; Kerr, the leader; Hughes, the long-haired opportunist; and Tueart who liked to scamper round the flanks like a voracious puppy. The team was on form and their flair for beating such teams as Manchester City prompted David Miller in the *Sunday Telegraph* to tip them to beat Leeds.

The great majority of sportswriters could not envisage Sunderland gaining the upper hand against the cocky, strutting Leeds. I, for one, queried Miller's brave optimism at the time, because Sunderland's opponents were famously consistent and as a team of all-round internationals were fully aware of every speck of grass on the old Empire Stadium pitch. Could Sunderland really raise their game sufficiently to withstand the concerted barrage that would undoubtedly be hurled at them on the day? Could Stokoe's Second Division crusaders find the stamina and fire power to breach one of the most feared defences in England? Could they shake off their tingling nerves and blow a red and white raspberry at the men from Elland Road? Sunderland's devotees, in their massed, happy numbers assembling on the Wearside start line on the road to Wembley, were in no doubt that their club could do all of these things – just as Raich Carter and his rejoicing heroes had done back in 1937 when they won the Cup for Sunderland against Preston North End. But Sunderland were a talented First Division side in those days, playing First Division opponents – so the gap, on paper at least, was not so wide for judging the outcome. And yet this present Sunderland side, although in the Second Division, did carry enough team spirit to achieve victory in a competition notorious as a non-respecter of reputations.

There was still a puzzle or two on the faces of neutrals when they read the Sunderland team sheet on the morning of the match. Leeds hardly needed a glance down theirs to inspire instant recognition – Harvey in goal, Reaney, Madeley, Hunter and Cherry at the back, Bremner, Giles and Eddie Gray (as a retractable left winger) in midfield, and Lorimer, Jones and Clarke up front. Yet Sunderland, in the words of Geoffrey Green of *The Times*, had climbed 'over moonbeams' in reaching Wembley, and, as underdogs, the neutral soccer following took them to their hearts. While the manager who had come to them by way of Bury, Carlisle, Charlton, Rochdale and Blackpool, assembled his squad in a quiet southern headquarters far away from the hysteria back home, he proclaimed that Revie's team were due for a surprise.

So in the early afternoon of May 5, 1973, we travelled to Wembley Stadium needing galoshes or wellingtons to escape wet feet, for monsoon rain which had pounded down that morning, worked over the arriving fans from Yorkshire and the North East until their long strands of hair dangled like sea-weed on their sopping shoulders. But it was still 'HAWAY THE LADS!' and 'HAWAY THE MESSIAH!' from the indestructible Wearsiders. The Leeds fans had been to Wembley often, but for the Sunderland fans the experience was new and exciting and a great challenge.

The Sunderland fans dearly wanted to outmatch their haughty rivals and, once in the sacred stadium, they more than did so, draping their sections behind one of the goals in a cloak of red and white. At the Leeds end, the Yorkshire gathering adorned in white looked as regimental as fresh linen in a hotel suite. Shortly before the kick-off, the sun came out prompting Geoffrey Green to let out his famous battle cry 'Over the rainbow, baby,' as, adorned in a red and white Sunderland scarf, he let it be known which side his allegiances were anchored to on that day of David and Goliath.

When the teams eventually emerged, there was a minor surprise when the manager of Sunderland was seen to be wearing a vivid red tracksuit. By comparison, the manager of Leeds, wearing a city suit and a mackintosh as he trudged alongside, could have been an accountant on his way to a corporation hearing. Stokoe, compared with Revie, looked relaxed and happy, which could not in all faith have been exactly true, because he must have felt as if he were about to hear the brigade whistle ordering him to go over the top with his rum-in-the-tummy platoon. After being presented to the Duke of Kent, the players prepared for action amid a bedlam of noise, most of it from the Sunderland end.

Revie, a superstitious man, had put on his lucky suit, but once he had taken his seat at the head of the Leeds bench, he must have winced and uttered a little prayer. From the kick-off Sunderland went at their illustrious opponents with a fervour that clearly disturbed them. With the rain falling again to dampen an already greasy pitch, Clarke, the England striker, found himself an early victim of Sunderland tackling, Pitt winding 'Sniffer' with a thundering challenge which turned the victim's constitution into a frenzy of sparks and jets of shooting pain, the Wembley turf saturating his nostrils with the rich, turgid stink of unwelcoming earthy toast.

From the resultant free kick, Hunter – the same 'bites your leg Hunter' – pushed the ball to Lorimer who hit one of his specials past the Sunderland goal. Jim Montgomery, a long-serving player, who by the end of that season had made 412 appearances for Sunderland, was still trying to calm his nerves, nerves that cut into him like a shark's teeth, nerves that made him yearn for the comforting warmth of the dressing-room and mum's cuppa. It happens to all goalkeepers until they get the first magic touch, or first magic save, which allows them to calm down and settle into the fray. Hadn't big Frank Swift felt the same playing for Manchester City against Portsmouth in 1934? At least he had the intelligence not to faint until after the final whistle and City had claimed the Cup.

My own feelings in the Press Box, as one on-duty at a Wembley Final, were scarcely inaudible; the itch to get on to the telephone and call Fleet Street during the course of my running report for the first edition, expressed itself in wild clawings at the flex and muttered oaths, while waiting for the office to reply. Miller, my neighbour and experienced colleague, who had covered everything from a World Cup final to countless FA Cup finals before, calmly kept his eyes on the pitch while gnawing at an obedient apple. Sunderland, meanwhile, were obviously determined not to allow Leeds any favours at all: they chased every ball like whippets, and when Jones burst through their ranks, Pitt came to the rescue with another blazing interception. What a start this final had provided, and all along fuelled by a cacophony of rattling sound from the terraces.

Sunderland had begun to play the game of their lives, but Leeds, so knowledgeable, so electric, had one message in mind – to teach these brash Second Division upstarts a venerable lesson. In this atmosphere of tension and escalating, whirlwind action, it was difficult to concentrate on one's mission on the telephone, and the copy-taker had to strain to catch my urgent squawks amid the noise.

Suddenly the favourites were pushed back on the ropes with a viperish swiftness that must have surprised the old guard and Revie, staring intently at them from his seat. Johnny Giles, noted for his dislike of any form of sloppiness in his overlording role as navigator, made an uncharacteristic, unkempt pass straight to Hughes, who, in turn, found Tueart waiting with a greedy look out there in the great, wide divide. Chunky Horswill was there to meet the latter's delivery, but his shot was blocked on the edge of the penalty box. Then a pretty move involving Halom and Porterfield led to a searing volley by Hughes which bypassed the Leeds goal.

It was open, fairly even stuff, with the Leeds three front men – Lorimer, Clarke, and the ambling, muscular Jones – never quite being out of the picture. But what became more and more obvious was that Watson and Pitt had the advantage over Clarke and Jones in the air. Watson, in particular, was not going to give any ground away or lose any aerial challenge. He became more and more magnificent, and a total inspiration to Sunderland. While Leeds were trying to make up their minds about how to break down this challenging rival defence, Halom began to benefit from some astute service from the rear, the perception and athleticism of Hughes and Tueart giving him an incentive to beaver his way towards the Leeds penalty box. And Ian Porterfield, the son of a Dunfermline undertaker, showed he could be effective when using his left foot as a lever in midfield, an area usually dominated by Norman Hunter and Eddie Gray. But Gray had been out of action through injury before the final and there would be rare hints of the form he showed in the 1970 FA Cup final when he turned Chelsea's Dave Webb inside out.

The red and white zebras were happy to indulge in hefty tackling just as much as Leeds, who, curiously, were none too keen to reveal the skills which had made them such a formidable team. Billy Bremner was clearly perplexed as his team stuttered, lacking the drive and consistency that was the hallmark of their style. He tried to gee his team up with those expansive qualities the heavy metal kid from Stirling would show a year hence, in a World Cup match in Frankfurt, when Scotland all but beat Brazil. Sunderland kept attacking, however, and when Horswill shot past the right-hand post with Harvey off limits, the punters who had tipped Sunderland to win began to look confident. And they had every cause to celebrate when the unbelievable happened on the stroke of the 31st minute.

The roar from the Sunderland end had escalated into a fearsome bellow, when a corner was awarded them after Harvey, opting for safety first, knocked a centre from Kerr over the crossbar. The Leeds players massed around their goalkeeper as a limping Hughes prepared to take the kick. Over came the ball, and as Watson leapt in to make contact, two Leeds defenders were distracted, giving Halom the chance to knee the ball back low in the direction whence it had come – but this time not as far, because an alert Porterfield, cradling the ball with his left thigh, brought it down and volleyed the glistening match ball into the roof of the Leeds net with his weaker right foot. A blurred wire photograph showed the swoosh of that ecstatic moment, the Leeds players looking almost petrified as their fortress was breached.

There then began the long, drawn-out time when watch power took over the minds and souls of every Sunderland supporter at Wembley, not to mention quite a few outside punters as well. How slowly the hands of the clock moved as Sunderland's precious lead hung in the balance as Leeds, their pride dented, their second half challenge simmering hot; Jim Montgomery, between the Sunderland posts, sensing that his time had come. He was given warning enough when a shot from Bremner thumped against the goalkeeper's chest, yet Sunderland had not forgotten how to shoot when they were able to break out. A shot by Guthrie might have beaten Harvey had it been inspired by better direction, but generally Leeds had the upper hand, and they screamed for a penalty when Bremner was pulled down by Watson. The referee decided the dive was too theatrical. In the 75th minute, Leeds replaced Gray, the obvious candidate for an early bath, and the substitute, Yorath, pushed forward to harass Sunderland. Wave after wave of white shirts threatened Sunderland's goal, but again and again Watson showed his reluctance to give anything away. And during this heavy squall of Leeds pressure, there came a double save from Montgomery that has gone down as the greatest save seen in a Wembley Cup final.

Reaney, the Leeds right back, crossed a long ball to left-back Cherry, whose diving header at the far post was blocked at point-blank range by Montgomery. Then, heavens above, as the ball bobbed clear, like a sea-lion squirming to break free from a narrow gap in an amorphous cove rock-face, the lethal Lorimer emerged with evil intent in his Scottish eyes. A thundering drive would suffice: he measured his aim, found his target, and hit the ball from six yards towards the welcoming rigging. Leeds fans rose in unison, yodelling 'GOAL!' while in the Royal Box, hands were poised for polite, congratulatory applause. Montgomery, on the other hand, had other ideas, ungeared to the routine world of bowing to the expected. Taking inspiration from Watson's reluctance to allow Leeds water from a stone, the goalkeeper sprang to his knees, at the same time somehow launching himself into space, like Gordon Banks in Mexico three years before. The sudden flash of Montgomery in motion was more like watching a potential suicide's tumble from a cliff edge. There was a momentary silence, a shudder as Montgomery managed to turn Lorimer's shot on to the underside of the crossbar, and an almost hysterical scream of joy from the Sunderland end as the ball came down into play to be safely cleared.

In those frenzied seconds, the stadium quivered, not quite knowing what to make of such classic goalkeeping. Revie, who was about to hail the equalizer and probable extra-time, or indeed a probable victory, sank back into his seat. Stokoe, hovering aloft like a fluttering red moth, tried to grasp the magic fact that his team had escaped the burning of their windfall. And so play went on with the Sunderland element gnawing their fingernails as the clock ticked on so slowly towards time.

Leeds never looked as deadly again after the Montgomery 'miracle' and Halom had a chance to score Sunderland's second, but for a flying save from Harvey. When Mr Burns blew his whistle for the end, some veterans near me in the Press Box

Stokoe/Montgomery – Sunderland's goalkeeper hero, Jim Montgomery, relishes his after-match hug from his manager, Bob Stoke – Wembely, 1973.

could not disguise their misty eyes, while Geoffrey Green waved his red and white scarf happily towards the ceiling. 'Well done, you Stokoe babies.'

And there was the Messiah himself, with a mac over his red tracksuit, racing on to the pitch to embrace his saviour. Manager hugged goalkeeper, and then every Sunderland player was joining in. Sunderland really had become the first Second Division club to win the FA Cup in 42 years.

Years later, Stokoe recalled how he felt that afternoon when he was surrounded and kissed by all those dancing red and white zebras. 'I suppose I will always be associated with running on to the pitch and hugging Jim Montgomery. Everybody I meet always wants to remind me about it. I probably started the hooligan element who love to invade pitches.' Down in the dressing-rooms where we members of the Press were like sparrows for the hint of a quote, all the fun and laughter came from Sunderland's cavern as Montgomery, Stokoe, Porterfield, Kerr – heroes all – embraced each other, holding the trophy.

The photographers were insistent.

'Come on, Billy, one more.'

'One more, Bob, that's me lad.'

Meanwhile, Revie and his Leeds team mourned, not far away, in a dressing-room where they had often laughed in triumph before. They had to admit they had been caught by a sucker punch delivered by a Second Division team, and it hurt them deeply. But they were more sporting than they had been following the 1970 FA Cup final defeat at Chelsea's hand in the Old Trafford replay. On that occasion, they had refused to accept their medals at the presentation after the match. It was not to be a winning season that year at Elland Road. The Sunderland defeat ran in conjunction with only a third place slot in the First Division behind Liverpool and Arsenal, and defeat in the European Cup-winners' Cup final against AC Milan. The following season saw the Leeds side at their most ebullient, winning the Football League Championship; but that would be the last one under the Revie regime before he moved on to briefly succeed Sir Alf Ramsey as England's manager.

The master of Roker would take another three years to gain promotion, while the team which had done so well at Wembley began to break up. Tueart joined Manchester City in 1974, and

Ian Porterfield, who had been everybody's hero on Wearside following his king-size goal, was lucky to escape with his life in a car crash.

As for that magical afternoon at Wembley, it will always be fondly remembered by those sports writers lucky to be there. The Messiah and the Sunderland lads saw to that.

7
Fräuleins at Play

The 1974 World Cup was in full swing, as could be observed by the number of tam-o'-shanters visible at Frankfurt railway station. The tiny but efficient train which whisked me into the peace of the West German countryside one Sunday, seemed oblivious of all the fuss, humming along the tracks past soft meadows and rolling hills. The call of deadlines, and the roars of impassioned crowds from Hamburg to Stuttgart, faded away; for a brief time, I was free of the Press centre and my hotel phone.

It was a question of choosing the right hamlet to get off the train at, the type of pretty hamlet that has a good restaurant in the centre, and a straight tow-path along a river. I did not have to wait long.

The restaurant was Yugoslavian, very full, with a fruity carafe of red wine to go along with heavy sauerkraut served by a bumptious waitress. Yesterday's *Daily Mirror* warned that the German police were placing 'a ring of steel' around the Frankfurt stadium, where the Scots were playing their matches. Up till then, and subsequently, I never saw a Jock raise his fist in anger, while Willy Ormond's team played some of the best football they have ever displayed in World Cup finals. Subsequently, they were unfortunate not to make a longer go of it in that West German competition.

After lunch, I took a stroll through the town, and soon hit the tow-path by a meandering river. The sun was dazzling, and dragonflies cruised through water weeds with spurts of frisky colour; a river bench beckoned, there was nobody around, not even one plump male German. The peace seemed eternal; no distractions, except for one fly settling on my nose. I read a novel – and day-dreamed nostalgically for London town, a baby's cry, an open bathroom door, an urban rose, a stretch of bare limb, a female hairbrush, the sound of washing up, a toy Snoopy dog.

Through the poplars, and across a range of spotty hills had appeared a giant expanse of bloated black, conquering a vast backcloth of blue sky, the sun seemed to flicker and recoil as the storm approached. It wasn't fair – I would have to leave. But what sound was that across an adjacent field about 400 yards away from the river? It sounded like the thump of a football being kicked, in collusion with a moan of agony.

I made my way towards the field which was hidden by a tall spray of unfriendly hedgerow – the sound of babbling, surely female, had increased – grunts and sighs, yells and a muffled bellow of protest. An open gate revealed the subject of my interest – a female football match between two teams of fräuleins was progressing with hectic combat on a lumpy, soggily-grassed pitch. On the far side was a small stand full, it seemed, of men imbibing beer.

Even as I skirted one of the goal-nets, the Blues struck at the Whites' goal; a straddling, colossus of a centre forward with blonde locks flowing down the back of her shirt, obscuring the number nine, had darted through and placed the ball with heavily motivated zeal into the folds of the net. The pace of the ball which swished into the ragged rigging was quite overpowering. The goalscorer let out a screech of ecstasy – and descended into the arms of her bosomy pals. The fallen goalkeeper swore in German. In the stand, the big fellows with the flagons of teutonic beer raised their glasses. One or two, supporting the Whites, simply frowned.

I approached the stand and found a small bar open by the adjacent dressing-rooms. A comely fräulein served me a quart of brown-black froth; outside it was still hot, and a space was found to watch the match. 'Sehr gut, Eva.' A sliding tackle by one of the Whites' mid-field players propelled one of her boots high up into the exposed and ample thigh of one of the broader members of the opposition. A stud sliced into flesh. 'Swine!' The fallen hero collapsed in agony – and two or three members of each team joined in unison to slap and punch, kick and swear. The male referee, a reedy German with immaculate black and white uniform, disguising his under-nourished, office-harassed frame, dived into the middle of the scrum. There were howls of laughter from the male spectators; they chortled, they danced on their big feet. I saw open mouths like deep caves leading down into an eternity of bubbling beer froth which lay inside their gargantuan bellies. The fight was eventually stopped, but now there was a new hazard approaching. The black storm cloud was suddenly overhead, and plonks of rain water descended, as thunder and lightning crashed around us. It was very Wagnerian – the teams raced for cover, already soaked to the skin.

The open-plan dressing-rooms were separated by a thin partition – and the players were soon slumping down on benches, smoothing the wet off their thighs, and tossing their seaweed-wet hair in all directions. They looked exhausted, the majority of them, except for one nimble nymph on the Whites' side who pulled down her socks and began a series of prodigious exercises – bending and stretching. In contrast, the fearsome number five on her side stretched back on the bench, pulled up her shirt and scratched a steel-cupped brassière. Yawning, she looked at the ceiling, then disdainfully at we men gathered around the bar at the far end of the hut. It was revealing to see that some of the fräuleins who had pulled down their shorts to ring out some of the wet, were wearing elastic protectives around their groins.

The storm was now at its height, rain pinging down ditty-de-ditty-dee on the corrugated roof – the referee was elsewhere, no doubt having a calming smoke in the toilet, away from the storm he had confronted on and off the pitch.

A visibly tipsy male clutching his beer slid over to me, being the stranger in the pack. His eyes wobbled slightly as he examined my city suit and shy appearance. 'You a visitor?' he asked, switching from German to almost perfect English.

'Yes, sheltering from the storm.'

'You here for the football?'

'Yes, the less important games, the World Cup ones.'

He laughed hugely. 'You're an Englander – we beat you in Mexico. And we should have beaten you at Wembley. That Hurst goal was never over the line. It was that crooked linesman, that Ruskie peasant who allowed it.'

I was already being pressed back against the wall by the speaker and his thrustful friends. But the malice did not remain for long. He raised his glass: 'To all Englanders,' he said. 'To the Queen of England.'

After the loyal toast, which I assisted by toasting Willy Brandt or some such person in power, I asked the score. The Blues were apparently winning by two goals, it was a cup semi final, a very important match, and many of the male companions had wives or girlfriends playing. The tipsy man even went so far as to say that one of the muscular Blue members monsooned on a bench was his wife.

'We had a row this morning. She kneed me here,' he said, pointing to his groin. 'It was torture.'

Our hut was now engulfed in waves of water, the pitch turning into a lake.

'Will they go on?'

'Of course they will go on. They haft to, they haft to go on.'

More beer flowed, and one female crept away from her dressing area to take a gulp from her burly man's glass. I noticed the girl who had been sliced by that crude tackle was rubbing a purple-coloured ointment into the grotesque wound. She looked disillusioned, unconfident of carrying on to face the challenges that lay ahead.

The storm abated as suddenly as it had begun, the sun burst through on the green landscape, turning rain puddles into shimmering diamonds; birds twittered in unison. 'We haff half an hour to go,' my companion said. 'We haff a very difficult half hour to go.'

The referee emerged, blowing his whistle to summon out the teams. But suddenly there was a rumpus from the Whites' corner. A combined female moan that seemed to rock the hut. 'What is happening?'

'The Whites – Hamsburg, that is – they will not go out. They say the pitch is too wet; they say the Blues are too dirty.'

The referee approached the captain, ordering and pleading for her to lead her team on to the pitch. The Blues were already out, splashing a football through a pond of water. But the Whites would not budge, sitting firmly on their benches. My head humming from the strength of the ale, my in-built alarm system began to sound warning bells.

Suddenly, the loveliness of the landscape turned into an impending war zone as the Blues' captain marched into the hut. She stood there like a tyrant, her blonde locks attached to her bullet head like a steel helmet. She almost snorted; her boots went tap tap with impatience on the wood floor. Then she approached the Whites' captain, a smaller, but more muscular female, grabbing her brunette mane and tugging it without mercy. Screams rent the air, and male hangers-on began to swap punches near me. I decided a quick retreat was very necessary, and slid out of the hut door. The referee was caught up in a ferocious contest between the two parties – but, then, as suddenly as the storm had abated, the fighting abruptly stopped – and the Whites reluctantly decided to come out and play.

I strolled over to a vacant corner flag away from the throb of hostility surrounding the dressing-room/bar area; the referee had whistled for action again – players with scores to settle drifting warily towards each other like boxers who have lashed each other for 12 rounds and have little to give for the last crucial three. The storm had produced many puddles on the pitch, the water, translucent and dazzling, quickly drying in the serious heat. By the corner flag, all was peaceful, except for the cries of the girls, and the odd boom of laughter from the bar. Bird life predominated; birds of vivid colour rose twittering in the air and made for nearby water meadows. They were finches; a kingfisher would have been a luxury.

'SEHR GUT!' I half spun round in surprise, shaken by the sudden arrival of my tipsy friend, holding two enormous glasses. 'Trinken,' he said. 'We haff had a gut afternoon. You see, in Germany, we take football seriously, specially the women.'

'It does seem so.'

'The Blues will win. We haff a good team.'

'They look the stronger.'

'Mein Gott – they are the stronger.'

After a few more scything tackles, the referee suddenly decided to take offensive action; he stood over a Blues' culprit, trying to look official, but in retrospect only looking comic. Struggling with his breast pocket, he produced a soiled red card and waved it theatrically in the pastoral air. There was a growl of discontent as the offender trudged sulkily towards the dressing-rooms.

There were 20 minutes to go, and the Blues looked safely through to the final. Their chief scorer, who looked like a female version of the Argentine striker, Mario Kempes, again charged through, but was nearly garrotted before she could reach the penalty box. Again, the referee decided a red card was necessary, sending off the Whites' offender. 'Sehr gut,' my friend howled, taking an enormous sip of ale from his glass.

Frau Kempes took the free kick herself and curled in a vicious outswinger, which this time failed to fox a flying goalkeeper's fiery dive; at the last second, a pair of well-chewed fingers made contact with the ball as it dropped brutally towards the far corner; for a second, Frau Kempes protruded a bulbous pair of lips in appreciation of her strike, but the ball burbled away now to safety, to the relief of the Whites.

For some minutes, I had been watching the stylish activities of the nimble nymph who had spent her waiting time doing exercises back in the dressing-rooms. She became increasingly authoritative, knocking the senior and far more mature Blues' players out of their imperial stride. She moved in and out of their ranks like a young Wilf Mannion; she won possession of the ball over and over again; she moved forward offering threats that had not been posed before. There were eight minutes to go when she first struck. After Frau Kempes's effort had been saved, the ball was struck downfield, and the nimble nymph appeared in a space up at the left near our corner flag. With a certain arrogance, she put her foot on the ball and ordered her puffing colleagues to get into the goal-mouth. The Blues' right back came storming in with a leg-breaking tackling which our nimble nymph carefully avoided, surging forward with a stunning burst of speed which took her wind-surfing through the rain puddles to find an exposed position just on the angle of the near six-yard box. The Blues' right back was still struggling back when the nimble nymph belted a devastating strike into the exposed cage.

This sudden moment of supreme insolence acted as the stimulant the Whites needed, and especially the nimble nymph, now the conductor of a match rarely free of physical challenges and flurries of feminine motivation in which three or four players of the same side would steer the ball forward with the protectiveness of mother eagles returning to feed their offspring. I tried to imagine what profession or job or school or college the nimble nymph dedicated her working hours to. Perhaps one day she would marry a chemistry professor in Frankfurt and settle down with three children, and a giant Bavarian hound; or perhaps she was a simple baker's daughter with a menial job working in a store; or then again, with her pallid features and beaky nose and cropped blonde hair, she might have settled into a nursing groove, tending the sick during night hours, and having a brief flirtation with a student doctor; or then again, perhaps she was studying for her exams, and playing football to stay relaxed – if this was the type of game you could relax in, that is.

My tipsy friend had sobered up with a jolt when the nimble nymph's goal went in. He kept looking at his watch in apprehension. 'We haff to win this game. It is necessary to win this game. It is necessary to reach the final.'

There were three minutes to go when the nimble nymph struck again. The Whites' goalkeeper lofted the ball downfield and it plopped into a drying puddle just over the half-way line. The ball stayed there for sometime, the Blues' defenders staring at it, reluctant to make contact; not so, the nimble nymph – she ran over, took possession and swept away downfield with the Blues' girls yelling and screaming and near frothing at the mouth in their efforts to catch her. There was only one person in the world now who could stop the nimble nymph and that was the chubby Blues' goalkeeper, her bust ample and projected, stuck forward as some kind of threat. Two large arms prepared to envelope themselves like giant crab's claws around our heroine.

The inevitable happened. In a flurry of movement reminiscent of two zebras tangling in some distant waterhole, the nimble nymph was axed to the ground. She lay for a while, savouring the moment, her ears pricked for the shrill blast of the referee's whistle. It took a long time happening because his point of departure was yards behind the fallen sprinter; at last, the huffing and puffing was eliminated, he claimed his sentinel and blew long and hard. 'PENALTY!' My tipsy companion threw the remains of his Alt on the grass in disgust. 'Nein, nein,' he bellowed. Then he said something about the nimble nymph being a whore of an actress.

Inevitably, the nimble nymph was invited to take the kick by her excited companions and with commendable maturity, she accepted the challenge, sweeping up the ball into her thin fingers like a young mother plucking her slumbering baby from a small pram. The kick, on reflection, was firm and almost too accurate, the ball striking the underside of the crossbar before bustling down into the folds of the netting. The Blues let their heads sink in dejection, the Whites squealed with delight – a replay was inevitable, there being no extra time. When the referee blew for time, all the gas, wind, rage, animosity, teutonic jealousy and cunning bullying evaporated – the two teams put their arms round each other and lumbered off. One of the Blues homed in on the startled referee but only to bow and offer a polite hand to shake. The Blues' champion took off from our quiet haven and made for the dressing-rooms behind the disappearing girls. His long bushy sideboards bristled with the intensity of new-found disappointment. His direction was not exactly geared to a straight line. For a moment, he swayed, but then righted himself and reached the dressing-rooms without further mishap.

I decided to take one more look before making for the town and the Bahnhof. Passing the open door, revealed a large red curtain drawn across the centre aisle, blocking off any view the imbibers might have had of their women friends tearing off their muddy gear. I half-waved to my Erasmus of women's football, but he was now a member of the male post mortem team, the papal inquisitor into what had gone wrong with the Blues.

I left behind those who had played, and those who had not; a subtle difference, for those who had played had no connection for a time with the outside world, the immediate momentum being the game just passed, a game which the Blues justifiably felt they had thrown away, while for the Whites, it was a raft suddenly spied arriving over the crest of an ocean in the nick of time. It was easy to imagine the emotion which rapidly intensified as the girls washed their kneecaps in a tiny twin shower and powdered their faces for their clucking men the other side of the curtain. But for a time, the men had no say in the thoughts of the female players; sulking, half sniggering, pouting, petulant, swearing, scoffing, sniffing, staring, scratching, snorting, armpit tickling, they went about their business of preparing for the world off the pitch.

The brawls which had dominated the match before the storm, played no part now in the general palaver of where and when the replay would take place. A vision came to mind on my walk back along the river into town of the tipsy man and his craggy wife enmeshed in their own post mortems later that night, in some large beer hall where men hold their titanic flagons high and boast of great white whales they have never seen. And the tipsy man's wife staring down into her own brew and swearing vividly about that 'pissing ref' who should be shot, that eunuch with a big square head and no brains!

There would be drinking that night in town, a secret faction made up of different teutonic parties, and repercussions galore. Perhaps our nimble nymph would put on a new pair of stockings and a party gown and steal away into the urban sticks, the recent triumph strictly hidden away from whoever she was dating for the night.

I took a slower train towards Frankfurt and became part again of another, more immediate world of high-pressure soccer with banner headlines sprouting from the front pages of my neighbours' newspapers about the progress of Helmut Schoen's West Germany team towards the Munich final. But it wasn't easy to put aside the events of the afternoon, drifting along to the clanking throb of a train on rails with strong ale galvanising the euphoria of admiring the greenery of a passing rural landscape.

At some point, I changed trains, and, while waiting, observed a fight in the bar between two Turkish immigrant workers. One of them took a punch high up on the forehead, which split flesh and sprinkled his yellow shirt with a mass of blood. A policeman appeared promptly to stop the feud, his pistol waggling ominously from his stocky waist. The brawls of early afternoon seemed a long way away now, as voices were raised and Moslem rights unleashed on the uncompromising law. Through the swing doors now emerged my colleagues, Colin and Peter, up from the South after an unruly match concerning two teams from Europe and South America. For a moment, they thought I was part of the commotion, standing back in some bewilderment, as blood flowed, and words reached gibberish point. Our new connection arrived promptly, and as German trains don't wait, we leapt aboard.

'Where have you been then?' Peter asked. 'Beating up innocent citizens?'

'No, watching a female football match in the country.'

'Bloody hell, Colin, the lucky bugger's been watching a girly game. No bloody aggravation.'

It was worth a laugh.

8
Bruising Tale in Brontë Country

Easter is a time when many unpaid acting footballers journey abroad on misty weekend tours with their clubs. Paris, Amsterdam, Ostend, Dieppe, Cherbourg, and countries even further away, like Portugal, host an annual invasion by bands of players of various sizes and odd shapes carrying suitcases stuffed with football boots without laces and football strips the colour of a Highland dawn.

But one year my club, Battersea Park AFC, decided the time had come to tour at home, to offer our services in combat to speakers of the English language, instead of going to Normandy. The site named was Yorkshire in the South Pennines, well out of range of hefty, victorious salvoes being fired off at that time by Leeds United in the East and Liverpool in the West.

It was an unpublicised experience, which drew little attention elsewhere, but as football tours go, any prevailing optimism that four spring days in the north of England would go strictly according to plan quickly evaporated when two of Battersea's more bruising defenders were detained for questioning at Victoria coach station by Special Branch officers, on suspicion of being ringleaders in some diabolical threat against the state. The two players, to be absolutely honest, did look as if they had recently arrived from an expedition deep into the heart of Peru with their long, streaky hair, and bushy whiskers fanning out from long sideboards. The Special Branch men diligently searched their suitcases, delaying the other passengers, and causing a near eruption from impatient inhabitants of Keighley wanting to get home for the short holiday. In the confusion, all that was found in the suitcases was one deflated football and several pairs of honking, unwashed socks. The two suspects

were eventually released, and sent on their way north, their
suitcase contents causing one or two occupants of the coach
to place scented hankies over their nostrils.

Tours of this nature need a great deal of diplomacy, not to
mention the clever trick of being able to con the welcoming
committee into thinking you are far better than you really
are. This had been counter-productive on previous tours; for
instance, Dieppe, who were so overawed by our presence and
stature that they put out their first team and beat us 6–0.

Our base in Brontë country was an old millhouse at Lumb
Bank where some of our team members including Tony White,
John Hinds and Peter Doherty were helping to restore a new
arts centre on a site owned by the future Poet Laureate, Ted
Hughes.

Poetry sessions, however, had little to do with our emerging Easter holiday, the sheer, necessary process of keeping
one's limbs in respectable battle shape outscoring a desire
to write casual sonnets or pen odes to Charlotte, Emily and
Anne Brontë. For somewhere out on the moor, we felt another
Norman Hunter was preparing to bite our legs and buffet our
bruised frames. It was with these sombre fears that the party
took to their camp beds amid scaffolding and drying paint
after an evening's exploration of the local ales at a village pub
in nearby Heptonstall.

The occupants of this West Riding hamlet on the road above
the Industrial Revolution's pride and gem, Hebden Bridge, were
not unduly surprised to find a bunch of London grizzlies in their
midst having long played host to legions of tourists exploring the
rolling, windswept landscape so favoured by the Brontë family.
The sight of our 'brass', at any rate, was not displeasing to them,
even if Louis, our metallic midfielder, disgraced himself on the
first night by insulting a group of American visitors, his language turning their Salt Lake City cheeks into ruby-coloured
Cox's apples. 'Out you go!' the landlord said simply but sharply.
'And don't come back.'

Louis was to be seen during the rest of the weekend skirting
Heptonstall, on the way to a suitable tavern which would
accord him an audience and an ashtray for his long Dutch
cheroots. He was in many ways the victim of his own tongue,
having trodden the boards of many a fringe theatre in London.
And Yorkshire bitter does have a kick comparable to a square
cut by Geoff Boycott.

Heptonstall, a picturesque village of stone weavers' cottages and rambling streets was forever poised on the edge of a moorland ridge, and around Lumb Bank, at least, the rocky landscape leading down to Hebden Bridge bore traces of a Swiss landscape. It was on the next morning that the tour commandant, Tony White, had it in his mind to test our fitness by running us up a painfully steep track – an idea which nearly required a hospital ambulance for one or two less lively members. But for those women present in the party, the sight of gawky males flopping down on the roadside with their tongues hanging out produced a rattle of cruel, female laughter. We muddied oafs, so boastful of our achievements on Hackney Marshes, were human after all.

Later on that morning, we rounded up our players for the journey over the moors to Keighley, a somewhat difficult task because tour footballers are not noted for keeping a strict timetable, wandering off, like Louis, to unknown watering-holes and staying put until pulled out of a cosy public bar by a peevish leader. We were scheduled to play four pub teams in three days and with a squad of only 13 players, four of them over 40, there was a doubt about our ability to survive the strain. A cold wind blew across Keighley and bored deep into our bones. 'Our best lad, our captain,' a beaming member of the opening welcoming committee said, offering pints of a lethal local brew. 'Leeds have watched him. They came here and watched him, they went away, and said they would come back and watch him again. And that's raht, they will an' all.'

'Where is he?'

'Over there, lad, he's the one with the crinkly hair.'

I beckoned Tony over, our leader offering a dazzling smile, which he sometimes produced to hide a certain apprehension at the outcome of the coming afternoon's ordeal.

'Look over there, that giant, you see him – Leeds have got him under observation. They want him to take over from Norman Hunter.'

The rival captain was indeed a giant, robust and well-built, and surely not long out of school. In football kit he would look even more fearsome. 'It's a shin pad, then,' laughed Tony, 'and two on each leg more likely.'

'That lad will make you run,' our Yorkshire friend said. 'He can kick ball like a ruddy mule.'

'Any more like him?'

'Quite a few, lad. They're dead keen young 'uns'.

We tried to explain, rather feebly, if memory is correct, that half our team were over 35, though some of them had been watched by Sir Alf Ramsey in their time. It was a good lie, and went down well at the bar. Another of the rival team turned up on a scooter and, to our horror, when he alighted from the saddle, stood up firmly in a stance far larger than the giant we had already seen. His bulging thighs and burly chest wrapped up in gleaming denim gave this youth a trace of rugged masculinity which the round, almost pimply face beneath a barrage of red curls barely deserved.

He literally towered above us, even Tony who was hardly a dwarf. With a robust pink fist, he held on to a gleaming match bag, favouring the colours predictably of Leeds United. It was time for us to counter this rude awakening by producing our own centre half, a bearded giant of six foot five in his country-music boots. He appeared from behind a curtain in the pub, a writer's writer, with James Joyce singing up his prolonged nostrils. The smaller of the two Yorkshire giants dropped like a piece of loose rock. Size for size, tit for tat, and wild laughter through the bar.

We debagged cautiously in a tiny box of a dressing-room, Louis's swollen head, reminding us of the perils that lay ahead, geared to making contact with our craniums every time the Red Fox brigade launched salvo after salvo at our penalty area. As a cold wind moaned across from the moors, fanning out along the small back alleys of a strictly urban, industrial setting, the rival team posed for team pictures, their yellow strip identifying them proudly with Don Revie's budding League championship team not so far away. Besides the two Norman Hunters brooding in the back line, there was a rugged, growling figure squatting on one knee in the front row who could very well have been a youthful Billy Bremner.

They rushed us off our feet in the first half, those eleven gleaming young men in canary yellow. They whirled the ball around, they pushed it everywhere we were not, they bellowed and cursed each other but only scored one goal because of the authority of John standing between us and a riot. A somewhat rotund figure from Fulham, he soared like a magpie, swept himself into all kinds of contortions between the posts as the ball dipped and spluttered on its way into a net recovering from recent frostbite. During one skirmish on the right wing, I felt what it was probably like to be hit by Norman Hunter when the taller of the giants laid me out grotesquely beyond the touchline, winded and full of disbeliefs in our regal game. It is in these moments of gross indignity that one feels the harshness of simple sport, which had its roots in the hacking confrontations of medieval rural England. My worried three-year-old daughter, Rosie, who was watching the match, named such violent activity as simply 'bumping'.

In the second half, the sun came out, and we astounded the Red Fox by quickly equalising. Paul Thomas, one of the few on our side who could match the opposition, chased through the middle of the pitch on to a pass from Nick Jack and planted the ball into the net. The home goalkeeper, after spending much of his previous time chatting to some younger friends behind the goal, returned the ball to the centre circle as if such happenings were an insult to the whole of the West Riding, let alone the Red Fox.

In the surprising event, we managed to hold out to draw. 'You never stopped running – even the one in the bath chair,' their committee chairman reflected afterwards. Our prizes or medals were Yorkshire pork pies which we balanced on our knees and chewed at the bar reception. Out of interest, I looked around for their two giants who had worried us so much at first but they had gone to ground, as many young teams do when their heads go down as the going gets rough. But they had sauntered away, probably in some disgust at their own negativeness.

Our Red Fox hosts duly drowned us in celebration ale and next morning we reported unsteadily for a match against the Brown Cow on the very same pitch at Keighley. Bless the brew! We ran them off their feet in the first half, with Louis assuaging his battered pride with a performance as committed as Brazil's Gerson. Perhaps it was our spirit of adventure and unceasing chatter which did so much to undermine this Yorkshire challenge – but our prize on this occasion was to go back to the dressing-room at half-time, a goal ahead, again from Thomas. Never has a cup of tea been more welcome, the sweetness of overloaded sugar going to the head like peach melba soaked in cognac.

In the second half, the home referee, a most loyal man as far as we had been concerned, finally decided we should be suitably punished, awarding the opposition an indirect free kick two yards from our goalline. Our centre half, Alan Horan had simply not called him a name. The Brown Cow netted after the kick, amid burbles of enthusiasm.

We went straight into another match at Hepenstall after the Brown Cow reception, and this time learnt our lesson. The word had got around about how brilliant we were and on a pitch covered by molehills and on a hideous slope we were properly found out. Our shame went unheeded by a party of American tourists in a nearby graveyard, visiting the grave of the American poetess, Sylvia Plath, and late wife of the Lumb Bank landlord. Hepenstall won by several goals.

The next day, after a barbecue at Lumb Bank, lasting most of a cold spring night, we took on the fourth pub and won by two penalties. The match was at Haworth where Charlotte, Emily and Anne lived in the Rectory, and Branwell Brontë enjoyed the local ale at the Black Bull. I somehow wish Emily had been around to record that match. Some of the tackling did sound like horse's hooves in *Wuthering Heights*. 'I would have sent him off,' the referee said, alluding to a tackle by Louis. 'But there weren't any substitutes.'

Like many touring football teams, we had run out of fresh limbs. There's nothing like a tour to find out what real soccer's all about.

9
Paris in Riot Time

The Church of England chaplain looked as if he had just returned from the First World War trenches after a routine night raid had inflicted numerous casualties on our patrolling Tommies.

Called out of his cosy bed to administer the last rites, he was now back at base camp, trying to soften another recent nightmare in the mud with a tot of stiff rum. But, in the company of other officers who had also returned from 'hell', he tried to keep his pecker up, despite the pain and disillusionment he felt in his soul.

This sense of trying to stay rational and mildly hearty, despite recent calamities, was very much the mood of the chaplain as we sat talking at three o'clock in the morning in the lounge of a hotel near Versailles as the players and wives of Leeds United FC executed one or two desultory wiggles on a nearby disco floor.

It had been a depressing evening, a near tragic evening, with the Leeds fans staging a riot at the Parc des Princes during a second half in which Bayern Munich had survived a fusillade of plastic chair seats, torn up and thrown by the rival supporters, to win the 1975 European Cup.

The depressing, frosty, aftermath, in which celebrations, as far as the Leeds party were concerned, resembled the slow drip of stagnant water, offered us many sullen post mortems. The players, dressed like café society pianists in their smart white blazers, sulkily concentrated rather more than their followers on the events of a game that had run away from them once Peter Lorimer's goal was disallowed for offside.

For the many others – journalists, travel agents, men of God, visiting city councillors, and general hangers-on – the manner in which the game had been won and lost had been completely overtaken by the mood of hate generated by the Leeds supporters, a bloodlust which only the strong presence of the Paris riot police prevented from turning into an orgy of destruction.

'It really was sickening,' the Rev Eric Allen said despondently, as Norman Hunter, described by the French press as a 'brute with a tender heart' jogged manfully about the disco floor. The chaplain to the Lord Mayor of Leeds, was obviously in a deeply depressed state – but he emphasised his eagerness to forgive his ailing Leeds flock by searching, not for obvious excuses, but for reasonable explanations into actions that other more militant members of his congregation might have deemed suitable for 'a raht birching'.

'We only had an allocation of 8000 tickets,' the chaplain said knowledgeably. 'Some of them must have got into the wrong hands. We don't usually have much trouble from our Kop.' His pronunciation of 'Kop' sounding in the early hours remarkably like 'flock'. Somehow, however, this sounded an empty statement – the 'don't usually' rendered like a priest's endeavours to play down the criminal record of a Lower East-side hoodlum. But perhaps he did have a point then – the Leeds fans were still putting their act together, their worst acts following the Paris riot coming in the years ahead. But now the Rev Allen had switched his tack – reminding me that normally it was the Manchester United fans who tended to be the chief offenders when it came to crowd trouble.

One had to agree, at this stage of football history, that he was talking sense. 'It was, nevertheless, a terribly sad occasion,' the Rev Allen added, looking around the lounge into which the first rays of a late May dawn would soon set a beam on the vulgar tapestries of a luxury French hotel. 'Obviously something will have to be done when we get home. We can't very well hide the incidents away under a carpet. I will certainly have to remind my own congregation of the dangers such wicked acts can create in society.'

Norman Hunter came off the dance floor, leaving Allan Clarke twisting with rather more venom that he displayed against Bayern. 'It was the first Bayern goal which finished us off,' he said, to anyone who would listen, the nearest being the Rev Allen and myself. 'It was not their second, the second didn't matter all that much. We knew we had lost when Roth scored.' Paul Reaney came over, looking a trifle sardonic. 'Peter's disallowed goal was deflected by a Bayern player on the way in – but the linesman did not see it.' 'It was still a terribly sad evening,' the Rev Allen murmured again. 'It was at that,' Reaney added.

We stayed on until 5.30 am, leaving the Leeds members who had not tottered to bed still discussing a night which had gone sour for them not long after it began. 'And to think it looked like being a classic game, a game to savour . . . and now we must dig around the rubbish and find the right post mortems,' Colin said as we drove through the daylight of early morning Paris in a grinding taxi to our own hotel. I thought back to the morning before when, in perfect weather, Paris had bestowed a traditional heroic blessing on the participants who would be celebrating the 20th anniversary of the European Cup in perfect, sunny weather.

I thought of the optimism that had gone into the earlier celebrations, when over a glass or two of champagne, memories came back of other romantic times in Paris when being in love ran concurrently with worrying about the price of the next bistro meal. From our observations, on that lovely day before the riot, Paris was going about her business as normal without a staggering fan in sight. It had begun with a plaque unveiling in our hotel to celebrate the anniversary, and there standing in the general throng were the masters of their craft offering the benevolent glances of heroes in the know.

It was around 11 am at the UEFA hotel when these heroes emerged for inspection, holding comforting, long, slender glasses of Bucks Fizz, mingling with each other like old companions, once, in many cases, having been fierce rivals . . . there was Alfredo di Stefano, cocky, as he had every right to be, predicting a win for Leeds. 'It should be a treat tonight. Leeds have some very good players, good quality players like Bremner, Jordan and Lorimer.' There was Ferenc Puskas, tubbier than during his playing days, enjoying the canapés and hero worship being lorded out by white-jacketed French waiters. Had it really been 15 years since di Stefano and Puskas slaughtered Eintracht Frankfurt in Glasgow to win yet another European Cup for Real Madrid? Fifteen years since I and my recent bride observed the shuffling arrogance of these two maestros from our floor mattress in Chelsea basement?

Then out of the crowds forming for the reception emerged another hero, Raymond Kopa, the French wizard of the 1958 World Cup in Sweden, the Rheims jackdaw, chain-smoking

Gauloises. 'I would love to be playing tonight,' he said, following the single-track mind of a great sportsman who craved for the arena again but knows his legs have irrevocably gone. And pray, who was the familiar debonair figure in a conservative dark suit moving through the throng to shake the hand of di Stefano? Sir Matt Busby needed no introduction; players, so many great players around him, stood back in respect as the Argentinian and the survivor of the Munich air crash recalled old memories of Real Madrid and the Busby Babes during those epic struggles in 1950 before the tragedy. There was sudden silence, and a short speech by a UEFA official speaking in heavy French rhetoric: 'The European Cup has broken down barriers and given the game soul.'

In the slightly oppressive, crowded atmosphere, Sir Matt looked as if he would welcome a good mop of his brow with a handkerchief. But he remained poised and dignified as welcomers pressed round him. 'It's a tremendously nostalgic occasion, seeing all these fine footballers here. Seeing di Stefano and Puskas on parade takes one back to those wonderful days of Real Madrid. And, of course, Puskas being cruel to poor old England at Wembley. I hope tonight's game lives up to expectations. It should certainly be a cliffhanger.' Sir Matt was sucked back into the crowd of players, journalists, officials, FIFA and UEFA members, autograph hunters, fringe football magazine editors, and one or two potential pickpockets. I left with a group of German journalists who were taking a taxi to the Left Bank.

They reported in an expansive, Bavarian-tinted, guttural way that the Bayern manager, Dieter Cramer, had gone out of his way to do his homework about Leeds. He had spent a small fortune on buying English newspapers and periodicals for news about Jimmy Armfield's formation. He had also been staying up until dawn combing through press reports about their matches. As the taxi swung past the Hotel Crillion in bright, absorbing sunshine, I was informed that Leeds scored most of their most important and fruitful goals in the first 25 minutes. Without a goal after half an hour, they tended to become frustrated. The Bavarian reporters told me, as we crossed the Seine, that they expected the Swede, Andersson, to mark Bremner tight, and possibly not in a very friendly manner either. 'I think the Swede may think he'll have to kick Bremner,' said one of the Germans. 'And I don't think Herr Bremner likes being kicked.'

I was meeting an American writer in the Café Floré, and he

was already seated on the outside terrace reading *Le Monde* with
a glass of Campari and soda at hand. 'Hi,' he said, 'welcome
to Paris. What brings you here during the wonderful buds of
May?'

'There's a football match at the Parc des Princes tonight. An
English team against a German one.'

'Well, I see the Yankees haven't been doing too well. But I
hadn't read anything about a soccer game in the *Trib*.'

'There was a line or two – Leeds are a rather good team.'

'Leeds?'

'In Yorkshire.'

'Ah, that's Brontë country, very beautiful. Where do you say
we have lunch – Chez Alligator?'

Chez Alligator was a favourite family restaurant down a narrow street near the Floré. Peter was a regular customer, enjoying
the fruits of a long, French country cooking menu. I knew he
was hungry because he always looked hungry when he took
off his granny glasses and licked his lips. 'I guess you'll need
a grand feast before you go out to the Parc. What about a royal
flush of escargots to settle you down before the ball game? I
must apologise for having a sore head this morning, there was
a soirée last night on the Right Bank for a visiting Korean poet
who claimed his piles were giving him hell. He kept on wincing
as his admirers fawned around him. I think they thought he was
being rude and feeling bored or something, but his piles, he told
me, felt like red hot chestnuts.'

True to form, Peter did take 20 minutes to order from the
extensive carte as voracious Left Bank academics scoffed their
gigots around him in the crowded bistro, hell-bent on getting as
much down their throats in one hour flat, before tearing back
to work. 'I once saw Mickey Mantle hit a homer in New York
. . .' Peter's concentration on the selection of one or two of
his favourite dishes, including boudin, wandered for a moment
into the portals of the Yankee Stadium, but just as I was about to
pin him down about this particular slug from a Yankee genius,
Peter took off again on another tack, which involved an article
on Georges Seurat he was writing for a glossy American art
magazine. 'I'm beginning to see Seurat dots in front of my eyes
in the shaving mirror. It's all that afternoon staring at his art that
does it . . . it sprinkles my eyes with dotty dust.'

Lunch slipped by in a congenial way, as they always did in
company with Peter. 'By the way,' I asked, 'did Mantle really

hit that homer?'

'Well, I guess he did, the ball seemed to go out of the ground and on to Manhattan. I remember the crowd screaming.'

The soccer game at the Parc des Princes was fast approaching now, and after leaving Peter sauntering away to add another thousand words to his lengthy Seurat thesis, I took a cab back to our hotel where a Press bus was scheduled to take us to the stadium. There was no evidence at all in the taxi ride across the Seine, or in the coach going to the Parc des Princes, of any crowd violence to come. Near the stadium there was the usual jostling to make the match on time, the Leeds fans waving their white, yellow and blue banners, the Bavarian fans letting go on their hunting horns in a throng of red.

It was not until three-quarters of an hour before the kick-off at 8.15 pm that I heard the first evidence of violence outside the stadium. Ernest Hecht, the publisher, with an almost insane passion for Brazilian football and Pele, reported that he had seen some Leeds fans beating up some ticket touts. 'They look very drunk,' said Ernest, as a kind of warning. 'They've been drinking red wine all day in a nearby café.'

But the final got away on time without any undue anxieties about what would eventually engulf the match. Where the smell was in the early stages was on the pitch, where one or two appalling tackles from Leeds did cast the first fuel on the unlit bonfire. One of these, by Yorath on Andersson, was such a crippling one that the Swede was carried off the pitch.

'A penalty, it's got to be,' the Leeds Press corps near yelled when Clarke was brought down by Emperor Franz Beckenbauer. It certainly looked like a penalty, but to Clarke's astonishment, the French referee gave Beckenbauer the benefit of the doubt.

Leeds had every reason to feel hard done by at half-time, but there was still a mood of optimism among the English and resident Leeds Press corps members that Bremner and company would eventually wear down their opponents and win through. And the likelihood appeared cemented when Lorimer's shot blasted swiftly past the Bayern goalkeeper, Sepp Maier, to give his team what looked to everyone apart from the referee like a worthy goal. But the referee, to the astonishment of the Leeds fan club, disallowed the strike, apparently for offside against Bremner. And the linesman confused the issue by running back to the halfway line as if signalling a goal.

It was too much for the inebriated members of the Leeds clan sitting behind Maier's goal with a deep, waterless moat providing what would be a highly necessary barrier. They began ripping their plastic seats from their foundations like Nile baggage carriers snatching up suitcases to earn prize tips. No sooner than they had armed themselves with plastic, than they ran riot, hurling their lethal objects towards the Bayern goal, and all the time spitting obscenities at the Germans, and the most unpopular man present on the night – 'the fucking frog ref'.

One of the riot police, wearing sausage-shaped tracksuits, on duty near the moat, sank to his knees after being hit by a missile whirring down like a flying saucer. He was dragged away a little too enthusiastically by his colleagues, who were now facing a major riot on this sublime early summer evening. A Leeds fan managed to make his way across the moat, which was a ridiculous decision because he never stood a chance with the police waiting eagerly for a scapegoat to punish with the maximum amount of pain in the shortest possible time. They caught him, pinned him to the ground on a layer of broken glass, pummelled him into something resembling a rag doll before hurling him back into the bottom of the moat. 'That's one broken leg for sure,' muttered Barry Foster of the *Yorkshire Post*.

All through this depressing, sinister period, in which more and more seats whistled towards a courageous Maier's goal, the game went on, the plastic seats mounting up in layers within the Bayern goal-net. The situation was not helped by Bayern scoring their two goals which were greeted by the crackle and explosive smoke of thunder flashes being thrown by victorious Bayern fans opposite their rampaging and out-of-hand Leeds rivals. To the noise of the crack of seats being ripped off their hinges was now added the sound of German thunder – somehow, the process of watching a football match had completely disappeared, the expectation, the cut and thrust on the pitch, the sudden form change when one team revives to punish the other, such factors were obliterated by the noise and clamour behind both goals – as Leeds, so disheartened by the events of the night, seemed quite happy to pack matters in.

A Niko-chained photographer emerged, reporting somewhat breathlessly that many of the Leeds culprits were middle-aged men. 'Some look as if they're throwing stones into the sea at

Blackpool. But there's hate in their eyes.' Jimmy Armfield, the Leeds manager, pipe in mouth, sat on the bench. He looked a lonely man, his vision of a match with which he had become progressively disillusioned was becoming more and more obscure with the arrival, out of the players' tunnel, of the dreaded Paris riot police, the CRS.

In 1968, during the Latin Quarter student riots, many of these representatives had gained a reputation for not taking prisoners. But, on this occasion, they chose not to launch themselves into the crowd, which was fortunate for the Leeds fans. These sinister, black dragonmen with their heavy riot gear and malice in mind may have been cuddly at home in front of the telly, but out on the boulevards of their capital city, they could be deadly, if need be. Their arrival may well have frightened many of the Leeds fans as their armoury of seat ammunition began to run out, but those of them who were too drunk to know about anything, kept the weary process going. In the Press Box, I sensed a look of disbelief, disgust and incomprehension on the faces of some of my English colleagues, a range of emotions which was to escalate by 100 leagues ten years later at the Heysel Stadium, Brussels.

When the referee eventually blew 'finis' on his whistle, the Leeds players ran towards the mayhem at their own supporters' end to try and diffuse the sitution because there were rumours that the environs of Auteuil were already in flames outside. Bremner stood like a pug dog, his paws held aloft, thanking those Yorkshire ranks of muddle, chaos, threatening hatred, and hard done by bitchery for their loyal support through a long season. Bremner may not have known then just how grotesque the night had become – a night that would provoke a long ban in Europe for the club in European competitions and participate in a decline at Elland Road in playing standard, plus an escalation of hooligan strife, and racial abuse. As Bremner lowered his weary arms, the light seemed to go out for one of the country's most valid and exciting teams in recent years.

At precisely 10.01 pm, Don Revie, Armfield's predecessor and so successful in his time, rose from his seat in the Press Box and made his way towards the media interview room. Chaos now reigned, with reporters shouting down their phones and tubby men with deadlines trying not to trip over cables on their mad rush to the telex room. 'I blame myself for this,' Revie, the new England manger, said almost wearily.

I have often pondered subsequently what Revie meant. Was he alluding to his own heyday at Leeds when his precious team achieved an escalating momentum on the football field through ruthless, formidable teamwork, attached to more than a random shot of sour gamesmanship? This had led to Bobby Charlton in later years scolding Leeds for their humourless behaviour, despite the presence of his brother, Jack. 'Revie's Leeds could play marvellously,' he reflected, 'but they always seemed to be on a tight rein. I never got the impression they were enjoying themselves. They were sour, winning was all, and they were paranoid about criticism . . .'

Charlton's words went a long way in summing up what Revie may have felt was his own doing. His own, sometimes devious behaviour when in charge at Elland Road, could not be condoned – his cynicism when it came to tolerating the goodness and flair of other squads was passed on down the line to the supporters themselves, and finally into the hands of a growing hooligan element who just could not tolerate defeat. So was Revie allowing himself a whopping, self-inflicting knock on the head when he spoke those famous words to me? Was the guilt sinking in now he was in charge of the national team? It may well have been so. I, in turn, ran down the Press block steps to see the effects Revie's former flock had achieved by their shameful conduct.

It wasn't a pleasant experience – that meeting with the unremorseful rampagers as they streamed forward on to the adjacent boulevards. A photographer I knew walked by with his cameras dangling like hand grenades. 'There's a Leeds bloke over there with his eyeball hanging down on to his chest. A French cop whacked him across the head.' Verbal Yorkshire sanctimony was everywhere as the crowds pushed past, uttering oaths and swearing at any strangers they thought might be German or French. A CRS detachment marched past looking distinctly smug, ready to knock more than a few heads together. A Leeds woman with a pretty knitted beret, was ready to explain, voluminously: 'It was the metal bits on the plastic seats. They cut like glass. I don't condone what happened. But the French ref. was bloody awful.'

Many mouths, expostulating hate and grievance, pushed themselves in my direction like the expansive spread of a toothy pike's grin. It was difficult to comprehend all that was said, but it all added up to frustration and mortification. 'If we had Manchester United out here, we'd do 'em proper like,' a sweating youth in a white T-shirt grumbled. A passing Bayern fan spat on the pavement, lucky to retain his feet in a sinister situation.

The cantankerous river of departing discontent began to dwindle as rival fans met in ambushes near the approaches to the metro stations bordering a slumbering and leafy Bois de Boulogne. The sound of police sirens blared through a sinister urban dusk merging into real night; a searchlight waved across the skyline as a message of goodwill to all newcomers to Paris, while those Leeds armies of the night still capable of talking and walking without stumbling and belching, made their way warily on foot back to the small hotels where they would be greeted without compassion by severe-looking madames on the desks.

Colin Malam, and I managed to find a taxi to take us out to the Leeds hotel for the wake – a nightmare journey, so it proved, in which the driver took us round Paris twice before reaching Versailles and the appropriate hotel. My meeting with the Rev Eric Allen was thus to come much later on, when post mortems began their sombre and weary tattoo around a disco floor.

After an hour or two's sleep, I rang my old *Evening Standard* friend, and doyen of Paris correspondents, Sam White. The British ambassador in residence was preparing to make a formal apology on French State Radio for the behaviour of the Leeds fans. Sam growled out his thanks at this piece of information. 'It seems, *mon vieux*,' he observed, with that rich sandpaper accent which developed by way of Russia, Australia, England and Paris, 'that Yorkshiremen never got over Don Bradman's batting against English bowling at Headingley before the war. They just couldn't take it. That 300-odd by Bradman obviously still rankles. Some of them last night were obviously not thinking about football at all, they were still sore at Don.'

Sam's wisecrack was a gentle nudge at many Yorkshiremen, not born to be good losers. How it must have griped the Leeds board of directors to eat humble pie and formally say 'sorry' for their hooligan element through letters to the Mayor of Paris, UEFA, Bayern Munich themselves, the English Football

Association and the French Football Federation. It was hardly a time for rejoicing in Yorkshire.

My own lasting memory of a night when the Parc des Princes experienced the outrages of mob violence was of a prim, middle-aged Leeds woman fussing about a hotel foyer before going home, saying: 'How would you like someone smashing up your home? Shame on 'em!'

10
Double Take

A Euston backstreet November dawn does not have much association with the lively, noisy atmosphere of a crowded Italian trattoria. It certainly did not occur to me on a drab early London morning in 1976 that this would be precisely the setting I would find outside an otherwise sleepy row of houses.

There on the pavement was a group of Italian waiters, restaurateurs and chefs waiting for a coach to pick them up and take them to Luton Airport. I had been invited to join them for the day to watch a football match in Rome. It was a chilly morning, but Luigi, whom I knew from Soho as a diner at his hospitable Dean Street restaurant, Giovanni, Antonio, Sandro and the rest were already in a gregarious mood, murmuring, rather than bawling, in respect for all those slumbering parties behind brick above us: 'FORZA ITALIA, FORZA ITALIA'. . . 'FORZA CAUSIO'. . . 'ITALIA 3: INGHILTERRA ZERO'. . . 'FORZA ITALIA'. The group looked like small boys waiting on a railway platform at the end of term. They had every excuse to have their heads in the clouds, having grabbed only a few hours' sleep after leaving their salons and kitchens of work, but already the thought of cheering their country on at the Olympic Stadium, Rome, in a few hours' time had planted a kindergarten enthusiasm on their faces, something they would not lose until the early hours of next morning.

Some of the Italians had brought along their wives and girlfriends for the big day, the majority conscious of a day out in the Roman capital, heavily made-up and wearing their favourite winter coats for the journey. Their faces looked oddly fragile in the street lighting, dolls with painted cheeks and lipstick. The men hovered beside them attentively, their solid overcoats and polished shoes striking a strong chord of masculine Neapolitan domination.

'FORZA ITALIA,' Luigi whispered behind me, drawing on his first filtered cigarette of the day. 'You, John, you are in for a big disappointment today. Italy will be far too strong for your team.' Luigi was already getting into his stride, tapping a bollard with a sudden display of impatience frequently observed when things went wrong in his spaghetti hall. 'That bloody bus driver, he always keeps us waiting. Last time, we almost missed the match, he was so late. We had to take taxis to Luton. All the way to Luton.'

On this occasion, Luigi's impatience was quickly abated with the arrival of the coach, snorting and chuffing as it drew up beside our party. 'FORZA ITALIA, FORZA CAUSIO. . .' Through the empty urban streets into the environs of motorways we would soon be swept, this reporter contemplating, despite an irresistible desire to doze, why on earth he had agreed to a day trip which would be totally biased in Italy's favour.

If this had been an early morning coach ride involving English supporters, the kind who behave themselves, that is, the hour would have been far too early for conversation, or general sleepy small talk. Not so my Italian friends. They chattered and chirped and sometimes chanted in the black dawn, they wailed and giggled, smoked, and occasionally burst into song. Please not 'Volare' at that crazy hour! I thought about events in Rome which was the reason for being on the coach, and the England team sleeping uneasily in their beds before the pressures of a difficult afternoon confronted them in front of a frenzied Italian crowd. I thought of their manager, Don Revie, and his famous dossiers, which he handed out to every member of his squad; dossiers full of weird and technical information about their Italian rivals, dossiers that many of his players admitted later totally confused and dumfounded them. Some of them declared they would rather have read the 'Beano'.

What was at stake in late autumn Rome that day, were vital points needed by both teams in their World Cup qualifying group as security to reach the finals in Argentina, two summers hence. Revie had been heavily criticised by the English Press for failing to produce a settled side for this important occasion. There was a nagging doubt about the defence which became sorer as the Berkshire countryside began to light up translucently through early daylight, doubts also about the back

Revie – Don Revie on duty as England's manager, 1976, equipped with 'dossiers full of weird and technical information . . .'

four, playing together for the first time. It looked increasingly likely that I would return to Luton in the early hours next morning wearing a loser's cap, and perhaps one for dunces to boot. But time would tell, and we were not off English soil yet.

It was a surprise to meet the actor, Peter Cook, waiting in the airport lounge, a member of our party for the day as a 39th birthday gift from his wife, who had decided not to come. Peter, known by me from his Cambridge days, which led to 'Beyond the Fringe', and the founding of the Establishment Club in Soho, was equally surprised to meet another Englishman in the party. But being an ardent Spurs fan, he soon launched into his evaluation of the coming match with that clipped, authoritarian take-off going back to his early satirical days. 'Have you heard the pilot is called Bowles?' he said, scratching the number five printed on his purple T-shirt. 'With Stan Bowles in our side, that must be some sort of omen. I think the result will be a 1–1 draw.'

'Never on your life,' Peter's Hampstead friend, Giuliano, gently mocked. 'If Italy lose, I will give you free spaghetti for a year, both of you. But we would like the game to be a clean game, a good game, otherwise!'

Ever sedulous, in keeping with his role as a devoted owner of a trattoria where the famous actor could devour his pasta in total privacy, Giuliano made sure a busy brigade of yellow and black uniformed hostesses kept Cook's glass well primed. After all, it was signor Peter's birthday – and no prohibition orders had been nailed to our flight. 'The weather in Rome is fantastic,' cooed our travel agent from the pilot's cabin. 'We welcome you aboard, and trust you will have a wonderful time in our famous capital. And Italy give England a lesson.' He spoke in English, no doubt appreciating that most of his customers spoke the language of their chosen workplace daily on the restaurant floor.

'BOO!' the famous actor exclaimed, jerking his head up from the sports pages. 'Italy zero, England 3.' A woman passenger nearby was too engrossed with choosing perfume from the duty-free trolley to care either way. A buxom hostess allowed her some free squirts, and the woman sprayed a plumpish forearm with various samples, sniffing and snatching at the exotic smells invading the cabin. Her husband obviously ran a prosperous joint – her wrists were over-indulged with rings of gleaming silver and gold, her coiffeur raining down on a pair of pasta puffy cheeks screeched in waves of black horse tails.

We were soon flying down the western Italian coastline towards the Eternal City. My two companions next to me, Giovanni and Antonio, confessed they were both from Coventry, ran a restaurant, and on normal mornings would have already returned from the market. Italians are very fastidious and wise about the preparation of food, and in this, they tend to be rigorously partisan, their own cuisine comparable to the Vatican in comparison with the rest of the world's tables. So, when Antonio mentioned they had included a masterpiece of British game, the pheasant, on their menu the previous week, it came as a bit of a surprise. 'It was our speciality dish, very good,' Antonio added. 'With blackcurrant jelly, brussel sprouts, sauté potatoes, and a 1968 Chianti to wash it down. Bellissimo!'

It was a trifle early to talk about such grand dishes served with Neapolitan delight in the west midlands of England, but Italians love to talk about food, even in the process of being taken prisoner of war. A friend of mine who was in the Middle East during the war told me his own Eyetie catch discussed the power of pasta all the way to the cage. But then they were so happy to be captured.

Now we were flying over Rome, the toylike Vatican rising from below through the soft autumn pastel pinks and greens, and then the Olympic Stadium, embossed by two tiny white goalnets perched on a green leaf. 'Viva Italia, Italia weeen.' The sight of the stadium aroused a bedlam of noise in the aircraft's cabin. Waiters, managers, chefs and checkout girls combined in homage to their favourite capital, and their prize stadium down below – but Bowles, the pilot, refused to wait, soon putting our jet eagle of the skies down with a bump on the runway of Leonardo da Vinci airport.

In the coach going to the centre of Holy Rome, Cook declared he was worried there might be some trouble outside the Olympic Stadium, recalling a nasty incident at Old Trafford, Manchester, when United had the dubious reputation of having the worst supporters in the country. It was another item I could include in the growing pages of my war football journal.

'The last time I went to a football match away from White Hart Lane, I was beaten up in a Manchester car park,' Cook said, laconically, directing the memory of his plight to a sympathetic Italian audience, bored at watching pine trees lined up in rows along the passing highway. 'Spent two weeks in hospital with wounded kidneys,' the actor added.

'But why you, Peter, what had you done?'

'These people are animals,' a voice murmured, becoming angrier.

'I was just walking away after the match, and zoom, somebody hit me from behind,' Cook said, 'it was unbelievable. I think what enflamed the United louts was that my pal decided to have a go. I'm afraid it was like goading a bull. To tell you the truth,' the actor added wickedly, 'if there's any aggro today, I'll be the first to throw a brick into the Sistine Chapel.'

'You wanna help, we'll help,' cried an Italian admirer.

'I am quite capable of carrying out the task myself,' Cook laughed.

We had an hour or two to spend in the centre of Rome before moving off to the stadium, glasses of vino and jolly conversation occupying the attention of the male fraternity, while the females went off shopping and gazing at some of their favourite monuments. It was November, but one could still sit outside, watching the Rome traffic roaring past in mad bursts of murderous metal, traffic police imitating opera house conductors with their frenzied instructions waved on high. A full-scale dinner had been arranged after the match in town at a restaurant owned by a friend of one of our members. 'It will be a great occasion,' the travel agent cooed, 'lots of pasta and vino.'

Contrary to Cook's fears that we would be met with a hail of Roman rocks outside the Olympic Stadium, the scene could not have been more affluent and geared to aristocratic diplomacy. The majority of the men walking quickly towards the entrances wore traditional green overcoats, while their women, not long back from Capri with their children and nannies, had not worried too much about nearly bankrupting their husbands through excessive spending at the autumn collections. Viva Gucci.

Our Italian friends had, nevertheless, been excessively protective towards the four or five English members of the outing. 'Italy, yes, but any trouble, we help you,' Antonio said, as we climbed up solid steps to our block. There the Anglo–Italian mob formed a small square, wagon-train fashion, as all around us noisy Romans began to wave banners and chant 'FORZA ITALIA'. The sight of the interior of the Olympic Stadium can be overpowering, seen for the first time. It engulfed the emotions of the athletes when the Olympic Games were held there in 1960; it engulfed the emotions of many an international soccer team who had lost there in the past; the essential Roman theme, with white amphitheatre buttresses standing out at one end against a range of gentle woods, lined with pine trees, dominating a goalkeeper's view in the furthest away penalty area.

There was no doubt the crowd around us intended to be hostile to Revie's team, their Roman intolerance rising towards a greyish sky through a cacophony of shrill whistling. Down in the dressing-rooms, I could imagine Revie waving his dossier in the face of every member of the English team. There was no time now to adjust the plans for the afternoon. The referee had nearly called the two teams to arms. The reception the two teams received that Roman afternoon was in no way different from some of the other momentous afternoons involving these two countries in the past. Fanatical heraldry for the Italians, derisive whistling for the visitors. Tommy Lawton once told me how intimidating the Italian sound had been in Turin in 1948 when the England team played there.

The sound had clogged the senses of Lawton and his England colleagues as their captain, Frank Swift, leapt, dived and somersaulted to keep the ball out of his net. There was a discipline about that talented England team though, which Revie would never be able to rely on in the team we were about to see 28 years later. Gifted players like Wright, Franklin, the imperial Matthews, Mortensen, with a goal from an incredibly wide angle after only two minutes, Lawton, Mannion and Finney disregarded that intimidating reception by rolling up their sleeves in the sweating heat and winning 4–0. It was, according to Tom Finney, scorer of two goals, 'one of the greatest games of football which I had the pleasure to play in'.

The pride and purpose that great England team showed at the Communale Stadium, Turin, all those years ago, had no part in the proceedings we small band of English followers watched in Rome. It is difficult for me now to recall who was wearing the white shirts of England, without reaching for my *Rothmans Yearbook* – although memory does recall Stan Bowles, perhaps with his mind on the winner of the 2.30 at Plumpton, playing a solo, time-wasting ball juggle by a corner flag, at a stage when his team were two goals down and trying desperately to redeem a pathetic show.

What Cook, myself and a spruce Scouse who happened to be a brother-in-law of one of the chefs, did not know was that the Revie era was floating on the rocks; he would soon disappear to lucrative pastures in Arabia, with England's chances of reaching the 1978 World Cup finals in tatters. The famous dossiers did appear to work in Rome, because the players played so squarely and regimentally that the fluent Italians said 'grazie', and took off into enviable space. All we could do, high up in the stadium bowl, was to suffer the humiliation the England players must have felt themselves. Kevin Keegan, for instance, who did so much to win the European Cup for Liverpool the following summer, in the same stadium, suffered a red face when Antonogni's drive bounced off his legs past Ray Clemence. The sound of celebratory thunder around us was more in keeping with a Roman bistro at peak hour. It was even worse when Bettega scored Italy's second with a delicious header. I was rained with blows on the head by a female supporter waving a bamboo banner – Luigi nobly came to my assistance, grabbing the banner and shouting: 'My leetle darlings, Italee.' Bettega must have spent five minutes on the ground being embraced by his team-mates before the referee could get the game moving again.

By now, Peter Cook was doing his best to imitate one of his famous television roles in which he sat forlornly on a park bench with Dudley Moore, squeezing a cloth cap between his knees, and moaning about life in general. Ahead of us, mercifully, was the 'après-soccer', when the majority of our party would let their hair down and celebrate a stirring victory. While England dithered, Enzo Bearzot's team began to reveal the skills which would take them into fourth place in Argentina, and to the eventual winning of the World Cup in Madrid four years later.

'I thought Causio and Greziani fed us to the lions,' Cook said, as the coach steered us through the excited crowds leaving the car park. 'Didn't you feel ashamed to be English? Revie has totally failed to achieve a settled side.'

'He was a very good club manager at Leeds,' said the spruce Scouse, 'but being a great club manager isn't the same as being a great England manager. Give him the boot, I say. And give Bob Paisley or Brian Clough the job.'

The Italians almost swooned with pleasure, chattering with delight at their win, though gracious to their humble English friends, trying to defy defeat. Causio, in particular, was sin-gled out for extravagant Latin praises, and, in retrospect, his insidious form on the pitch defied a jaunty, almost awkward

Kevin Keegan – 'red faced' when Antongeni's drive bounced off his legs pa Ray Clemence in Rome.

appearance in keeping with a singing waiter. But once in possession of the ball, you felt he could control it like a dexterous
hand holding a serving tray in a crowd.

It needs no saying that the party afterwards was a masterpiece
of Latin hospitality, with bottles of Belle Amarone at £10 a fling,
going down very nicely with chatter, chatter, natter, natter
all the way and the woman who had sniffed all that duty-free
perfume becoming more and more like Sophia Loren in a fruity
state of mind, as bedlam and singing took over under rows of
hanging hams and salami. Peter Cook's voice, as he thrilled
to yet another toast on behalf of the losers, had lost some of
the authority it had conveyed earlier – it now sounded like a
hacksaw boring into timber – but then all of us, inspired by
Sandro's rendering of 'Goodbye to Sorrento', felt a little less
inclined to follow a conservative code of diction.

I felt myself burbling pompously and ineffectually to my
neighbour about 'England's lamentable *puffamance*' as another
mound of pasta was put in front of us. But Antonio squeezed
my hand. 'We are all pals here, Italian and English,' he said,
'Volare, ohohoh, Volare, deedeedum.' 'The trouble is you don't
have many footballers, great ones in England,' Antonio said,
'Keegan, maybe, yes, but you do not have a Bobby Charlton or
Bobby Moore now. It shows.'

The pasta began to make one's belt bulge. 'Si, si, si, it shows,
prego, it shows. Pass the vino, pal.' 'Ladies and gentlemen,
signors and signorinas, a toast to sunny Italy,' Cook pronounced, seemingly on the way to the stars, or to the ceiling.
He was on his chair, and we gulped in homage accordingly.

The flight home ran concurrently with the party, there seemed
to be no transit, until Luigi and I shared a taxi back to London, in
time for me to take Rosie and Leo to school. We managed a bit of
sleep on the plane, despite an Italian voice crying: 'WAKA UP!
Waka up. . . you lot, wake up! Italy beat leetle England. You tell
it to the customers, lads. You tell it. We're proud of our team,
you bet we are. Waka up.'

11

On the Track of the White Fly

'Have you heard of the Malvinas, John,' Julia asked, as we walked beside the River Plate one misty Buenos Aires morning in June, 1978.

I turned, half-captivated by my Argentine companion. 'The Malvinas? No, not offhand. Where are they?'

Julia and I had been out on an ornithology patrol, searching for an imposing South American bird called the Cardinal, which, with its Vatican-style red-head crest, fully earned its title.

'You call them the Falklands – we call them the Malvinas. I'm very afraid our two countries will be going to war soon over who owns them. Our leaders, the military, believe Argentina have the right of sovereignty. It is very worrying.'

Standing there alongside that huge expanse of murky river water dividing the World Cup hosts, and future winners, from the first 1930 winners, Uruguay, the idea of a war between Julia's countrymen and women and my countrymen and women seemed almost laughable.

'The Falklands? Oh, where the penguins live,' I answered flippantly. 'I don't think your people are really very interested in fighting a war over them.'

'But they are, some of our leaders, I mean. They would be very happy to invade. I think your own government must be very careful.'

'I suppose it will all be settled eventually by the United Nations. The Falklands are an outpost with a few Brits loyally doing their duty alongside the penguins,' I said, trying my best, in fourth-form geography terms, to trace the right wee red blob on the map.

'We will see, but I'm terribly worried.' Julia was not a woman who spoke in idle, café society gusts about such matters – she had the ear of many influential people in Buenos Aires, as did her husband, and it was more than chilling to think that such a contest between Argentina and Britain could be on the cards. But first we had the World Cup to see to, and the prospect of Argentina winning. This was a prospect which now enthused Julia as we continued our stroll in search of a missing bird, and it served to detach her from her anxieties about what seemed a tiny area of the globe down south.

'Do you really think we can beat Peru and reach the final? How exciting that would be. And if only England had been here to play against us on Sunday.' This born Anglophile, geared to riding horses freestyle across the Pampas, her freckly countenance beautifully groomed, was caught up in a sport she normally shunned through her teenage son's preference for rugby.

'It very much depends on how Brazil get on against Poland in Mendoza. Argentina will have the advantage of knowing what they have to do tonight in Rosario in order to win Group B. I think Brazil will win, but they'll need to score a lot of goals to reach the final.'

'I think our Mario Kempes is gorgeous, so good-looking,' Julia reflected. 'He really knows how to score goals. Daniel says he's the best goalscorer he's ever seen, and he goes to watch football a lot.'

I had met Julia and Daniel shortly after my arrival in Buenos Aires, at one of the many receptions given for the visiting media by citizens of Buenos Aires. They had invited me to a barbecue at their house in a smart quarter of the city where there were maids and butlers and Porsches in adjoining garages, and leather riding gear and gaucho hats in wardrobes, and squash rackets in hallways, and smuggled long-playing recordings of 'Evita' which was due to open in London during the World Cup. Daniel looked the epitome of a successful Buenos Aires businessman with his blue Harrods blazer and grey slacks to don in recreation hours, and his knowledge of football was fairly formidable, especially when it concerned matters involving the River Plate club. 'We have in Daniel Passarella a very striking defender. He is also a remarkable captain for our club and his country,' he said, taking a thin slice out of his gargantuan T-bone steak fresh off the spit. 'It will be wonderful for our country's morale if we manage to win the World Cup.'

'Is morale that low?'

'Well, it isn't exactly high.'

Neither Daniel nor Julia, being devout Conservatives, were inclined favourably towards their nation's military regime, having both been brought up through numerous political upheavals since the Peron dynasty. But once or twice, Julia would say almost in a whisper: 'It is very sad what is going on here. People disappear, you know, people come and take them away. I know one or two people who have been kidnapped. It is alarming.'

Covering World Cups does not provide enough time either to get the true feeling of a regime rumoured to be rotten, or, indeed, become acquainted with the lifestyles of the inhabitants; whether they be rich, like Julia and Daniel, and own horses, or peasant Indians living out on the great, brown, baked plains the other side of the Pampas, who own nothing. It was with this in mind that I had taken a 17-hour train ride impulsively from San Martin railway station in Buenos Aires to Mendoza to watch Peru play Poland in a Group B match in Mendoza, having spent so much time holed up in the fortress Press Centre in Buenos Aires, or a quaint bistro frequented by members of the British Press called the White Fly. Nothing much could be seen of the White Fly under the dim street lighting but inside it was a cauldron of noise with everyone from Ron Greenwood to Denis Law locked in conversation over their formidable-sized steaks.

'I'm taking a train tonight,' I said to Pat Collins. 'To Mendoza.'

'By train? Well, you better take a good book. It's only 24 hours from Mendoza, they say. And the trains travel at five miles an hour.'

'They say it should take only 20 hours, and after all it's Sunday, and we don't come out for another week.'

Pat, and my colleague Colin Malam, who was writing a book about these finals, had come out before me to witness Scotland's ignominious elimination in Cordoba through a defeat by Peru and a draw against Iran which not even victory over the eventual finalists, Holland, could rectify. Ally MacLeod and his fated 'Tartan Army' had gone home early, with newspaper headlines stinging their retreat like wasps.

I had woken up in my sleeping chair in what seemed a surrounding coffin of cotton wool waving outside the carriage windows. The cotton wool, as it turned out, giving evidence that we were on the Pampas, was waving grass. The train trundled on out of the dawn into cattle country, with the temperatures progressively dropping as we advanced cautiously towards the Andes. A young couple, who could speak English, asked me to join them in the restaurant car for a bottle of local red wine, and they talked about their plans to get married. 'We are living in difficult times here,' the girl said cautiously. 'We want to get married – but if we do, we will go and live abroad. Some of our friends have not been seen for months in Buenos Aires. We believe they have been taken away by the Junta for their Socialist views.'

'You are here for the World Cup, very good,' the boy said, raising his glass of fruity plonk. 'Our leaders are very happy to stage it, it keeps people's minds off other matters. And if Argentina wins, they will be full of joy, you see.'

This young couple, both clad in suede jackets, shared a refreshing outlook on life which contrasted with those of their sullen countrymen seated in the restaurant car. As the train neared San Luis, the feeling that one really was in the real Argentina began to click in the mind. Five thousand dissidents may have disappeared from the major cities, but here rural life seemed to go on unhampered by bullies or soldiers, the odd Indian with a battered nag pulling stacks of firewood across scrub-land.

'Tell us about England, and the Changing of the Guard,' said the boy. And happy, for once, not to talk about football, I launched into toytown fantasy about the lives of our Royal family. The couple, who both held clerical jobs in Buenos Aires, were in no doubt about how lucky I was to be living in a democratic country, free of the suppressions and monetary chaos which engulfed them.

Now, nine years later, I wonder what fate lay in store for them and whether their uncommunicativeness allowed them to continue their freedom through the last years of the Junta.

A few hours later, I was in Mendoza, relieved I had brought my jacket, because it was real winter now, as I drove by taxi to watch Peru play Poland. Poland, in fact, won 1–0, but it could have been ten, so repetitive was their attacking. But one it was, and as the sound of a bumping tango blasted out over this pretty stadium after the match, the cleaners put down their brooms on the terraces and began to dance very stiffly together.

There was a far more relaxing atmosphere in Mendoza after the tensions of Buenos Aires, although a strong military presence in which companies of paratroopers paraded for interminable hours, wearing pudding-basin steel helmets and holding carbines suggested a hint of repression elsewhere. How many of these young men, I wonder, ended up in the Falklands four years later? But such a prospect then still seemed a novelty. Eager to butter up the visiting Press, the Mayor of Mendoza had given a wine-tasting on the roof of his chambers in bright sunshine, proudly inviting us to taste his local vintages, of which there were many. From the roof-top terrace, there was a clear view of the road to Chile blocked by the snowbound Andes. And, far below, came the constant chant of youth, marching through a shopping complex chanting 'ARGENTINA! ARGENTINA!' The run-up to the final had begun, and the Junta must have sighed with delight at this new-found passion which had fallen straight into their hands.

Just as I was becoming acquainted with one of the Mayor's more fruity Mendoza Rosés, and admiring the environs of an outwardly gentle city, which had similarities with a French Midi township, with bright walls, narrow streets, fountains, and the odd barking dog, a hand touched my shoulder and a Scottish brogue unleashed the most inarticulate of questions in the direction of my quivering right ear.

I turned and found myself looking at a fresh-faced Scot with red curls brooding over a narrowish forehead, and segments of brown chaff disguising an overall florid complexion which was offset by the saucepan lid of a Highland tam-o'-shanter thrust on the back of his football-shaped cranium. A black suede jacket partly obscured the obligatory Scottish National team shirt worn by so many of his fellow fans, while below one expected to see this robust figure thrust into a pair of much-travelled jeans and battered trainers – and inevitably one did. The Glaswegian accent slowed into a pace that was easier to understand as Jock came to grips with a highly-chilled Mendoza blanc, hurling it back, and with a wink, asking for more.

'Do ye ken the wee Mayor? He says we were a wee bit unlucky to lose out here. But I told the wee Mayor we were a bloody disgrace, mon, and that Ally should be shot, understand shot, or strung up on top of Hampden Park. And hear this, mon, I'm from the *Troon News*, do you ken?' My new pal winked.

'I understand, the *Troon News*. You all seemed so keen on Ally when you came out here. Called yourselves members of his Army. Aren't you being a bit hard on him?'

'No, no way we are, mon. He can go and stuff his wee self, for all I care. And that Willie Johnston popping pills like a prancing poof sucking smarties. What a friggin' lot we were, all on the booze, and no football until he was more than a wee bit too late. Archie Gemmill, I forgive, mon – he got a special beauty against Holland, but all too late. Gimme another wine, mon, that's a favour. It's a change from Argentine beer. You can smell the fresh air here – like Troon on a spring day when the chill comes off the sea, and you can smell the seaweed, frosty cold and smelling of oil and salt.'

A bit of a poet then, this warrior from over the Borders – I asked him what he had meant by the Atlantic Ocean. He replied ambitiously that he was going to thumb down a passing banana boat at Mar del Plata and get home that way. He had taken a banana boat to Montevideo from Glasgee and it had taken weeks it seemed before he got the ferry to cross the River Plate. Now he was off home, maybe getting to watch the final on the way, if time and generous drivers on the road to Buenos Aires responded to his signals for a lift.

In fact, they did. Jock's tam-o'-shanter proving an irresistible attraction, he found no difficulty in thumbing rides across the Pampas, and we would meet again before the final in an Irish pub in central Buenos Aires, Jock now in company with two new Highland pals. They had already booked a boat passage out of Argentina and had no intention of staying on, unlike some of their comrades in 1967 who had settled permanently in Portugal following the euphoria of Celtic's European Cup victory against Inter Milan in Lisbon.

'It's home we're goin' to give MacLeod a V-sign up the Clyde.'

Julia did find a cardinal bird for my inspection that morning by the River Plate. This large South American finch with a bright red crest settled amiably on a branch singing for all its worth.

'It's singing a song for Mario Kempes,' said Julia. 'I have seen them much bigger than this one out in the country.'

'Now I know I've seen one before.'

'Where?'

'In a small zoo in Battersea Park, near where we play Sunday
football. Funny to think of a cardinal bird living among our
London sparrows.'

Julia gave me a lift out to the River Plate Stadium where
Holland were due to play Italy for the right to play in Sunday's
final. The inhabitants of Buenos Aires were more preoccupied
with the games in the other group involving Brazil and Poland
and Argentina versus Peru, but they marshalled a fair convoy
on the roads leading to that huge bowl. As there was plenty of
time to spare before the kick-off, Julia made a deviation to show
me the residence of the head of the Junta, Lieut-General Jorge
Rafael Videla. Behind the high walls, there were the customary
clues of the fortifications, needed to keep the leader safe from
all those dissenters, still around, and hating his guts: barbed
wire and patrolling police and troops, the odd armoured car
discreetly hidden behind a hedge, a sense of living on an ants'
nest. There were no singing cardinal birds here. 'What do you
think of this Videla?' I asked.

'I think it was necessary for this country when he took over,
because the country was in a chaotic state. But now I believe
he and his Junta have made themselves unpopular with the
ordinary people. He is married, you know. But his wife very
rarely comes out. She seems to be shut in all the time.' Julia
spoke even more guardedly. 'I am a hospital visitor and I wish
she would come and see the horrible state some of our hospitals
are in. There is a shortage of everything – and patients have a
dreadful time inside.'

Julia had turned the car into a wide boulevard where platoons
of orange-bedecked supporters and their blue-clad rivals from
Italy were trudging towards the stadium, waving banners and
blowing trumpets. 'I found one old man who was dying, lying
in bed alone last week,' Julia said, ignoring the football advance.
'He had not seen one doctor or one nurse during one whole day
and night. He needed some comfort. It was awful. He died soon
after. They were sorry – but they were too busy. The doctors
work long hours, sometimes it is not their fault. But this is an
everyday happening in Buenos Aires.'

'The fifth most populated city in the world, they tell us,' I
offered. 'Over ten million inhabitants.'

'And one of the saddest. But tonight, if Argentina reach the
final, we will have the biggest party ever on the streets here. You
will see most of that ten million come rushing out to cheer.'

Julia dropped me off near the stadium. 'Come to our house if Argentina win – we'll take you out for a celebration drive. I hope Italy win this game – they have many Italians in this city, and they'll be noisy this afternoon.'

In fact, Italy, four years off winning the World Cup for the third time, were beaten 2–1 by Holland through two corking blunderbuss shots from Brandts, who had scored an own goal in the first half, and Haan. I can still see both those shots driving past the Italian goalkeeper, Dino Zoff. Both these goals somewhat redeemed some atrocious tackling by Holland in the second half, tactics which were the reverse of some of the classic total football employed by Johan Cruyff and his team-mates four years before in West Germany.

Rep, for one, and a member of the Munich squad, was lucky not to be sent off for two brutal challenges. The Italians claimed Holland were lucky. Their manager, Enzo Bearzot, was bitterly critical about the Dutchmen's second-half tactics, and, indeed, had young Rossi's header gone in during the first half, instead of just over, Italy might well have reached the final. But their time of glory would come in Spain, and especially for Paolo Rossi.

So Holland went off for a quiet drink to await news of whom they would play in the same stadium the following Sunday. Brazil's 3–1 defeat of Poland in Mendoza had all the mathematicians working out what had to be done on old envelopes – it was simple and very straightforward. Argentina had to beat Peru by four goals in Rosario to reach the final. Now it was time to find fingernails long enough to chew, and a bar equipped with a television to observe the local population's agonies of tension. Some of us took a taxi across town to the Irish Club where a congenial host had promised an evening to remember.

The interior of this Walt Disney caricature of a Dublin ale-house, beside the River Plate rather than the Liffey, revealed not the bookish complexities of a Synge reunion but rather the Ramboesque camaraderie, prevailing from a crowd of muscular, gaucho-looking men lined up against the bar drinking Guinness. The large television set mounted for their convenience at one corner of the bar by Dublin expatriate, Paddy Bushmills, was already winking with the floodlights of Rosario, but the sound was drowned, not only by the frenzied chanting of the Argentine followers within the stadium, but also from a passing brigade of supporters marching past the pub chanting 'ARGENTINA, ARGENTINA!' Their banners floated backwards and forwards

Mario Kempes, World Cup-winning darling of Argentina's Junta – Buenos Aires, 1978.

outside the tavern windows. Some of the fans burst into Paddy's bar and within minutes of our arrival, you could hardly move or speak for the gregarious explosiveness which was summoned out of stout froth.

A British colleague leant against the bar talking about something well away from football, which if his feelings were emotionally right then, was about the recent break-up of his marriage. His wife had gone off with one of his best friends after he had found them almost comically linked in passion at the family homestead. He spoke slowly of the incident, as if numbed by the memory. And I remembered the dictum of the sage of stoicism, Seneca: it did not matter a hoot where one went in the world, for the agony of a personal crisis would never be erased.

But the match in Rosario had started and with Argentina needing their precious four goals, the gauchos and Rambos around us began bellowing and blabbering and shouting and nagging and expostulating as Kempes and company began marauding around the Peru goal. It took 21 minutes for Paddy's bar to receive its first jolting salvo delivered straight into the central orchestra pits, an enveloping cacophony of burbling bedlam. 'GOL! GOL! GOOOOOOOOOOOOOOOOOL!' My ears pinged, my head danced. Kempes had emerged out of the dancing floodlights, after exchanging passes, delightfully, with Luque, to score. 'GOOOOOOOOOOL!' bellowed the commentators on the verge of a goggle-box orgasm. Three more goals were needed to do the trick. We held our breaths and waited for more. My colleague said: 'I'm beginning to forget about what's going on at home now. This is just the right antidote.'

A second goal proved a long time coming with the commentator, backed by our own screeching audience, entreating Kempes to get in there and belt the ball home. Luque hit a post, and snarls from the 40,000 crowd at Rosario signified that the French referee had refused to give a penalty when Bertoni was brought down. At last, with half-time imminent, a corner floated over and as we craned forward, Taratini emerged to power the ball home with his bonce. Fresh bedlam, and with the stout frothing over, a faint smile appeared on Paddy's lips. He was, after all, making a small fortune.

Two up and two to go, to pass the magic mark. Argentina soon scored another, through Kempes, after half-time and then, only a minute later, in the 52nd minute, Luque summoned a soaring, diving header from a downward pass from Kempes. The explosion of joy from within our cave matched the explosions of joy which had stopped the traffic of Buenos Aires. Now the Peru side had started waving their opponents through like affable Spanish travel cops, and, from then on, this became the match coated by the stink of 'FIX!' Two more goals, by Houseman and Luque, completed the scoring, but their arrivals were hardly noticed by the fiesta-gibbering, nationalistic, flag-waving volcanic eruption taking place all over Argentina. The Junta purred even more. Their prize team had reached the final.

To escape into some hidden alcove of sanity, we made for the Plaza where the rich socialites and country club members were already raising their vodka martinis in celebration. The emotion was so intense that I felt a trip out to Julia's would provide a much-needed escape route from all that gloating rumbustiousness. But I was quickly proved wrong, after arriving in a taxi. Julia and Daniel's house and garden were ablaze with light, the swimming pool empty and abandoned on this first day of an Argentina winter. The place resembled an advertisement for plush suburban living, South American style. Julia raced down the steps and gave me what was meant to be a formal kiss.

'We've done it! It's so wonderful, really wonderful. Do come in and have a champagne cocktail. We are all going out for a drive round the city. Everybody's out in the streets. Daniel is ecstatically happy, and all the children are here.'

This was no overstatement – Julia's barbecue lounge was thronged with the young, middle-aged and old, all piping out their pleasure over drinks and snacks. A passing maid giggled as she almost slapped champagne into my glass.

'Come on!' Daniel roared. 'We'll take the cars, and drive and drive.'

Goodness knows how many people squeezed into Daniel's open sedan, but space was found for my own unslender girth in a back corner seat, cosily placed next to Julia. Daniel had placed a large blue and white Argentina flag on the bonnet. No sooner had Daniel opened up the throttle, as we roared out of the sedate environs of this select residential district, than the flag began to flutter wildly in the murky evening light before we hit a main boulevard and turned left to go downtown. Julia, by now in her claustrophobic position, seated between one large man and two large boys, had lost all the serenity and poise which normally went with her position as a do-gooding, horse-riding Buenos Aires socialite. She had acquired an Argentine scarf and, with a voice which had now risen to the level of an owl's screech, delivered her own pronouncement on the night's proceedings: 'ARGENTINA! KEMPES, ARGENTINA, KEMPES, ARGENTINA, MENOTTI. . .!'

And so it went on as we joined up with a convoy of other cars, all plunging towards the Playa de Mayo. Forget the Mad Mothers and their weekly protest against the disappearances of their loved ones; forget all those patrolling policem'zen, and their packed cells discreetly hidden from US media men and tourists; forget Videla and his Junta – this was the night for the football fans of Argentina and in that cauldron of sound, as more and more citizens packed the wide avenues or flung ticker-tape out of the windows of towering blocks, manager Cesar Menotti and his team had suddenly become gods of 'footee'.

Daniel found himself constantly held up in traffic jams and during these waits, when hysteria could have melted blocks of butter, I noted a certain restrained impatience in his disposition, an impatience which certainly would have boiled over had this been a routine Buenos Aires traffic foul-up. But he restrained his temper, becoming increasingly more nationalistic and passionate as we forged our way into the city centre.

During one snarl-up, as the mobs roared us on at every street corner, Julia jumped up on the open backdrop of the sedan, and invited me to join her. Soon we were waving and saluting the mobs who yelled us on, my own moustache disguising the fact that I was a mere Englishman at large in one of the biggest celebrations Buenos Aires has ever seen. The urge was to imitate Charlie Chaplin's Great Dictator, holding one's arms aloft and encouraging the unleashed cheers of a long-suffering race. Julia almost cooed with joy, and the crowds pressed nearer and nearer until they almost engulfed Daniel's motor.

We lingered, and we lingered; we lingered outside packed cafés and on the steps of fountains near Daniel's car, which he drove somewhat frenziedly on to grass curbs to park; we lingered amid all the jubilation mustered by those blue and white armies of the night; we raised more than a glass or two of Argentine wine; and, back at the Plaza, a bottle or two of champagne, to the likes of 'Fix' Ubaldo Filliol – the local goalkeeping hero, Daniel Passarella, Osvaldo Ardiles, Mario Kempes, and all the other Argentine employees of the chain-smoking Cesar Menotti due to play Holland on Sunday.

Julia and Daniel, surrounded by their rejoicing party, seemed distant now from the more restrained emotions of a passing stranger, and yet one could not condemn their patriotic celebrations. Hadn't we more reserved English danced the night away after England had won the World Cup in 1966, a night when Harold Wilson sucked on his pipe, warming to the smokescreen gained by this rare triumph when the state of the pound was critical?

Our party went on towards dawn, until we wearily split up after a last fling at a café by the River Plate, a café which during the summer would have been frequented by small children with ice-cream cones, but now harboured a company of bellowing Rambos preaching the gospel of Menotti. I slipped away, as Julia and Daniel did two days later, to their ranch outside Buenos Aires, where they would watch the final on television. 'You must come and see us. You are most welcome,' Julia called out as I piled into a taxi. 'We will win,' Daniel added, 'I know it.'

And so Argentina did, but not before extra time, and the kind of suspense which nearly led an Argentine journalist on my left into a state which required him to be lowered into a deep grave, in the peace of some urban cemetery. It happened at the end of normal time after Nanninga, a tall substitute for Rep, had headed an equalizer for Holland eight minutes from the end after his team's long trail behind Kempes's opening strike. In the final hush of activity as Holland mounted one last attack, Rensenbrink foxed the Argentine defence and planted a shot against the outside of Filliol's right-hand post. There was a sigh next to me, and my stout companion fell forward holding his head in his hands. Quickly, he was taken away by numerous first-aid men and women and I thought of what Julia had said about the state of her Buenos Aires hospital – though, almost certainly, his newspaper would give him all the welfare and privacy required if he were to escape the condition of never knowing whether his beloved country had won the World Cup or not.

I heard later that his condition was not quite as awful as it had seemed in the electric chair leading into extra time, and the victim was able to resume work again having survived a mild turn precipitated by the clanging of alarm bells caused by

Osualdo Ardiles from Buenos Aires triumphs at TO-TT-EN-HAM.

Rensenbrink's cheeky run and unlucky shot. A Dutch friend subsequently told me that the whole of Holland, from Texel to the Belgium border, had come to a stop as the ball loitered tantalisingly towards Argentina's net and then settled almost amicably against the wrong side of the post. The pent-up Dutch frustrations, which had been simmering since their national team failed to win the World Cup four years before in Munich, were ready to explode into an Orangeman's fiesta. But it never happened – Argentina went bananas in extra time and scored twice through Kempes and Bertoni. Bertoni had looked offside when he exchanged passes to score. But who was going to persuade that timid Italian referee, Signor Gonella, to blow his whistle in face of all the unrestrained provocation and nationalism of South Americans, who regarded football stadiums as their rightful place for blowing their tops in the nastiest fashion allowable from the deep caves of their palpitating throats. Signor Gonella rarely disguised his simmering nerves, and when the teams had lined up at the start, his spindly knees were literally knocking. But at least he did not appear to be drunk, as was one FA Cup referee in one Wembley final not too far away.

Mario Kempes was now hero number one, and deservedly so – as my colleague Colin Malam wrote in his book about this World Cup: 'I think it is fair to say Holland would have destroyed Argentina if they had Kempes. Not only because of his skill but because of his leadership.'

Now it was up to President Videla to hand over the magic trophy to Passarella, almost angrily shooing away a covey of armed policemen who strained to form a protective circle around members of the Junta. I wonder if he now recalls the majesty of that moment as he languishes in a prison made available for him by a new democratic socialist system. On this occasion, his almost fragile frame, topped by an ordinary tight-lipped face, acquired a military stance as if he was on parade in front of a squadron of passing cadets.

It was time now for many of the Press Corps to go home, after quickly filing their stories home. For me, there was time to linger a day or two in Rio while in transit. It was there, in that sublime city, that local mobs had burned an effigy of their manager, Claudio Coutinho, for failing to bring back the World Cup. Passions ran high, but, then, on the way home across the Atlantic, there was ample time to look back and wonder at the almost compulsive effect football has on South Americans.

In Argentina, we foreigners had been astonished by the friendly outlook of ordinary men and women going about their normal lives, an attitude they did not always convey once inside their own football stadiums. But that is all to do with football, and football is something else in South America. It was almost four years later, when Argentina were still under a military dictatorship, that I read the headlines about General Galtieri's ill-fated mounting of the Falklands War. And I thought of what Julia had said about the threat of war in the Malvinas, and the walk we had that winter morning by the River Plate.

12
Pele

It was in the sheer, hyped-up luxury of the Giants Stadium at Meadowlands, New Jersey, on a grey afternoon in October 1977 that we bade farewell to the greatest footballer ever to don a pair of boots. Edson Arantes do Nascimento, nicknamed the 'Black Pearl' and known as Pele to you and me, was bowing out from the game he adorned with such passion, grace and prodigious scoring flair.

The occasion in which his former club from Brazil, Santos, were matched against his other club, the New York Cosmos, playing on their home ground, mattered little as a contest over-awed as it was by the Meadowlands' family weepie in honour of the King. In matters like these, the Americans can be more than useful at making syrupy hype sharpen the dazzle of the tinsel, at the opening of the 1984 Olympic Games in Los Angeles, to name one classic example. Everyone was at Meadowlands that afternoon, bar Mickey Mouse and Donald Duck. It was possible to marvel at how the old-fashioned game of soccer had progressed and prospered under the auspices of the Madison Avenue ad-man.

So thorough was this nostalgic send-off in which Pele played one half each for his club sides, that an announcer made it his duty afterwards to tell all and sundry of the length of Pele's tear flow at the end of the match. 'Pele cried uncontrollably for 30 seconds. He is now recovering in a private room with his wife. He will be with you soon.'

A dark-suited Muhammad Ali, who had won a near-run world heavyweight championship fight against an unlucky Ernie Shavers at Madison Square Garden earlier in the week, crossed the Hudson River with a covey of the usual hangers-on to pay homage to Pele. He was standing formidably, large as a small skyscraper in the centre circle and then turning to Pele to administer two smacking kisses on the Brazilian's cheek. And with a slight trace of modesty, the world's greatest heavyweight added: 'PELE AND I are the greatest in the whole world.'

The crowd cheered, the crowd clapped, some of the fans cried. Pele's own tears were seldom far away – as when we talked once three years before, in his Frankfurt hotel room, when he declared what it felt like to be missing the 1974 World Cup. Immaculate in a pink sports shirt and Gatsby white slacks and gleaming casuals, his mood had become particularly sombre: 'Once in a while, watching these matches here in West Germany, I get a strong feeling, deep inside, that I want to be out there playing again. Particularly when they are doing the things I think they ought not to be doing.' There was ample evidence during that tournament that Pele might have galvanised a Brazilian team determined to play it the European way, more by kicking than skill. They had fallen in confrontation with the magic Dutch, who then blew the final in Munich against West Germany, despite the entreaties of the man Pele thought had the divine right to wear his own crown: Johan Cruyff.

It was not long after our meeting in Frankfurt that Pele decided his astounding goal tally of 1216 could be added to in the colours of New York Cosmos. It was a decision which did much to promote soccer in the United States – although the years following his retirement would prove that it takes more than resorting to such gimmicks as changing the rules of the game to suit artificial surfaces to win round an American public weaned on baseball, popcorn and the gridiron game. But still, all was not lost, and with soccer flourishing at college and high school levels, and the Olympic soccer tournament played in front of full houses in 1984, FIFA at last gave the United States the nod to stage the 1994 World Cup in their country. Pele, as the elder statesman, very much approved of that decision. The former shoeshine boy from São Paulo was now waving his Coca Cola hat as a true world missionary of soccer.

It was as 'a missionary of soccer for 22 years' that he had been described at a United Nations presentation before the Meadowlands match – as the world's leading player, he enjoyed the accolades of the world's sporting press that week in Manhattan while his friend, Ali, had to suffer the slings and arrows of wrathful columnists, not only because of his lax performance, but also his own reluctance to step down off the stage. Pele had decided enough was enough, so fine, give him a slap on the back. The guy was making a noble exit with statements like: 'That's life. Some time you've got to stop.'

Ali still had years to go, leading up to his pitiful final fight against Larry Holmes – but the warnings were there already on a day he hastened from the Waldorf Astoria hotel opposite Madison Square Garden to bid his farewell to El Rey. 'The truth is,' Red Smith wrote unkindly in the *New York Times*, 'Muhammad Ali at 35 has only one thing in common with Cassius Clay at 20 – the mouth.'

'The Mouth' did his level best to make a weeping Pele's farewell party the success it deserved, without forgetting his own entitlement to tell the whole world he was still 'the greatest'. 'Pele here is like a little boy,' he said. 'A great soccer player. Men like Pele all come to see me when they are in town.' The ringmaster, Foreman's conqueror in the rumble in the jungle in Zaire, hovered around as 353 reporters and 168 photographers clambered, not for him, but for Pele, weeping down there in the playing area. 'It's a bit crazy, isn't it?,' my old friend and *Daily Express* colleague, Jim Lawton, exclaimed. 'Walt Disney should be filming this. Where are Snow White and the Seven Dwarfs?'

Eventually Pele managed to hide his emotions which had first erupted when he scored a typical whirlwind goal from a free kick. The Black Pearl's cheeks were streaked with wet; it had been the same when he first burst on the scene at the 1958 World Cup in Sweden; it had been the same when he scored his 1000th goal.

Many of the reporters who grilled Pele and his team-mates that afternoon during the fall were girls: feminists wearing trainers, with so much to ask that El Rey began to tire rapidly. Did he wear pyjamas in bed and did he fancy yogurt or cereal for breakfast? What books would he be reading in retirement? Could he cry just once more for 'our Ernie's Rolex'? Franz Beckenbauer and other members of the Cosmos team continued to take casual showers, despite so much female presence, so intense for us limeys who were only used to seeing a pioneering Julie Welch of *The Observer* in our rustic Press boxes. 'Say, are you into junk food?' was one question sidefooted away with the reply, 'Well, I guess I chew gum.'

With a huge fiesta going on inside and outside the two dressing-rooms, it was possible on one or two occasions, when he was allowed air to breathe, to marvel at El Rey's physique, with the closely-knitted muscle, formidable thighs and legs linked to a flexible frame which had been the scourge of so many defenders. One was reminded of instances such as when Morais of Portugal in the 1966 World Cup resorted to the lowest form of tackling, which reduced Pele's legs to bleeding hunks of bruised bacon.

'That's life. Some time you've got to stop.' Memories of Pele came back, of goal-mouth wizardry seen on television and live in the simmering stadium of Mexico in 1970 when he perhaps reached his zenith in probably the most formidable international team which has ever assembled for a World Cup final. Somewhere up there, in middle-priced seats at the Aztec Stadium, Mexico City, as heavy rain turned to grey cloudy humidity and then into bright sunshine, we England supporters were left to marvel at a personal performance from Pele against Italy, which gained fire increasingly, once he had taken wing like a golden eagle to head Brazil's first goal. Much later, much later, after Italy had equalised, and Jairzinho and Gerson had regained the lead for the South Americans, Pele laid on that nonchalant rolled ball forward to his captain Carlos Alberto, who had exploded an angled shot far into the net. That was a time for firecrackers, and beating, throbbing drums. Bill, a blind Englishman who had made the trip from Surrey, sat beside me savouring it all. He really could tell when Pele had the ball at his feet: 'The vibrations sound different, a symphony of movement; with Jairzinho, you hear the pounding of his boots up the wing, with Pele, the vibrations have a meaning of their own.'

According to Bill's calculations, Pele's natural control of the ball was navigated by that awesome spring in his heels, causing vibrations which the blind man would pick up eight times out of ten. It was uncanny. But then Bill, being a fanatical football fan, was determined that his white stick would not prevent him enjoying the exploits of his beloved England. Pele he imagined to be a descendant of another hero of his youth from listening to Olympic results on his crackling wireless: Jesse Owens.

To have made the trip to Mexico to pay homage to Pele was something the average spectator with average sight could not fully comprehend – while many more belligerent Mexican hotel

The great Pele. Farewell weepie at Meadowlands, New Jersey.

staff members, weaned on the harsh way some of their brothers treated the physically handicapped south of the Border,
felt his presence a chore. It was during his last few days in
Mexico City, leading up to the final, that Bill found himself
alone in his hotel room, with only a bedside telephone to link
him with the football fiesta going on outside. In the chaos
of cactus transition from Guadalajara to the capital, he had
lost his chums, and for one day went without food through
the neglect of his hotel minders. He was eventually rescued
after getting through to the British Embassy, reunited with his
friends and taken to the great final. On my return to Mexico
City in 1986, I happened to pass the same hotel which had
been a cruel cell for Bill, but now it was a shell, obliterated by
the recent earthquake.

That extraordinary summer of 1970 seems long away, though
those of us who watched and thrilled to Pele's performances,
and, in Bill's case, sat and listened, can still tune into our
flickering memory sets of sights and sounds, like Pele strum-
ming a guitar at his team headquarters outside Guadalajara, or
mesmerising the Uruguayan defence with an eel-like, one-touch
run, which just failed to make the goal of all-time.

Perhaps those who admired Pele most of all were his immediate opponents, like Bobby Charlton: 'It was impossible to pigeon-
hole Pele. He was certainly a great goalscorer, the most prolific
of his time. But he could also create, organise and inspire.
Eyes set remarkably wide in a strong face accounted for the
extraordinary extent of his vision. Only five feet seven inches
tall, he gave the impression of being much larger in the colours
of his country or Santos.'

England's favourite footballer had been only too aware, often
in opposition, of Pele's powerful muscles which 'provided him
with murderous pace and his imagination, allied to great natural gifts, never failed to thrill. Pele invented ways to play the
game. . .'

Charlton's views summed up the true abilities of a genius who
began his football career kicking a bundle of socks around in
the town of Bauru, round the corner from the port of Santos.
This emerging genius had begun to flower under the light of a
Brazilian moon as Pele – a nickname which when translated
means that long-abandoned Edwardian expression 'urchin' –
began to knit his own inventions by coaxing a ball of greasy
wool.

At Meadowlands, on that famous farewell day, it was still possible to identify him with the heroes of kings, presidents, popes, dictators, prime ministers and presidents with such humble but exciting origins. As Pele sat, looking almost boyish despite impending retirement, his reluctant words rang out clear for the world to hear: 'That's life. Some time you've got to stop.'

13

'Is this what they call an Irish Joke?'

The centre back of AC Milan and Italy stood naked in the showers, shaking from what could best be termed a fit of the giggles. Romeo Benetti held his head back and let a thin drip of lukewarm water, courtesy of the nearby River Shannon, drip into his mouth and plop hesitantly into a pair of formidable dragon's nostrils. His giggles increased so that the wooden walls of the dressing-room groaned from the vibrations. We observers, pressed around him because there was not enough room inside to welcome a single donkey, laughed as well because we had witnessed an afternoon's entertainment in deepest Ireland far away from the swank opulence of AC Milan's San Siro Stadium, far away from the expansive boulevards and highways of northern Italy, and far away from the luxury dressing-rooms Benetti was used to every week in Serie A football.

Benetti grabbed a towel and moved a yard or two into a tiny, steamy stall where some of his team-mates were tearing off their soggy, boggy, stripey kit, their boots caked with the type of bog mud only an Irish playing field can unleash on a visiting innocent. The Italian Press piled after him, wild with rapid questions the Irish media could not understand but reckoned they knew the gist of. The man from the *Irish Independent*, who could speak a bit of Italian, having dallied there once as a Rome correspondent, was soon telling us what they were saying, letting loose a caustic Blarney laugh as he did so.

'For Jazus sake,' he mocked, scribbling a line or two in a prodigiously sized notebook. 'They're asking Benetti why the Danish referee didn't give them proper protection against the Irish heathen. They want Benetti to say the Danish referee stank. But he can't stop laughing because he says the whole thing

143

was a pissing joke and they'll murder poor old Athlone back in Milan.'

The fact that mighty AC Milan did take on the humble Irish side, Athlone, by the banks of the Shannon one damp autumn afternoon, had to do with the magic of the UEFA Cup draw which demanded that this improbable event take place. The venue at St Mel's Park might normally have seen a scattering of fans to witness a pedestrian afternoon of Irish League football; but the visit of the Italian party unleashed an almost frenzied display of Blarney anticipation in which discipline, once heavily enforced when the town was a British garrison in Victorian times, totally vanished as grown men sang in the streets and grown women sank more than the pint or two of Guinness which they might normally have consumed in a lunch hour.

I had travelled by train across Ireland from Dublin on the morning of the match, in company with a Gucci-attired band of Milan supporters. We were chatting in the bar of the orange and black train when it suddenly bumped to a halt in open countryside, supremely green and affluent.

'You'd best be comin' away from the windows,' an arriving ticket inspector barked. 'You don't want to get shod, do you? Bless me now. They're out there, and they've got their sights on you.'

'Shot?'

'Yes, young man, shod.'

The Italians were nonplussed, until the inspector kindly told them in strong Blarney, much of which they did not understand, that the house we could see 800 yards away was being controlled by terrorists who had kidnapped an unfortunate Dutch businessman. It was the subject of major headlines in our newspapers, and police could be seen ringing the house, from our advanced outpost. There was a reluctant move away from the nearside windows, our thoughts once reverted to the budding football match now directed towards a man in distress. There was no explanation as to why the train had stopped, though a police Land Rover, passing through a level crossing, seemed a likely explanation. We remained in the direct line of fire from the silent farm for some time, then lurched forward towards Athlone, where a state of beery mayhem was under way when we arrived.

Having booked into Athlone's most plush hotel, I joined the company of the great grandsons of military ostlers in sizing up the chances of their beloved football team against the San Siro aristocrats.

'Oi say, we be lucky to escape a drubbin'. And what about another point, then?'

'Go on, Kerry,' a friend said to a speckled ruby nose. 'There's a saying in this part of the world that there's no place like Mayo to bring yer down a peg, even if you are so flamin' high and mighty.'

'Well, go on then. But it'll take a couple of goals from our Tony Daly to do the trick.'

Tony Daly, may I explain, was Athlone's local football hero, a dribbler with the looks of George Best and an ability to run rings round a covey of wide-hipped, cumbersome full backs.

A reporter from *Corriere della Sera* emerged from the bar to tell me in a tone, somewhere between a chuckle and a sneer, that a star Athlone player would not be turning out; he had to stay home and milk his cows. This turned out on later investigation to be entirely untrue, but it must have read well over coffee in the Vatican.

Now on my way by foot over soft meadows to Athlone Town's wooden hut stadium, I soon regretted not having purchased a pair of wellies used by anglers to fish by the Shannon. The surface we plodded over, keeping well to the duck-boarded pathway, resembled yellow porridge, creating a Daliesque scene. One spruce Milanese accidentally put a shiny Gucci shoe smack into the middle of a juicy cowpat. The Athlone pipe band was in full, cheek-puffing swing, as the crowds rolled up to join the fun, and there were 10000 on parade that famous day. Some kind Athlone official had cut down a hawthorn hedge to provide more room for the fans, who crowded the sidelines, baying their contempt for the Italians as they ambled out into the mud to warm up. Their goalkeeper, the gangling Albertosi, who had seen far more spacious surroundings as an international custodian, earned a fair whack of Blarney scorn as he stretched down to pick up the first arriving practice ball. He let it slither through his fingers into the net, and my yelling neighbour sprang on Albertosi's apparent aimlessness with total scorn: 'Warm up boyo – you're going to get more than a few to tickle 'ee.'

The barely disguised cynicism of captain Benetti and his team-mates mounted as Athlone tore at them like members of

the Light Brigade. Many an unfortunate Irishman, that afternoon, found himself dumped into the mud by violent means,
pausing to taste the grime of a murky Blarney afternoon. A
strong wind blew in off the Shannon, which didn't help matters,
but mighty Milan were ill-prepared for a sudden decision by
the Danish referee, Henning Lun-Sorenson, to award Athlone
a penalty before half-time. Scala was the culprit for fouling the
tricky Daly, though plainly the rest of the Milan side felt the
Dane had suffered a touch of the bacon, and chastised him
verbally. The swarthy Benetti was a picture of malice, his red-
dish cheeks bulging like a jay's with an egg in its mouth.

'Get on wid it, then. Go home, you Eyeties! Go on, there.' The
home crowd, though delighted to have a home penalty in their
midst, resented the delay. Meanwhile, some of us from the Press
Corps made for Albertosi's net where the penalty execution was
to take place. The wind blew stronger and the ground grew
squelchier. John Minnock looked paler as he prepared to take
the kick. For a moment, he seemed in two minds what to do after
placing the ball on the spot. Did he yearn for an afternoon's sea
fishing off Galway, or the sanctuary of a cosy village bar? Soon
he must have done because with one aimless stride and kick, he
shot limply out of harm's way.

Minnock's wasted kick sent the Italian green overcoat and
fur coat brigade thronging the little stand like members of a
Tzar's railway carriage exploring the sticks, into an avalanche
of titters. Minnock, the unfortunate Minnock, was singled out
for abuse like a tenth-rate opera singer at La Scala. And on the
pitch, the swarthy Benetti could hardly suppress a backhand
chuckle as the ball was placed by Albertosi for a harmless
goal-kick.

To the Athlone crowd, Benetti was arch-villain number one,
and one of his bludgeoning tackles on a winded opponent sent
St Mel's Park into a frenzy of rage. The Danish referee, so kind,
so diplomatic to one and all, spared Romeo the red card, which
prompted a large wink directed at the Milan bench becalmed
on a mudflat. Athlone, too, were hardly angels, and the home
captain, John Duffy, somehow survived after a wild boar lunge.
In truth, the AC Milan players did not bother too much, because
they knew they would win the return leg comfortably, which
they did, although only by a modest three goals. A goal for
Athlone would have been a treat, but though they performed
heroically at times, there was always a feeling that Benetti and

Italy's World Cup star, Romeo Benetti.

company could contain them through tactics more brutal than fair.

The referee was given an abusive reception as he left the pitch afterwards, enemy of both teams and both sets of supporters who were waving walking sticks, umbrellas, soiled tweed caps and hip flasks in their disgust. The Dane slipped quietly away with his linesmen to a sanctuary safe from the mob, to await the next morning's train to Dublin. Most of the rest of us descended on Molloy's Bar in the heart of Athlone where the home team were to host a party, which wasn't quite a wake, but by two weeks' time would have been.

'Those Milans were tapping their heads and telling me I was crazy,' captain Duffy reflected from an outpost on the bar. 'They were saying I was an Irish cowman, and I didn't deserve to be playing a team like theirs. Roit, I thought, I'll take you for that, and I did, roit up the arse.'

'But now, John, you had a great match, that you did,' a friend pointed out letting the froth of his Guinness pile up on a pair of two piacular lips.

'I said to their interpreter after that we wanted police protection in Milan,' Duffy added. 'Otherwise we'll get one hell of a kicking. It stands to reason, like, that they'll want their revenge, if you could call it revenge for the way we went at 'em. Shook 'em up, we did. 'Twas a pity we missed the penalty, it was a roit blow to us.'

The Milan team had made off by coach, winking all the way to Shannon Airport. Their own newspapers next morning would not only mock the Blarney setting at St Mel's Park, but hurl abuse at the Danish referee. 'The Milan players were offered to the lynch mob of Athlone under the couldn't-care-less gaze of the Danish referee. . .' But there was no fear now for Benetti and company as they flew away into an autumn sunset. The rich pickings lay further on, beyond the second leg; although, as time would tell, Milan would not reach the UEFA final that season, FC Bruges knocking them out before losing to Bob Paisley's Liverpool in the final.

At the Athlone supporters' club dance, later that evening, a large proportion of the whirling inmates were in acute danger of becoming inebriated on stout, chased by buckets of Irish whisky. Somewhere in the jogging throng, I ran into Terry Daly, Athlone's wizard of dribble, modestly reappraising a match in which he had constantly worried the renowned Milan defence.

Yes, he did look a bit like George Best, with his longish locks and jaunty stance, but far less guarded in his appraisal of a match which could have become a bloodbath. 'They were hard all right,' he said, enjoying the sight of a freshly emerging pint. 'They were hard, indeed. They kept whispering at me about seeing to me in Milan. I had to laugh. They were whispering all the time. Whisper, whisper, whisper. That Benetti couldn't stop talking, and it wasn't a captain's lingo.'

The next morning, a blustery, grey Shannon morning in County Mayo, I met up with the Danish referee on the Athlone platform. Having read the Irish press reaction, I felt I should offer him some protection just in case an Irish dowager in a gig rode up to give the unfortunate man a good horsewhipping. The donnish-looking Dane had not bothered to pick up a newspaper at the kiosk – and who could blame the poor fellow. There were headlines on the back pages with long quotes from the Athlone manager, Amby Fogarty, blaming the referee.

'The referee should pack his bags and go home and forget all about the game of soccer. His handling of the game was disappointing, to say the least. He should have sent off four of the Italians. I was like an altar boy in my day compared to what the Italian players got away with. We knew they would be tough but we didn't expect the treatment we got. They were more suited to a rugby pitch or a boxing ring.'

I joined the Dane for a coffee on the way to Monasterevin – where the Dutch captive was still imprisoned behind a solid Irish wall. After we had again been warned to keep our heads down which Mr Lun-Sorensen for a moment thought had something to do with his own retreat from the Emerald Isle, he spoke candidly about how it felt to be out there in the cauldron of a ground no bigger than a greenhouse.

The Dane looked very like a visiting don at Trinity College, Dublin, as he analysed an afternoon which had given him an infinite amount of trouble. 'Both teams are entitled to their opinions,' he reflected, as the Curragh Racecourse surged past in oceans of rolling green. 'But I handled the game as I thought it should be handled. It wasn't an easy game to referee by any means – and you can say I am mighty relieved that a Romanian is refereeing the return. Take that Benetti on the Milan side. He has played many times for Italy and he should have known better because he is a class player. He and his team got up to many tricks again, as they usually do, but had I blown for every trick, it would not have been to Athlone's advantage. I could really have sent four or five players off – but that would not have made it a game, would it?'

As we shook hands on the platform in Dublin, the Dane smiled, a little reservedly, as if longing for the peace of a pint in a Cophenhagen ale-house, with only the lilt of 'Wonderful, Wonderful Copenhagen' booming from a street organ to disturb his peace. 'You know, this was the most extraordinary game I have ever refereed, the atmosphere was tremendous.'

He sauntered away to find a taxi to the airport, Irish gremlins from the news-stand headlines haunting him all the way.

14

Pride for Dad, Sardines for Mum

I had ridden over the causeway at Faro in a jolting taxi, feeling tired and edgy after a sleepless night in the Algarve capital. Left-wing fanatics, who had taken over the town hall, had regaled all and sundry through crackling loud-speakers. This being post-revolutionary Portugal, there was a Marxist urgency about these constant declarations wafting over the waters of the port towards my dawn-lit, cosy hotel room.

It was a relief to leave Faro and make for the ocean where our tiny-tot Fulham football team, Chalham, were camping out on the beach with manager, John hinds, and assistant, Dave Banks. The smell of bacon and eggs wafted over to me as I left the taxi and trudged towards the camp-site. John and Dave were the acting, unpaid chefs.

'Morning, commander,' John said, lifting a long streak of glistening bacon off a sizzling mobile barbecue slab. 'Good night in town?' His tone suggested I had spent most of it battering my kneecaps in a sleazy disco. 'You bet he has,' Dave added quizzically.

'I had a quiet night,' I replied. 'At least I thought it would be – a quick dinner, a few drinks in the hotel bar, and early to kip. Then I went out into the central square for a walk. The armoured cars were out protecting some moderate Government officers. They threw a captain out of the windows of the town hall, and he broke his leg. Then the armoured cars turned their turrets on the onlookers. We ran. I've never run so fast; well not since a bull spotted me in Normandy. A woman kept telling me they were going to open fire. It was like running with the bulls in Pamplona. People were screaming and shouting. But

151

they didn't shoot in the end. Mind you, the left-wing buggers are still in the town hall.'

'Well, you better have some breakfast, commander,' John answered, playing down my recent adventures as if they were no more than rush-hour at Waterloo. 'We've got a game on here, revolution or no revolution. The boys are out on the beach training. Call 'em in, Dave.'

'Come on, you lot!' Dave roared towards the thunder of the surf, 'Grub's up!'

The Fulham boys, aged between 11 and 13, came loping off the beach after their early morning practice match, their hair windswept, their fresh-faced features speckled with Faro sand, their eyes spread to the novelty of their new environment. As a visiting scribe on a short recce to the Algarve, I was treated by the boys as a kind of mystical pastor met on a wagon voyage across the Prairie, someone of immense age who should be treated with reserved respect. As for John, manager in chief, and Dave, general nanny, cook, babysitter, camp supervisor and referee, they were the ones to listen to, to obey, respect and honour the rules of the trip based around the kicking of a football.

We tucked into Dave's solid English breakfast, the wind off the ocean blowing our hair into twisted, tufted knots. The boys ate with gusto, jangling their eating irons and spreading creamy egg round their insatiable lips. Before leaving on the tour which John had arranged through the sponsorship of British Airways and the Portuguese Tourist Board, still yearning for visitors after the disturbing effects of the Revolution, the boys' parents had been given clear instructions about the gear to send along with the lads: no bovver boots or stupid gear; football kit – West Ham shirt, white shorts, white socks; other items included plastic soup bowls, pyjamas and dressing gowns. Also in the package were packets of frozen beefburgers, sausages and bacon, chewing gum and a good selection of comics including *Beano* and *Roy of the Rovers*.

The soccer-boppers of Chalham FC had every reason to feel excited from the moment they stepped down from the steps of the TriStar at Faro Airport; few, if any, had been abroad before; some, coming from under-privileged families, had never left the Metropolis. One of them told me brashly, as he scoffed his fried bread: 'I ain't been nowhere before, mate.' It was difficult not to believe him – those long, unending summer holidays spent roaming weedy, open urban sites for a place to play football; days spent loitering outside cafés, betting shops and pubs waiting for dad to come out and give out a good clip on the earhole. Then along comes 'Father' Hinds with a chance trip of a lifetime – it was, so to speak, 'real magic, mate'.

Hinds took the boys off later for another busy tactical talk while I helped Dave clear up the cookhouse, army style. 'One or two of the lads have been homesick already,' Dave said. 'They wanted mum, and their teddy bears. Real shame. It made me almost want to cry. Bloody hell, can you see me crying?'

'Not really, Dave. It's not really your theme in life.'

We strolled over to join John's party busily and clamorously going through a one-two passing exercise. When a ball broke loose, I broke into a walk to return the leather to the circle.

'Take it easy, commander,' John shouted. 'We might need you as sub.'

'No fear.'

'Go on, it's better than being shot at.'

We stayed on the beach until it was time for the coach to arrive. In the best tradition of post-revolutionary Portugal, the coach was half an hour late. By which time, John was fretting about the uncertainties which lay ahead. 'I haven't got a clue who we're playing, or where we're going. The courier just says to allow him to direct the coach driver somewhere over there towards the Spanish border, and they'll give us snacks at a nearby café.'

I asked the courier if the opposition were going to be under 13 and he just shrugged. 'Wait and see'.

We drove around in circles skirting the same areas of Faro three or four times until we reached the Farense Stadium, glistening white under a warm autumn sun. There were few signs of the disruptions I had witnessed the night before, most of the post-revolutionary citizens relieved to go about their businesses in peace, without fear of the former dictator Salazar's secret police. Clusters of camouflaged troops, with bristly chins and long hair under their brown berets, gave a hint of the recent upheavals which had sent so many British restaurateurs and landlords packing, back to Blighty. And where were all those ardent golfers now, who had packed every green with a hole in it over recent years? Their scampering figures in union with local caddies were all too obviously missing.

When we alighted from the coach, there was a scramble among the boys to seek out the dressing-rooms. But John and the courier signalled that snacks were laid on at a café over the road, where tables had been booked by the Tourist Board. The scramble now was for beefburgers and coke, and to hell with the running to follow. Dave raised a glass of beer in the homely café where a plump lady owner fussed diligently over the welfare of the soccer-boppers. 'A referee is not the same without a pint,' he said, with evident satisfaction. 'I've polished up the red card in case any of those Portos get shirty.'

When we got back to the stadium, the shirts of the senior team, which had been given a hard time the previous Sunday against Benfica, were hanging from a clothes' line in the car park. It has often amused me on visits to the stadiums of top teams in faraway countries to see their welfare conducted on the most austere levels possible. Once, in Romania, out in the sticks where Count Dracula loved to roam in the blackness of night, I saw a group of peasant women ironing the strip of a First Division football team with what looked like their bare hands.

A wiry man approached me, and grabbing my hand, asked if I knew Billy Wright. He said he had played against Billy in some friendly match a while ago. 'A wonderful man, a wonderful captain.' And I thought of Billy when he was manager of Arsenal at the famous seat of Highbury, where you definitely don't see washing hanging on the line.

When Chalham eventually ran out into the arena two hours later, there were 1000 fastidious and gregarious Portuguese spectators to clap them on. Our Fulham boys looked tiny, and when goalkeeper Graham Walker took his place between the posts, the goal looked the size of Marble Arch. It was quite alarming when the Faro youth selection came out, because they surely had disregarded the under-13 rule set by Hinds. Some of the swarthy players towered up towards six foot and the goal-keeper must have had his first razor the previous Christmas.

'It's the prestige business,' Dave commented acidly, now adorned with a magnificent referee's outfit gleaming black and white under the sun. 'Look at their keeper. He's got hairy legs. He drove up in a Jaguar with his girlfriend.'

In the event, the Chalham boys did remarkably well, losing by only three goals and putting their stocky frames about with bravery and guts. Goalkeeper Walker was given a double ration of sweets afterwards for pulling off a string of saves which the sporting Portuguese applauded loudly. The Portuguese players were a strong bunch, which was not surprising, because they were generally a head higher than their opponents. But they felt the pygmy stings of some of their rivals' tackles, and Dave Banks once or twice nearly had to produce the yellow card.

After the match, as the boys made for the communal bath, I was surrounded by some admiring Portuguese who were anxious to talk about the performance of Chalham's vice captain, Anthony Wilson. Anthony had played a colossal part in his team's honourable defeat, and it was significant that while the rest of his team were chattering in the dressing-room, he slumped exhausted in a corner.

Anthony came from a footballing family: his brother Robert played for Fulham Schoolboys and elder brother Patrick for Watford Juniors. Robert eventually went on to play for Fulham and Millwall. Anthony, with his long blond hair and slim build, was endowed with the gifts of a natural player. But now he occupied himself with the delights of a candy bar.

John Hinds, being a fastidious manager when it comes to running a youth team, was not entirely happy with some of his players, whom he accused of shirking their duties. 'That Delroy, he's tall and flashy and gifted, but he won't work hard enough,' John said caustically, as our coach took us back to the beach. 'A big Portuguese bloke was comparing him with Pele, but he was too often knocked off the ball. Delroy's got to work harder in the five-a-side tomorrow.'

'There was quite a lot of needle,' Dave reflected, contemplating the large seafood banquet we had been invited to by the Tourist Board that night, with a barely suppressed lick of the lips. 'There was that Ali brute of a left back the Portuguese had. His knees were like burning bushes. Almost gave him the red card on one occasion, then thought, I don't want a post-revolutionary lynching on my hands, or round my neck.'

The Chalham boys did very well in the five-a-side competition along the coast at Albufeira, winning their match by nine goals. Hinds was particularly pleased because his son Jonathan, an ardent Sunday footballer in years to come, was exceptional. Father had said a great deal from the line that night. 'Use the open spaces, you lot – pass,' while his rival on the bench held his head in his hands, almost weeping, as Chalham goals rattled in.

The Chalham boys, who had little chance previously of leaving the asphalt jungles of south-west London, enjoyed their first taste of orange trees, juniper bushes and a trip out in a colourful

Algarve fishing boat. Their own pocket money was spent on buying toy fishing boats, and cans of sardines for Mum. By the time I bade the group 'adieu' and made for the airport, peace had returned to Faro, with the left-wing extremists nowhere to be seen. As tiny tot ambassadors, the youngsters of Chalham had been far more popular.

15
Karen

Karen told her mates she was a refugee from south London; abandoned as a baby outside a Tooting phone box before dawn by a distressed mother 16 years her senior, whose casual liaison with 'flash' Ted after a Dave Clark Five concert had led to an unwelcome pregnancy.

The abandoned child had grown up in foster care, unruly and disruptive from the time she left the cradle. Karen's early appetite for violence was revealed when she clawed the face of a female social worker who had accused her of using foul language. Her schooling was equally tempestuous, geared to running away from the foster home on a number of occasions and landing up eventually with custodial sessions in Borstal. Eventually, the King's Cross area of London opened its seedy, destructive arms to a shaven-headed kid with an army combat jacket, rough jeans and hefty bovver boots, looking like a boy and wanting desperately to be one.

In other circumstances, she might have succumbed to a life of drug peddling in the West End, or joining those many new volunteers attached to members of the world's oldest profession. Karen wasn't interested, however, in either of these escape routes; in her world of petty thievery, she had one burning desire – to conquer the male domination of soccer hooliganism and become, if not the leader, a queen bee, with enough sting loaded in her fists to create havoc on Saturday afternoons.

'It was all I ever wanted to be. Join the Leeds Inter-City gang,' she muttered to me once during our meetings on the fast upline express to Leeds on Saturday mornings. Her presence as a gatecrasher in the first-class section always made one feel distinctly uneasy and uncomfortable; the round, bullet-like, intrusive head, and pouting lips painted the palest of pinks, screwed on to a flamboyant Leeds scarf. Her bovver boots would be thrust ominously on to the opposite seat without concern for a fellow passenger looking nervously towards the communication switch. Karen would emerge from the buffet car clutching a can of lager, because alcohol was still allowed during that era in the late 1970s, leaving some of her boy pals to make it a liquid sleigh ride into Yorkshire.

Karen's devotion to Leeds was not what one might have expected – surely Chelsea, with an escalating and unpleasant record of violence from an expanding hooligan fringe, or Millwall, with a fan club happy to confirm they had started football hooliganism in the first place, might have secured her primed devotion. But asked why Leeds, instead of these two London teams, she would sneer: 'Chelsea, shit; Millwall, shit; Leeds, inferno – Leeds inferno.'

But how did this inferno begin, this passion which sometimes made this adolescent swell into a belligerent, pouting, tit-beating, prospective maimer or even killer? Her knowledge of the tactics of soccer, or its long history, was almost non-existent, and she only had the vaguest idea of where the city of Leeds was anyway: somewhere on a vague line from London to the North Pole; somewhere a long way away from the team she hated most, Manchester United.

Passing meadows and hedgerows, horses and cows, church steeples and canals, brooks and woods, ploughed fields and rooks, made no impression on Karen. She would sit, staring at her lager can and telling all who would listen about her battle plans for the day ahead. It was not the game of soccer she was interested in – she professed once that she hardly watched 'the fuckin' ball being kicked 'cos I wanta kick one of them near me' – but rather the aggro dramas before, during and after the match. Taken along by a Leeds fan she had met late one night outside King's Cross Station as a reward for allowing him to bite her left ear, she had never looked back. Leeds had apparently won a contest against some Arsenal fans on her first ride and Karen blessed the day she had taken up this new hobby. She kept in her jeans' pocket two fragments of an Arsenal supporter's tooth booted on to a dog-fouled Leeds pavement.

Karen's tenures in the first-class area were only brief, if duty policemen were on the train; but often on the return journey she would survive all the way, regaling her audiences with tales of blood and thunder, and broken heads. 'They've put me off the train, at Peterborough mostly. Took my boots away once. Had to walk a mile, then two blokes picked me up and drove me to London. Had to nick a new pair of boots.'

'Why did they put you off the train?'

'I kicked a Paki woman right here. She was preg. She screamed. Some shitty bloke reported me. They put me off the train. But I hurt the Paki. Normally, I don't kick women, but I kick women Pakis. The boys like kicking the Pakis, 'specially the Pakis in Birmingham. You just pick 'em off. Then turn their shops over. It's great.'

These statements were delivered to shock, and they certainly offended numerous elderly ladies and weekending couples trying to hide their gazes sheepishly behind their newspapers. The arrival of the ticket collector on upward journeys would prove their salvation – Karen would be escorted back to the second-class area, grumbling oaths. The sight of random fields passing, acted as calming therapy against Karen's hostile world – I and my colleagues knew that what awaited beyond Leeds Station was a battleground in the mile or so of walking space that lay to Elland Road.

Karen's battle plan, discussed with her pals in the buffet car, was to try and break away from the wary eye of the law in Leeds City Centre and create as much havoc as possible with anyone connected to the visiting team who dared display their scarves in alien urban territory. Sometimes the fighting would begin on the up-train itself, if there were no police on duty and the London branch of Manchester United with their long hair and leather jackets sussed out that there were some 'Leeds scum' on board. Karen loved these pre-match scuffles in which she could select her targets through a periscope of brooding animosity, the victim caught later in a station toilet with his jeans halfway down and ready for a fierce kick in the groin. Karen never let the 'GENTS ONLY' sign prevent her from barging ferociously forward like Joan of Arc, going into the breach with her mates, with more than a taste of English blood on her lips.

'Why do you enjoy all this violence? What can possibly be gained by hurting other people?' a colleague asked Karen almost sheepishly, one rampaging night when the Leeds fan club had taken over three-quarters of the first-class section. Karen and her colleagues were hanging over us, waving their programmes like opera fans as they 'fuckity, fuckited' their sentences in relation to a nasty bit of butchery at Littletown Lane near Elland Road.

'Well, mate, it's a kind of magic kicking other supporters, especially if they're fat. The boot goes in more easily, see. There was a fat bloke at Stoke, we got 'im on the ground and the geezer was screaming for mercy. Kept kicking 'im and kicking 'im and a bit of blood came out of his mouth. It was like red honey.'

'But why, for God's sake, why?'

"Cause we're Leeds fans and we're the best, and it's our manor, and shit on the other teams who go there. Shit on 'em.'

'I remember the Stoke shit,' one of Karen's pals added, picking up my colleague's pink football edition, rolling it up and banging the paper down on our table. 'We got 'im in a corner and shut his gob for 'im. He wouldn't forget that bashing. It bust his gob.'

'The fuzz came up eventually, but we got away. Heard later it was a hospital job,' Karen said. 'That was the time I got this brick on the terraces and cut a bloke's head almost in 'alf.'

'She's a real raver, Karen, when she gets going,' another male fan added, with suitable aplomb.

'Yea, I'm full-time now. No time for nuffink else. Saturday and Leeds, Leeds and Saturdays.'

The trouble was that the majority of the Leeds fellers could never really accept Karen as anything more than an egregious stranger from the world of Oz who, by being a girl, could never really be accepted into the clan. The more outrageous her behaviour became, the more they closed ranks and encouraged her to stalk alone. A few of the more mindless elements worshipped this bullet-headed freak, never daring to suggest that there was more to this world than knocking people about – like for instance going out to the cinema, or a disco, or having it off on Dad's sofa, or simply walking along a canal bank hand in hand and minding one's own business. 'It was a bit of a liberty having her around,' one Leeds fan observed, after she had suddenly and mysteriously disappeared off the rail scene. 'We usually do the aggro bit for a bit of a giggle, but that tart was different – she was a real vampire, a bit of a witch, that cunt. She wanted blood. In a war, she'd be a raving killer. No prisoner, she. She didn't know the difference between a football and a pingpong ball, but she knew all about busted bollocks. And not blow-job busted either. She was loony.'

'Where did she go?'

'Dunno, mate, somebody said she packed up and went Bristol-ways. They've got some right daft supporters down there, I can tell you. All that cider shit. The smell stays on you all week after giving 'em a going over.'

Karen's world, as far as we were concerned, lay the other side of the ticket barriers dividing King's Cross and Leeds from the iron railroad. It was in and out of the urban alleyways that she thrived on her brutal missions – but sometimes, the game backfired on her, and she would take a beating, proudly exposing a raspberry-coloured graze on the train home. A trace of dried blood showed where her enemy's boot had sliced through her defences.

'You better watch that.'

'What? It's nuffink.'

Karen's devotion to Leeds arrived when they were on an irrevocable slide towards the Second Division, a weary conveyor belt of managers after the departure of Jimmy Armfield, including Jimmy Adamson and that old scoring hero, Allan Clarke failing to prevent the inevitable. Revie's glory days had long gone, and adding to the despondency came an increasing penchant for violence and racial abuse from a section of the supporters. Karen eagerly tagged along, but her knowledge and love for the game remained a barren subsidiary to her cantankerous daydreams.

'Leeds got a useful point today,' I might say, engulfed a few feet across the carriage aisle by her bott-straggling presence. 'They should have won in the second half.'

'We woz robbed,' Karen stuttered. 'We had those United fans fish-sliced across the barrier, coins, ballbearings, can tops, I gotta bit of brick, then the fuzz broke us up, the bastards. But we licked 'em, the shits, in the city centre after.'

'But shouldn't Eddie Gray have scored from close range? He only had Bailey to beat. Leeds can't afford to miss chances like that.'

'What?'

'Tickets, please. Laddie, this is only a second-class ticket. I would ask you to move, please.'

'The sod thinks I'm a boy,' Karen said in triumph, moving sulkily back to her friends.

Karen could sometimes display her childish insecurities, and even, if only occasionally, a certain sweetness that lurked somewhere deeply camouflaged within. Once, when a pert Harrogate spinster was having trouble in controlling her poodle, Karen moved in and picked up the springy, woolly, vaguely stupid, yapping canine and deposited it on the top of her denim covered thighs. Somewhat alarmed, the matron made no protest; in no time, the poodle called Kooky, settled down in the presence of such a comforting stranger. We had to laugh. In those moments of near domestic bliss, before the roar of blood and thunder between overweight men and one girl on the terraces, Karen looked as if she had just given birth to a bouncy baby, the poodle staring up at this round bullet head lulled by a pair of pale blue eyes, tinted vaguely red, with an underling's respect.

'Always dug dogs,' Karen said, as the poodle almost swooned with pleasure. 'That's why I never kick those fuzz dogs. Even when they try and bite my legs. They seem to calm down anyways when they sees me. I had a little dog once called Whistle – a boy gave it to me for Christmas, but I had to give it away – moving all the time, see.'

It was to be hoped that Karen's sudden disappearance from the railroad show meant good things – perhaps she had met a young soldier outside King's Cross, and been wooed away westward to some married quarters in Wiltshire or Northern Ireland, following a whirlwind romance, a baby soon to follow, a wee pug dog to escort on trips to Tescos; in many ways, an improbable prospect, but one could only hope.

As it was, the duty police seemed to know all about Karen's suspect side – and some of her enforced absences probably meant she was being confined by Her Majesty's law officers for a short, sharp duration behind bars. 'She's a bit of a nut-case,' a plumpish policeman said once on the way to Leeds. 'We've turned her off the train many times for causing trouble. She's been in and out of trouble for years. She just can't settle. But who knows, there's always a silver lining.'

So Karen continued with her passion which began as Elland Road slipped by and the train ambled on to slip warily into Leeds Station. The city of Leeds – her shrine, her battleground, her excuse for the big wallop, the gross insult to unsuspecting alien supporters. By the time we scribes had alighted on the platform, shoulders slightly hunched in our mackintoshes as a form of defence mechanism geared to the perils of hooligan aggravation, deadlines, rationed telephones and taxis, Karen had gone her own way to scavenge for some lurking Lancastrian hiding behind an office refuse bin.

The secret, as far as Karen and her mob members were concerned, was to skirt the police-escorted visiting support-ers, lumbering along in a column towards Elland Road, then administer an unwelcome greeting through boots and knuckles by infiltrating the forbidden zone on the terraces. The reverse happened at away matches, when the Leeds fans found them-selves being marched to their own private cage, the taunts of Manchester United fans providing all the provocation the visitors needed. Karen enjoyed her battles in the London Under-ground with rival Arsenal, Spurs and Chelsea fans, she thrilled to these skirmishes, these flurries of hate conducted up and down the escalators.

'Wankers, wankers! We love Leeds, we do, we do. United are wankers, Leeeds great. Ooooooooo! Who's that black-faced United bastard, nigger shit? Throw 'im a banana!' The terraces were Karen's chapel, she worshipped the noise and the tension, the bust of cantankerous lung power, a sudden expedition by an enemy seeking to gain glory by breaching the rival zone. The crowds on the terrace would be parted suddenly to form a revolving hole, and then the police would go in and drag out the culprits. We reporters kept talking into our phones, trying to concentrate on what was going on in the match. If Karen did not return, she had probably been slung in the cells for the night.

Karen's short reign of terror in a Leeds scarf ended, from our point of view, around the time the Yorkshire club toppled into the Second Division. Trips to Elland Road became less frequent now that the club, as far as the national press was concerned, had lost its way and was worth only a quarter of a column on the sports pages.

The violent scenes witnessed regularly at Elland Road during Karen's epoch were generally suppressed, following the Heysel Stadium riot in 1985, when new laws relating to the banning of booze at football grounds and stricter control by police inside and outside grounds, not to mention 'dry' trains, and police galore trailing up and down the carriage aisles with their own form of mine detectors bent on rustling out a naughty individual sipping an illicit can. If she had remained on the scene, Karen would have found the going far less groovy from a point of view of making trouble. But I thought of her only the other day when a BBC news flash came over that 21 Leeds fans had been arrested after a disturbance in Littletown Lane, near Elland Road, following a Second Division match against Chelsea. The Chelsea fans had been kept behind 'for their own safety'. Maybe in some faraway urban ghetto, the news might have filtered through to housewife Karen, now approaching the tender age of 30.

Could the news have stirred up memories of Saturday thuggery for this former yeowoman of the North Stand? Perhaps as she struggled downstairs with a basket full of soiled nappies, her memory went back to the days when she sprayed an impressive message on a brick wall in the same Littletown Lane:

KILLER KAREN LEEDS FC WOZ ERE.

16
Gastronomy – Ipswich-style

You could tell the chairman and a platoon of directors had eaten well by the way they chuckled and pulled at their bulging belts when they entered the hotel foyer. Patrick Cobbold and his tweedy Suffolk team had been treated to a veritable *grande bouffe* at the renowned Frères Trois Gros three-star restaurant at Roanne before Ipswich took on St Etienne in the first leg of a UEFA Cup quarter final at the Geoffroy-Guichard Stadium.

It was one of those flying visits, back in 1981, when the delights of grand French cuisine bestrode the actual reason for being in St Etienne, which was to watch a challenging football match. While chairman Patrick and brother, John, could genially boast that they had been through a menu consisting of *Escalope de saumon à l'oseille* and *Boeuf dans toutes ses formes* washed down by a classic range of vintage Fleuries and Sancerres, the Press party members present fired off a few salvoes of their own about the beauty of the local oysters and the high quality of the *coquilles St Jacques* at the Restaurant Le Bouchon downtown. Added to these treats was a special Press lunch given by the St Etienne club for visiting Fleet Street scribes and their Suffolk brothers.

With one scribe down with food-poisoning after eating too many oysters, the remainder were left to keep a gallant tab on Bobby Robson's team from Portman Road, Ipswich. There was a genuine excuse or two to release an odd belch on a soufflé bed of rich food. But somehow words were found to warn of Ipswich's peril against a famous Cup-fighting team marshalled by the hero of the Rhone valley, Michel Platini.

'Mornin', Bobby,' John Cobbold bawled out gleefully as Robson, assistant Bobby Ferguson and the team made for the

coach on the evening before the match. 'Work 'em damn hard.
And keep the buggers off the caviare and champagne until after
we've won.'

I went down to the home of 'Les Verts' (St Etienne) with some
of the daily newspaper reporters to watch Robson work out his
team. Alan Brazil had been busily shopping in town earlier,
needing interpreters to assist him with a range of orders –
but now the Scottish striker was one of a tracksuited crowd
in the pouring rain as Robson and Ferguson conducted one of
the most vigorous work-outs I have ever witnessed on a football
pitch. There was a hint of a frown on Robson's face as he forced
the players through a range of sapping exercises. But he earned
the confidence of the players, who followed his orders without
resentment. For them the *grande bouffe* was a matter for others.
The game lay ahead the next evening with schools of card games
in bare hotel rooms to pass the time beforehand.

Back at our modern hotel which looked down on the sprawling industrial city of St Etienne, Tom, a Suffolk farmer with a
nose for good food, was championing the one-star meal he had
treated himself to earlier in Lyon. 'Frogs' legs, old boy, and a super pigeon salad. Very delicate and tender. And a bottle of 1975
Brouilly with a pungent sting. I'm afraid the cuisine knocked
spots off our old pseudo-French restaurant back home. But they
do their best. By the way, how are the lads shaping?'

'They look in very good shape.'

'Well as long as they keep off the old *soufflé glacé*.'

John Cobbold emerged in his usual exuberant form, demanding everybody have drinks on him. 'The St Etienne chairman has
invited us out to another three-star meal tomorrow. I don't think
our waist-lines will stand it. Patrick says he'd much rather go
fishing.'

I thought back to that magical afternoon at Wembley in 1978
when Ipswich beat Arsenal and took the FA Cup back to Suffolk for the very first time and John did not know whether
to laugh or cry or dance afterwards and his mother, Lady
Blanche, asked if she would like sugar in her tea, declared
she would much rather have a large gin and tonic. It had
been a great occasion for Ipswich, the Cobbolds and Robson,
and this contagious feeling of gravitation had stuck with the
club at Portman Road all the way up the line, through the
subsequent years to St Etienne. Robson's line-up on the road
towards the UEFA Cup final still rolls enticingly off the tongue:

Paul Cooper, George Burley, Mick Mills (Capt), Franz Thijssen, Russell Osman, Terry Butcher, John Wark, Arnold Muhren, Paul Mariner, Alan Brazil, Eric Gates; subs: Kevin O'Callaghan, Kevin Beattie.

The arrival of the two flying Dutchmen, Muhren and Thijssen, had made the team sparkle like a Bali sunset; although Muhren, the first arrival, had found it difficult initially to settle in. I remember his first match against Liverpool when Ipswich were thrashed and Muhren sat alone and miserable in the foyer of the hotel he was staying in, before moving into a house. 'I have never chased so many shadows,' he said. 'Liverpool never give away the ball.'

Now more mature, English League* indoctrinated, Muhren would play a vital part in the exciting proceedings which took place the following evening at the damp Geoffroy-Guichard Stadium.

It was with power defence in mind that Robson had decided to recall Kevin Beattie to the line-up for the match that damp evening. Beattie had been out of action after a number of painful injuries, but his zest and team spirit soon convinced the green-shirted St Etienne players that they were not holders of a free ticket. Beattie kept gobbling up the ball as the French team made their sallies towards goalkeeper Cooper. His inspiration roused the whole team.

Beattie had first appeared in the Ipswich first team back in 1972 as a full back, and his physical strengths soon had the fans raving about the arrival of a new Duncan Edwards. Bill Shankly, given the chance of signing young Beattie from Carlisle, dismissed the budding Anfield recruit as being 'unreliable' – and Beattie sadly went home to his labourer dad and four brothers and four sisters. Don Revie picked Beattie up during his short spell as England manager and the Ipswich man won nine caps which might have been added to but for the injuries which kept crippling him. So, nine years on, here was Beattie playing the game of his life out there in a daunting atmosphere ringed by layers of green favours and chirping Rhone voices.

Ipswich did go a goal behind in the first half, when that handsome Dutch veteran of two World Cups, Johnny Rep, put them

*Ipswich reached the UEFA Cup final after knocking Cologne out of the semi finals. In a two-legged final against the Dutch club, AZ Alkmaar, Ipswich triumphed 5–4 after the second meeting in Amsterdam.

ahead with a typical scene-setter. But Ipswich did not waver and Paul Mariner's header which equalised had the flavour of a Tommy Lawton special. The ball went whooph! into the net and there was Mariner, dancing away in delight, and the fervour was caught by my *Daily Telegraph* colleague, Donald Saunders, bubbling with excitement down his telephone. It was all too much for 'Les Verts' – they withered in the second half into pale straw, Platini making a number of uncharacteristic mistakes. Goals came the way of the plundering visitors: Muhren, who had done so much to inspire Ipswich in partnership with Thijssen, shooting in a devastating long ranger that shocked an alarmed St Etienne goalkeeper. In the end, the score was 4–1 to Ipswich.

After the visitors had been cheered sportingly off the pitch, the Suffolk party were treated to glasses of warm punch before the 'plane journey back home to Southend. Roger Roche, the St Etienne president, was so enthusiastic about Ipswich's performance that he flung his arms around a startled Patrick Cobbold, crying: 'Allez Ipswich, brava Ipswich.'

John Cobbold came up grinning. 'We're going to put a big marquee up at Portman Road for the return leg. And champagne will be on the house.'

Later we met the St Etienne manager, Robert Herbin, still wearing a tracksuit, his red Affro hair blazing up like a burning bush. 'Alors,' he said, almost gravely, reflecting on what had nearly been a Suffolk trouncing of his team, 'I compare Ipswich with the great Ajax team of the 1970s' (no mean compliment) – 'or the Liverpool side which eliminated us from the European Cup in 1977. They have a very solid formation, very dynamic, made up of very good technicians. It is very much a British side at heart, despite the presence of two Dutchmen. But their attacking style is more continental.'

Mick Mills appeared, all smiles, after his immense contribution, in a captain's role. Tom the farmer had long given up thoughts of flowing foie gras to relish the *grande bouffe* on the pitch. He shook Mills' hand avidly. 'Well done, sir, well done.'

And now it was time for Robson to make his entrance, as the hot punch flowed and the defeated Monsieur le President continued to rave about the victors. I had been witness to a range of Bobby's emotions since watching him play alongside Johnny Haynes in the Fulham Football Combination side at the start of the 1950s: I had seen his broad Geordie smile erupt, almost coyly, after he scored his first goal for the stiffs at Craven Cottage; I had seen his almost respectful private-on-parade salute of his first two goals for England at Wembley; I had seen him sour with grief when he was sacked as Fulham's manager after only a short spell in command, when he read the news in the *Evening Standard*; I had seen him reacting like a caged animal when confronted by plbzayer power during his early days as Ipswich manager: I had seen him reacting joyously to Ipswich's FA Cup semi final victory against his old club, West Bromwich Albion, which took his team on the victor's way to the final in 1978; I had seen him steely, in command of men in training; I had seen him, the Geordie miner's son, throwing his head back and laughing at a number of randy John Cobbold jokes, but I had never seen him as happy as he was on that night at St Etienne.

Compare that night with some of the soured Press conferences which took place in later years when Robson's face looked as if bolted in a 'damn 'em all' expression, faced by what he called unjust criticism in the face of major defeat – Class of 1988, West Germany. But seven years earlier, in a St Etienne directors' lounge, he would show what it was like to be a winner. And he made no secret of his delight. 'That was the best tonight. And I can tell you I have seen quite a bit of the best over the years. We were nearly faultless. But there is a lot of hard work ahead yet.'

And for farmer Tom, too, sitting near me on the plane back to Southend. He admitted he would be up at dawn, milking the cows. 'But I'll be dreaming of our great win, and the pigeon salad. You have to give it to the "frogs", they can't half cook. But bless us, can't we play football.'

17
Melia's Marvels

'If you ask me, mate,' the photographer said grudgingly, as we walked up a snowy meadow towards a Brighton Polytechnic soccer pitch perched on the Sussex Downs, 'we're wasting our bloody time out here. If Liverpool don't beat this lot by ten goals, then I'll eat my Rolex.'

The Brighton side, languishing at the bottom of the First Division that wintery February morning in 1983, were already playing a practice match when we strolled on to the scene of muscular action, our thin city casuals hardly protecting us from the slushy snow bordering the pitch. 'Jimmy Melia's playing,' I said. 'Best concentrate on him.'

'He'll get his desserts at Anfield, you wait and see,' the photographer chuckled, pulling his gear out of his camera box. 'Melia used to be a hero at Anfield. It'll be like going home for him.'

In retrospect, it did seem a bit absurd at the time standing around watching an apparently downhearted team training for what was undoubtedly going to be an FA Cup thrashing against the invincible masters, Liverpool. Brighton had been having a lean time of it under their caretaker manager, which had aroused threats of relegation. All that seemed to be required of Liverpool in that fifth-round contest was to lace up their boots and dawdle through to an easy victory. That is what the form guide suggested, and there seemed no reason to dispute it, while Liverpool were in one of their spells of Herculean form, in which their victims were merely out there to make up the numbers. With this in mind, I stood by a corner flag as the photographer snapped away, trying not to feel sorry for the players who would be required to offer themselves like Brighton sheep for the Anfield slaughter.

It was soon apparent, however, that the Brighton players were responding to the schoolboyish enthusiasm of Melia, the caretaker, who had only been working in this tenuous post since the previous December after Mike Bailey had been sacked. There was the balding buzzard so adored by the Liverpool Kop in the early 1960s when he feinted, schemed, shot, nodded, trapped, dummied, bellowed, shimmied, sprinted, all in the loyal service of Bill Shankly, reviving memories of the glories of those times when the Kop sang 'You'll never walk alone' and Melia was a name to savour, as much as the whiff of hops topping your first pint of the day. The trouble on this occasion, outside Brighton in the snow, lay in the caretaker manager's insistence that the beloved ball was to be controlled by him alone which meant that even some of the more experienced players like Jimmy Case, another former hero of the Anfield Kop, Steve Foster, Gordon Smith and Neil Snillie found it hard to get a touch, laughing with frustration as Melia sped away literally on ice, savouring every moment of boot touching leather.

'Gimme the ball, Jimmy.'

'Hey, Jimmy, up the right.'

'Jimmy, yer no giving us the ball, you greedy wack.'

'Nice one, Jimmy.'

'Shot, Jimmy.'

'Fuckin' hell, Jimmy, give us the ball.'

Melia weaved and spun, danced by the corner flag, took all the throw-ins, took all the corners, rammed home a penalty, and even tapped the ball to the representative of the *Sunday Telegraph*, which made him an automatic claimant to be an honorary member of Brighton's Cup squad that year.

It was fun, of course, and Melia's huge love for the action put heart into the team, who were well out of earshot of big brother chairman, Mike Bamber, fretting elsewhere over the need to revive spectator interest at the Goldstone Ground which had been in decline during the team's depressing record of only one League win in nine games. Could one really be cynical, though, about the chances of an honest bunch of triers faced with the demolition prospects awaiting them at Anfield? The happy-go-lucky atmosphere inspired by the wiggling, weaving Melia defied the enormous challenges awaiting them the following weekend. The relaxed informality surrounding Melia's training schedule had something to do with a message running through the back of his mind about the dangers of being too pedantic and lordly in company with a team of players, many of whom were old enough not to be lectured about the necessity of collective smotherisation in the face of lethal opponents such as Liverpool.

Melia continued dancing with the ball in the vicinity of a snowbound corner flag until a hard tackle from a committed Case, who had a penchant for angling off a Sussex brook, laid the boss flat on his face. 'That'll teach yer, Jimmy, for being so bloody greedy.' There was a cackle of laughter around the pitch. Melia rose with an evident chuckle. 'You reserve those for Kenny Dalglish, Jimmy wack.'

When it was all over and Melia dabbed down the sweat on his bald egg of a head, he obliged this reporter with some thoughts on the dangers which lay ahead for his club, not only at Anfield, but through the dangerous labyrinths of relegation problems, which could endanger his own slimline position at Goldstone. Melia, talking as he helped two apprentices carry the training goals back to their store: 'If you want to hear what my heart says, it's winning at Anfield and going on to Wembley. That's what the ticker says, and winning at Anfield would be marvellous. But the real test here on the South Coast is staying up. That's what I'm here to do. And in saying this,' Melia continued, putting down the goalpost, and staring over the icy Downs, 'I can tell you we are far too good to go down. The lads are confident and the team spirit is tremendous.'

Melia's convictions certainly seemed sincere. His mission at that particular time was to convince the missing fans that captain Steve Foster and his team were worth watching again. With average gates 4000 or so short of the 16000 Brighton needed to break even financially, Melia's energies were being funnelled into working some kind of Goldstone miracle, not the first time a manager had taken on such a forlorn-looking challenge. But Melia, who had stood on Liverpool's terraces as a school-kid from St Anthony's School, Scotland Road, was not without the qualities his mentor, Bill Shankly, had carried to inspire the Anfield club on their great run in the 1960s. 'We are taking 4000 fans to Anfield. The match has caused tremendous interest in Brighton and Hove, but we obviously need more support in the League as well.' The photographer came up and took another snap of Melia.

'Fancy your chances, Jimmy?'

'Never say die.'

'Well who says miracles don't happen.'

The players, wrapped up in tracksuits, prepared to drive off to Goldstone. Melia gave us a cheery wave goodbye. 'See you at Wembley, lads.' We giggled. George Aitken, Melia's assistant, emerged beside him to wring out one more inspiring message about the Anfield prospects. 'They said the "Titanic" couldn't be sunk. I know different. I was at Watford with Ken Furphy when we knocked Liverpool out of the Cup in 1970. Nobody expected us to, but we did. It was dead lovely.'

Dreams are divine, and we speculated about such Sussex optimism, the photographer and I, as we trudged downhill to his car. 'You've got to hand it to them,' the photographer said. 'They haven't a bloody chance, but they're brave enough.'

'What about some oysters at English's?' I suggested. 'Before I do a Goldstone recce.'

'No thanks, pal. I've got another job on in town – a Brighton murder enquiry.'

Jimmy Melia (left) and chairman Mike Bamber leading Brighton to Wembley, 1983.

The photographer dropped me off by the seafront and I went into a newsagents to buy the *Brighton Argus*. There was a tone of optimism in a club advert, rallying supporters to the Goldstone colours. 'The Goldstone Ground is the place to be. Support on the terrace and in the stands is vital to your club. We have said before that we can't promise to win . . . but we have shown everyone that we mean to entertain.' It was a nice little trumpet blast, and one could sense Melia's bustle behind it.

Later, walking up towards Brighton Station, the chances of Brighton winning against Bob Paisley's team seemed as steep as that steep climb, even though that morning had proved that Melia had won the confidence of the lads.

Brighton beat Liverpool 2–0 at Anfield, and went on to reach the FA Cup final at Wembley for the first time. After a 2–2 draw against Manchester United, Brighton lost the replay by 0–4.

18
Sambas along the Ramblas

Nobody in Barcelona could remember a hotter July than the one that blazed down through the narrow winding streets of the Ramblas, so that birds hanging in rows of cages from numerous, flower-bedecked verandahs felt their feathers singeing and their pretty singing thwarted not only by the rays of the sun but by a stunning throbbing erupting below.

It was the hour of the Brazilians in the World Cup in 1982. Argentina, having been beaten thoroughly at the Sarria Stadium, and Diego Maradona sent off, the Brazilian supporters rolled forward in happy waves towards their beloved Ramblas which, for some of them, was a precious pathway dividing the football stadiums with a large ocean liner which had brought them dancing and singing all the way from Rio.

There was no doubt in the Brazilians' minds as they snaked through the oven streets, drums throbbing, penny whistles shrilling, traffic jams blaring, that it was only a matter of time before they won another World Cup final; this time in Madrid. Their hotel reservations and match tickets were booked for the great day when Socrates, Zico, Falco, Junior, Eder and company would stand rejoicing on the pitch in front of the King of Spain. It was only a matter of time, with only a draw against Italy needed to qualify for the semi finals, before Madrid would turn into a carnival city, Rio- and São Paulo- made. And somewhere there, in the middle of all the noise and clatter and throbbing of drums and samba beat, was the great Pele himself, lunching out of sight in a restaurant near the port called the 'Seven Doors'. It was a famous visit, and they put a plaque on the wall where he sat after he left, saying simply 'Pele sat here'. He sat there with a vague frown, because he was worried about the hype that

Socrates, a qualified doctor, on the attack for brilliant Brazil. It was his team's defensive howlers against Italy in Barcelona, which deprived them of glory in 1982.

the Brazilian following were fanning around town because he felt Brazil had made mistakes against Argentina and the Italians would not be the walkover many of his countrymen supposed.

I had worked on a feature at five in the morning, in my Y-fronts, because the heat outside my hired apartment was already making sweat drip down from forehead to chest and even the orange juice taken from the fridge quickly warmed into yellow soup. Then the Brazilians passed by, 600 of them, rolling on in bobbing groups, their yellow and green banners stark against the ivy-coloured foliage protecting the inner, affluent privacy of the owners of grand apartments in this wealthy residential area. In the early morning, curious faces stared out at the happy procession, but there was not a policeman to be seen. After the first night of Brazilian carnival, they had stood around in groups, perhaps geared to fears of hooliganism which had been stirred up by English fans in Bilbao and Madrid. But they retreated after a Spanish newspaper criticised the police for letting the Brazilians go where they pleased. 'They are such a happy lot, and they bring fun and laughter wherever they go.' The law, in their paratrooper style berets, stepped aside and went back to their stations.

The carnival had been going on since Brazil's qualifying matches in the deep South when their team had beaten the Soviet Union, Scotland and New Zealand, in the Andalusian cauldron of Seville, and where we pampered scribes cooled off beside luxurious swimming pools, watching coach-loads of Welsh grandmothers arriving in a state of collapse, in knitted cardigans. 'They asked me if I wanted a room with or without swimming pool,' Paddy said, applying sun oil with gusto. 'I think the *Echo* won't mind if I turn into a water baby.'

The pressures mounted once in Barcelona, away from the frolics of the south, and the Brazilian players must have felt so, as they went about their serious training in the devastating heat. All the 'Olés' were for them, from the Spanish hosts now that their own wretched team, already beaten by Northern Ireland, had failed to supply the glory which was much expected of them. Scotland had departed early, which is their habit in World Cup finals, but England did have a chance of reaching the semi finals if they could beat Spain by two goals in Madrid. But these diversions were going on a long way away across a Spanish plain, and with the sun up high near noon, the Sarria Stadium began to fill again with blocks of blazing sunflower-coloured sheets thrown over battalions of Brazilian heads.

On the morning before the Brazil-Italy match, I walked down the Ramblas to the central post office to post my weekly newsletter to *The Times of Blitzkhan*, a noted Far Eastern newspaper which, with some alacrity, had asked me through their cricket correspondent to pen a few words to them on the progress of the World Cup. I could think of better things to do than queue in steaming Spanish post offices to express these letters east – but the correspondent was so pleadingly enthusiastic, and the fees generous, that I agreed to become, when time permitted away from my official duties, a servant of those remote lands lying south of Kashmir. It was a howling blunder – never was I to hear another word from those Kiplingesque editorial offices far away, or receive a fee for waiting in those queues fighting back Spanish two-step of the tummy. On this particular morning, the post office was engulfed with Brazilians sending postcards home, the drum-beat continuing inside, despite the threats of an emaciated and enraged official who looked as if he had never ventured out of the post office in his life, not even during the Civil War.

Once outside again in the sun, the fiesta was in full force as armies of Brazilians marched up and down the Ramblas, mocking the odd Italian waiter who ventured out in bright green, red and white scarves. The bottoms of the girls swaying up and down the flower-bedecked avenues rotated like small melons to the rhythm of their drums, putting a normally on-duty band of prostitutes to flight outside the Cosmos bar, possibly in awe of their South American rivals' golden looks.

Many of the Brazilian supporters were relatively poor members of their country's society, living in ramshackle conditions in less congenial areas of Rio and Sao Paulo. By working long hours, cleaning, scrubbing, darning and washing cars, they had put enough money away to get to Spain. Some of the more affluent men had brought their entire families, others were accompanied by wives or girlfriends. The Spanish took to them, especially the long-legged girls with bronzed complexions, who became the subject of wonderous stares from Juan and Antonio.

The Sarria Stadium looked in the heat of noon as if Vincent Van Gogh had put on his battered straw hat, tied an easel and canvas to his back and gone out and painted the squat stadium in all the colours of an Arles raging landscape. The

Italy's Paulo Rossi out jumping Falcao during the famous 1982 World Cup match against Brazil.

Brazilians had simply drenched the terraces with colour, while the Neapolitan elements were not far behind either. Such was the background set for one of the most exciting games I have ever been privileged to see.

If ever Brazil committed suicide, this was it; this was the stage for their wringing of their own necks, the stage when they were executed by the devastating firepower of an angelic-looking young man named Paulo Rossi. Rossi had not been particularly conspicuous in the finals up till then, not having scored, or shown the panache which had been a feature of Italy's progress to the semi finals in Argentina four years before. But there was something sinister about the way Paulo toed the simmering turf during the pre-match kickabout, a gesture that suggested that inside that lithe frame were goals bursting to get out. And so it proved after only five minutes, when Brazil's uncertain goal-keeper, Valdir, was beaten by an emphatic Rossi header. Now it was the turn of the Neapolitans to crow while the stadium seemed to erupt into a green, white and yellow foam bath.

This was all Brazil needed to press forward to claim the equaliser. But Gentile, who had treated Maradona with scant respect in the Argentina match, in a display of almost brutal proportions, now set his sights on Zico, cracking the shins of this exceptional artist whenever he could get near. It was loathsome to watch, as opposed to the wonderful football played by his colleague, Antognoni in midfield, a precious asset which would earn the applause of his manager, Enzo Bearzot, after-wards. Brazil soon equalised when that gangling medical man, Socrates, got through to squeeze the ball past Zoff just inside the post. A big mountain of a black Brazilian sitting next to me almost let his teeth rattle at the relief of it all. Then back came that elusive bundle of nuisance, Rossi, to punish a grotesque error by a slack Brazilian defence to put Italy ahead again in the 25th minute. My neighbour looked stunned. He mopped his brow, he crossed his beefy chest.

It took a suffocating, agonising period of Brazilian pressure before Brazil scored another vital equaliser – Falcao choosing the 68th minute to score a sumptuous goal which he celebrated by running back towards his own dug-out, his mouth wide open, his arms flung wide in ecstasy, his dance caught by the screaming adoration of the Brazilian supporters. My neighbour was now smiling like the Cheshire cat, gently cuddling my own head in his muscular arms, a grip which was so tight that the representative of the *Sunday Telegraph*, London, had to exert maximum pressure to free himself. All Brazil had to do now was to keep out of trouble, follow the example of Arsenal in the past, and put the shutters up. But what did they do? They pressed forward, leaving large gaps in the rear. It was maddening to watch, if one had any allegiances to the yellow and greens. And they paid the fatal penalty in the 74th minute when Rossi forced in another goal, a goal which would secure Italy a place in the semi final against Poland. I turned right to face my neighbour – but he had disappeared, perhaps to shoot himself, like the Brazilian fan who took his life with a Colt revolver in 1950 when he heard his country had been beaten by Uruguay in the final.

It was all very sad afterwards, unless you were an Italian; the Brazilians made a lot of noise outside the stadium but many were already in tears. Soon there were only layers and layers of paper outside the Sarria Stadium, a dog nosing a beer can along the tarmac in the wake of the last supporters trudging back into town. Up at a packed Press conference, Brazil's manager, Tele Santana, disguised the miseries of misfortune by generously praising Rossi. 'Rossi is a great player, intelligent, and very dangerous. There was no man to man marking in the match – and Rossi took full advantage of openings.' A growl or two from Santana? Not really – he was more interested in praising Italy than debunking his own defence. And his prediction that Italy would win the World Cup would prove spot on.

That evening I watched England fail to beat Spain, and therefore fail to reach the semi finals in Madrid; Keegan heading past an open goal; a sad experience in a darkened café, where the few customers stared grimly at a flickering television screen. So the semi finals would be between France and West Germany and Italy and Poland. Much of the fun had gone out of the competition now that Brazil had been thrown out. Down in the Ramblas later, the Italians had taken over in force from the Brazilians and were making the most of their operatic celebrations. My friend, Jim Lawton, was seated at a café table, smiling. 'There's no sign of our Brazilians. They must have all sailed away. The party's over, man.'

'Well, Rossi may have a few things to say about that.'

It was days later, on July 12, at the Santiago Bernabeu Stadium, Madrid, in the final against West Germany that Rossi and his pals abundantly proved their point.

19
Platinimania

The flamingoes were up early, and so was I, gazing out of my motel window across a stretch of oily water near Marseilles Airport to a distant splash of congregated long necks, based in the sanctity of their own smelly, very private creek. A jet plane took off from a nearby runway, en route to Africa, hovering for a moment in the early morning haze, before swinging left over the ultra blue Med. The flamingoes took no notice, their joint stance proud and lofty. My own composure, in reflection, was hardly so restful – I was suffering from pre-match nerves which encouraged an occasional crazy march across the sparse hotel room floor to snatch at a cup of coffee while holding a copy of that morning's *Provencal*. The sporting headlines were all devoted to the chances of France's national soccer team reaching the final of the 1984 European Championships, in Paris, the following Wednesday. All the tricolours had to do was to dispose of Portugal in the semi final on the evening of the hot flamingo day which had just dawned at the State Velodrome, Marseilles.

With so much time to spare, I went out to the poolside after breakfast. The choice of the hotel had not been mine, the London agent having offered the choice of what sounded like a pea-sized brothel in the roughest quarter of Marseilles, or the plastic offering near the airport a long way out of town. I chose the former, but on arriving, was met by a bristle-chinned, ex-convict-looking para-legionaire, reeking of garlic, whose form of greeting at his tiny reception desk was to snuggle up close so that his chin was near to connecting to my much smaller one and hiss, 'Allez, Monsieur, complet.'

'But you have my reservation.'

'ALLEZ!' His hint was one I wisely took heed of, because from behind a damp curtain guarding the peppery labyrinths of his kitchen, came the sudden warning bark of an infernal guard dog. Despite being so close to the airport, the haven I now found myself in was luxury itself, the thunder of passing jet planes bearable compared with the snorting, licking animosity of that fiendish alsatian downtown. I flicked over the pages of *Le Provencial* near the pool, half-distracted by two busty Air France hostesses in transit, who were about to take the plunge. So many odes to France's great captain, Michel Platini, had to be re-read, as a long leg attached primly to the tiny thread of a bikini, stretched forward to test the sparkling, running waters of a luxury pool.

'Oh là là, c'est froid!' Miss Blonde said to Miss Brunette. Their figures were rather too plump to rival those Concorde goddesses we had seen romping about the rooftop pool of Rio's Hotel Meridien when in transit on the way back from the World Cup in Argentina. Those goddesses, one felt, in total admiration, would settle for multi-millionaires as spouses. These two, in comparison, wouldn't feel out of place being married to an affluent vet. Two male stewards sitting back from the pool and looking almost comically spruce in their off-duty beach shirts and slacks had, judging from their conversation, been somewhere in the Pacific only hours before, and now were on their way somewhere equally romantic. But their thoughts and ambitions were on this occasion not fired by some swivel-hipped Conga girl or cheeky beach boy offering numerous favours, but by the challenge facing France that evening. They read their sports pages avidly as the two hostesses splashed around the pool, giggling and holding on to each other's shoulders with an avidity they rarely showed when going through the emergency lifebelt drill.

'Platini's wonderful, marvellous right now,' one of the stewards said. 'I once served him lunch on a short trip to Turin. He was magic then. He knows so much about football, it isn't true. And he has such a wonderful body, so firm, so muscular, though certainly not muscle-bound. And his face, so beautiful, so *magnifique*. Tonight, he will be our hero, he will kill Portugal, you will see, *mon ami*.'

'*Vraiment.* You make him sound like Superman,' replied his companion. 'I am more into tennis myself. Yanik Noah is part of my dreams.'

One of the girls climbed out of the pool, waving and twisting her head as she splashed water from her blonde hair. *'Bien sur*, Michel has a really positive make-up about him. Men can be so unpractical, but with him, you feel he has control of everything. On the football pitch, he is a commander, a leader. *Mon dieu*, would I like a date with him.'

'Isn't he married, Simone?'

'Peut-être.'

'With kids, *je pense.* But that doesn't deter Simone.' The two stewards laughed. Simone walked forward and with an almost graceful movement of one hand knocked a glass of coke into the more cheeky steward's groin. But now only laughter resounded, with Simone flailing down on to a lilo to soak up the overhanging, less bearable sunrays. 'This is magic,' Simone muttered. 'But then so is Platini.'

An hour or two later, this winged foursome were to be seen bustling around the motel foyer in their flight uniforms checking out, even though they had checked in only a few hours before. A mini-bus would pick them up to take them the short distance to the air terminal, Simone alive with her daydreams about Platini, as a nearby radio blurted out more and more information about the morale of the French team at their training camp. On the way down to the Vieux Port by taxi, I had visions of Platini and Simone doing a joint Julie Andrews by singing a duet on top of a distant Alps mountain ridge. Strongly jawed with a pert, efficient expression and immaculately made up, Simone indeed fitted into that class of female who considered Platini the man for them. If it was his ability to score exquisite goals from free kicks, and dominate a match with his audacious touch which attracted men, it was his charisma and style and sultry good looks which attracted women. And now Platini had really come into his own.

From France's point of view, he had been the supremo behind the tricolours' route to the semi finals from Group One. Two hat-tricks had been included in his symphonic repertoire, and his fellow players, like the crafty Giresse and the tigerish Tigana, had responded with typical tenacity to the maestro's baton. The type of football played by France, with their elegant midfield, against Belgium and Yugoslavia was technically supreme, giving the impression of long-term team understanding – though Michel Hidalgo, then ironically in his last term as team manager, had rarely been rewarded with such combined excellence from the Blues in the past. But the way his side, though obviously tiring, came back against Yugoslavia suggested a renaissance.

It was after the Yugoslavia match that I had run into the Northern Ireland team manager, Billy Bingham, who, like myself, was living out of a suitcase at those vibrant Championships. He compared Platini in a genial way with George Best; a formidable comparison, but not one to be scoffed at.

'Platini has improved considerably as an all-round player,' Bingham said, over an aperitif. 'This has certainly happened since he left France for Juventus. The way he has been playing in this competition has certainly reminded me of Best. Perhaps Platini is not as skilful with his feet – but he has the same full range of attacking perception.'

Jock Stein, Scotland's canny team manager, had been equally effusive about France after we had watched West Germany surprisingly knocked out of the finals by Spain at the Parc des Princes the Wednesday before. 'France have to win now that Jepp Derwall's team have been given the push,' he said, sitting in his shirt-sleeves in the Press Box. 'The other sides in this competition have had to work to win. France came out with their own script and Platini has been brilliant.'

'Big' Jock looked relaxed away from the personal pressures of steering Scotland towards the 1986 World Cup finals in Mexico. He had only just over a year to live, cut down by a coronary at the end of a World Cup qualifying match at Ninian Park, Cardiff, when the strains of seeing Scotland narrowly gain their finals' ticket, at the expense of Wales, through a disputed penalty, proved too much. But during that hectic June in France, Stein thoroughly enjoyed his freedom – like those other managers who bothered to make the trip. Ironically, so did four other leading managers on parade at Marseilles – England's Bobby Robson, Aberdeen's Alex Ferguson, Luton's David Pleat and Ipswich's Bobby Ferguson. For the wheels of fortune turned against all of them within the next three years.

Robson, sanguine and chirpy, had just returned with his England team from South America, having beaten Brazil in their den, helped by an outstanding goal by John Barnes – but the beauty of that occasion became more and more erased after Gary Lineker saved Robson's pride in Mexico and he fell victim to the marauding tabloid headline writers after England's miserable performance in the succeeding European Championship finals in West Germany. Ferguson was given the responsibility of leading Scotland to Mexico between his move from Aberdeen to Manchester United – but he, too, could not escape criticism as Scotland left Mexico prematurely. And what a cruel acid drop awaited the genial Pleat after he had joined Spurs from Luton, victim of a *Sun*-splashed sex scandal which saw him quit White Hart Lane to land up eventually at Leicester. And another Platini fan on that warm night in Marseilles was the chatterbox Geordie, Bobby Ferguson, Robson's former number two and now in charge at Portman Road. Time would see him become the first Ipswich manager to be sacked, and he landed up in the Middle East coaching, well away from the white heat of running an English football team.

Some of the English Press Corps who had returned from across the Atlantic had quickly become riveted by some of the football played in these championships, particularly by France and the happy-go-lucky Danes, who would face Spain the following day up at Lyon in the other semi final. David Lacey (*The Guardian*), Jeff Powell (*Daily Mail*), Don Saunders (*Daily Telegraph*), Bob Driscoll (*The Star*) and Brian Glanville (*Sunday Times*) – looking as if he had just arrived on his famous bike from down the Rhone Valley and bursting for a telephone – all thought Marseilles worthy of their presence and worth the long wait from a warm summer afternoon into an almost gleaming evening, in which the Corniches around Marseilles spiralled up in slabs of Milk of Magnesia white, and the colours of the yacht in the Vieux Port wove together in blotchy chunks, shimmering.

So we settled into our seats, either to report, or to enjoy the stage where Platini and his team-mates had vowed to reward their nation with a stunning victory against the less gifted Portuguese – and earn their rightful place in the Paris final.

The crowd, heaped in layers of blue, white and red, soon began chanting, 'PLATINEE! PLATINEEEEEEE! PLATINEE-EEEEE!' as their god from Nancy began strutting among the massed white armies of Portugal. It was not particularly surprising when the tricolours opened their account after the 24th minute, though the way it was scored was indeed surprising, with the laugh firmly on the sagging shoulders of the Portuguese defence. When France were awarded a free kick, the Portuguese lined up, fully expecting Platini to unleash one of his benders from outside the box. But in a well-prepared set-piece, the responsibility of shooting at target fell to a less-celebrated young defender from Toulouse, François Domergue.

Platini. A dramatic night in Marseilles. . .

It was some free kick, the ball whizzing over the top of Bento into the roof of the net. The stadium at once erupted in a bedlam of noise as France looked safely on their way to their first major international soccer final in their history.

The dummy that foxed Portugal had come from Platini, the killing shot from Domergue, who was celebrating his 27th birthday. Portugal did recover sufficiently to disturb France's rhythm in midfield with some of the cruellest tackling seen in the Championships, and on a par with their harsh tactics which put Pele out of the 1966 World Cup finals. One of the hackers was Lima Pereira, who was rightly booked for an atrocious foul. But the French showed they could mix it as well, and Lacombe was booked for a foul on the Portuguese player who did so much to revive his team, Chalana.

France had opportunities to double their lead but Fenandez and Giresse missed chances, lapses that might have been catastrophic but for the final, thrilling events of that night. Portugal did come back to equalize in the 72nd minute when Chalana completely outwitted the French defence for Jordao to force the ball into the goal. The Marseilles crowd looked sickened, and despite their pleas for Platini to revive his team, it had not proved one of his most illustrious nights in the face of some blunt tackling.

A masterly substitution in the 62nd minute in which the 34-year-old Benfica veteran, Nene, replaced Sousa did much to raise Portugal's morale, and when extra time came up in the silvery dusk, France had been made to look very uneasy. My own nerves had been aggravated through my running copy being lost in our Fleet Street office – though it turned out later that the messengers had staged a rapid strike to claim special fees for working a bit harder than they usually did out of the Kings and Keys. France could be said to have lost their way as well, in the face of a team they had been expected to beat comfortably, and Chalana, who had been carried off in a previous match against Romania, was a vibrant thorn in their sides. Soon Portugal were jumping for joy after a mis-hit shot by Jordao crept into the French net during the first period of extra time, and the faces of the many French journalists up in the Press Box began to grow longer and longer and longer and longer. 'Tiens! Allez France! Allez Platini!' The crowd nevertheless kept chanting and were rewarded in the second extra-time period when Domergue added his second goal in the evening's proceedings with a cracking shot which sent howls of relief bubbling around the stadium.

French relief, yes; joy, no – for the memory of how the tricolours lost their place in the World Cup final, through penalties against West Germany two years before, still rankled – and the prospect of another penalty showdown against Portugal sent more than a shiver down the spines of the resident faithful watching in Marseilles, or crowded around a television set in home, café, restaurant and rail or air terminal bars. My next-door companion, Brian Madley of *The People*, and I both viewed the emerging prospect without much relish, for penalty shoot-outs to decide who is admitted to the golden bowl can have no bearing on what has gone before. And picking up a queue of robots with numbers, intent on belting the ball past each other's rival goalkeepers, can be taxing after a long haul into extra time.

Thus the minutes ticked by to the final one, when Press phone receivers were raised ready for the score after extra time – 2–2. But one player had other ideas. He was the lithe Jean Tigana, a player never content to relax and call it a day, a player with the power to wriggle through the most fortified defences. Here he came, racing towards us, moving wide until his stride had taken him behind the Portuguese defence, before delivering the ball low across goal. All was suddenly hushed, the last gasp of a game depended on who would make contact with the ball first. Bento seemed hypnotised in the Portugal goal, his defenders wavered, and it proved suicidal, for now Platini was on the scene, his boot poised to make contact and score the deciding goal.

But wait – he stood there surveying the scene like a head gardener at Versailles engrossed with his first rose blooms of early summer, engrossed to the point of leaning forward and sniffing the dewy perfumes near a softly splashing fountain. Platini was in love with the ball – he looked at it tenderly based as he was near the edge of the six-yard box. He looked round at the crowd, like a triumphant matador raising two ears and the tail of the four-legged tauro he had triumphantly dispatched. He looked up at the Press Box and we felt he was about to make a speech. Everybody had stopped moving. Everybody had stopped shouting. Everybody froze. THEN PLATINI THUMPED THE BALL MERCILESSLY INTO THE NET!

For a moment the awful silence stayed with us, and then all was bedlam with Platini down there under his all-embracing team-mates, and the Portuguese walking away in disgust. I just kept talking down the phone until an incredible stab of pain engulfed my free hand. A disgusted Portuguese was trying to climb behind my seat, taking the opportunity to tread on my innocent palm, turning his sole circular fashion over every exposed finger. 'Prick!' I yelled. 'Prick!' 'What did you say?' the copy-taker enquired anxiously. 'Sorry, not you.'

A mildly bruised little finger was worth the subsequent fiesta which carried on around the Vieux Port into the early hours. Klaxon-sounding cars, covered in tricolours which streamed forth from their windows, were driven frenziedly to and fro along the tourist cruiser landing stages by drivers with wide open, palpitating mouths full of Gallic lip. Bobby Robson emerged to join our party of journalists, resembling a cleric who has just heard a very good sermon delivered by a visiting bishop. The café we sat in was crammed with revellers and Robson had to raise his voice to deliver his homage to France. 'France may have been a bit lucky tonight but overall they have shown how flexible they are as a team. And they have some electric players in Platini and Tigana.' One or two of the scribes jotted down a few notes before returning to the general euphoria, which saw more than a few local wines consumed before the coming of the dawn. By then, Robson had lost that slightly frozen, puzzled look he prefers in company of certain members of the Fourth Estate whom he feels might misquote him, and had become a fully-fledged Platinimania associate.

Eventually I took a taxi back to the airport motel, and as I drove through dazzling daylight I thought back to Simone's words about Platini's style, the way he had stood there in total possession of his faculties before scoring the winning goal. Most players, far less gifted than the man from Nancy, would have hit the ball first time and in many cases shot wildly wide. Platini simply showed that under extreme pressure, he still had time.

The flamingoes were still visible from my motel room nearly 24 hours later, although they seemed further away and less iridescent. The pressure was off for a few hours now, before I was due to catch the lunchtime PSV train up to Lyon to watch the happy Danes play Spain. It looked like being a roaster in Provence, and the newspapers would be going wild over France and Platini. It was, as Simone might have said: '*Magnifique*, chéri.'

France beat Spain in the final at the Parc des Princes the following Wednesday night. The winning goal was scored by Platini.

20

After Heysel

The guilty and the innocent who returned to Merseyside the day after the Heysel Stadium outrage in Brussels on May 29, 1985, did not have to wander far into the streets of their own city from Lime Street Station, Liverpool, to sense the mood of their fellow citizens. The big shun had begun.

Liverpool scarves and favours had been removed from the window of a nearby tourist office, leaving the Beatles in total command. The reason was given in a meticulously worded message from Ron Jones, a member of Merseyside County Council: 'As a mark of respect for the people who lost their lives in the Brussels football stadium disaster and as a measure of our infinite disgust towards those responsible, all local football souvenirs have been removed from sale until further notice.'

Many of the bleary-eyed Liverpool fans, many of whom were wearing Juventus shirts and headbands inscribed with FORZA JUVENTUS, pleaded to be heard for their version of the tragedy. Like oratory in an Arab market place, they rabbitted on about their innocence loudly, putting the blame on roaming Chelsea fans, National Front members, hostile Italians, or the brutal Belgian police.

There might have been an element of truth in some of their stories, as was certainly hinted at in subsequent investigations into a tragedy which had killed 39 spectators, mostly Italians, before the European Cup final between Liverpool and Juventus; yet the instant reaction of the citizens of Merseyside who had watched the carnage live on television from their armchairs in a mood of increasing horror was not sympathetic. Merseyside banter is noted for its caustic good humour, but on this occasion the silence was stunning – the Red Army walked alone.

Before touring Liverpool the night after the tragedy to test the reactions of those who had stayed at home, I ran by chance into my colleague, Colin Malam, who was on his way back to London from Brussels, via Liverpool, after watching the tragedy first-hand. Colin is a thorough-going Anfield supporter, but on this occasion he sat in the buffet bar at Lime Street Station looking stunned. He had toured the infamous stadium area where so many people were killed when a wall gave way through the pressure brought on by a mad charge by Liverpool fans.

'It was a nightmare,' he reflected. 'I toured the area later with Peter Robinson (Liverpool's chief executive) and a solicitor friend, Tony Ensor, and although the bodies had been taken away, clothes and shoes were piled up in a heap. The state of the terracing was so run down that it was easy for those responsible to rip up bits of concrete to use as weapons. The place looked like a bankrupt dog track. It was an awful trip back here. Joe Fagan (Liverpool's manager) was in tears. I've just come from the Press conference, where it was announced Kenny Dalglish had taken over from Fagan. We all knew about that anyway, and the appointment was not really in people's minds anyway.'

'Maggie Thatcher's in a fury. In this mood, she would like to ban football altogether.'

I left Colin on his sad way back home to write his piece on the tragedy, and took a night-time taxi ride into the outskirts of a grieving city, pausing to pick up a toothbrush on the way, having been sent north minutes after arriving at our Fleet Street office that morning. From leaving the chemists', the magnitude of an infectious gloom began to scrape on one's nerves. Even my first Scouse taxi driver, a member of a breed full of fun and laughter, was at a loss for words. 'Disgustin', disgustin',' he kept repeating over and over again.

In spite of such problems as massive unemployment, the citizens had kept their sense of humour, aided and galvanised by two beloved football teams, Liverpool and Everton. But now within the walls of that very city, they were confronted by a hideous shame.

At the Liver Hotel at Crosby, which was a regular watering-hole for devoted, well-mannered veterans of Liverpool's famous (and Bill Shankly inspired) Kop, the imbibers stared into their pint pots in a state of incomprehension. Edna Noonan, the trusty, affable landlady, noted for her sharp humour, was clearly distressed. 'We were expecting a party,' she said sadly. 'But instead, last night, we had people just drifting away without watching the game. It's a terrible thing to happen to Liverpool. In 21 years, the fans have been brilliantly behaved.'

The restored Cavern Club in Beatle city, where Paul, John, Ringo and George once performed in semi-darkness, going all the way to the top of the hit parade while Shankly was building a life and death side at Anfield, was closed for the night. Not that there were many people around anyway as darkness closed on the sunset of an early summer's heatwave. It was not a night for discos.

Pubs from Penny Lane to Anfield acted as inquest centres for the legions who had returned from Brussels and for many relieved relatives who had flooded the Merseyside emergency switchboard for news of the casualty lists. The park opposite Liverpool's ground at Anfield was not its usual noisy, boisterous, dog-sniffing, graffiti-daubed, litter- and shit-sprayed self – but then after reading stories told by Diane Massey in the *Liverpool Evening Post*, it was easy to see why larks weren't exactly twittering over the hinterlands of the old wharves, abandoned docklands and decaying post-war community centres where Eleanor Rigby found so much loneliness. 'A growing reputation carefully built over a decade is ruined. Now, for many Merseyside fans their hands are as red as the scarves they wear.'

Harsh stuff – and whether the writer now regrets her bitter criticism is a matter of speculation – but I doubt if she feels any real compassion for the ringleaders of an appalling evening. Elsewhere in the guilt-ridden city the night after Liverpool had lost the final through a penalty by Michel Platini – all totally forgotten, incidentally, in view of the previous events which was way out of context in a football-besotted kingdom – people continued to explain, to record, to bellow nasally 'not guilty' to any willing listener they could press against a bar wall. One shrill Scouse woman was convinced 'the Eyeties started the trouble. They pushed the wall down trying to get in. I was nearby. We were in good spirits, we Liverpool lot. But the Eyeties started attacking us, like.'

John Mullen, a building worker who had been on the scene, came up, unmenacing, in the face of my enquiry. 'I was snapping pictures near the wall. Then I saw dead people, many dead people. It gives me the creeps to think back on it. The Belgian police did not do enough to stop the trouble.'

Richard Sinker from Birkenhead, on the Cheshire bank of the Mersey, growled that he had decided to give soccer the elbow after watching the game for 25 years. 'What I saw in Brussels has finished me. I have thrown away my hat and scarf – they're in the bin now.' Very likely, being a fanatic, he went back and retrieved them for the new season. We'll never know.

I looked into a couple of pubs near Anfield – which were far from full, and conspicuous for that lack of bustle and noise prevailing on match days, no robust discussions about the welfare of the Reds; there were no trips down memory lane into the romantic world of Liverpool past, when smog swirled around Bill Shankly's beloved ground and the cheers from the Kop were for a chubby local goalkeeper called Tommy Lawrence, the man they nicknamed 'The Flying Pig' and the magic day he went soaring bulkily into the air to save an Arsenal penalty. And there was no recall of fond memories of the eras of Albert Stubbins, Billy Liddell, Ian St John, Ron Yeats, Tommy Smith, Jimmy Melia, Roger Hunt, Ray Clemence, Kevin Keegan, David Fairclough ('The Bionic Carrot') and many others adored by the Kop.

There was now only the enormity of a muffled silence, in which the odd game of pool did its best to trespass through balls cracking against balls. 'We don't want no excuses tonight,' a stout woman with a Bessie Braddock coal-scuttle hat pressed down on her head said, sipping a smouldering glass of barley wine. 'They put their heads on block this time. They should be ashamed of themselves, wack.'

Back at the Adelphi Hotel, I ran into a Belgian political journalist who was in town, doing a similar job to mine. 'The Brussels police must take a major part of the blame,' Marc Rozen reflected. 'They are far too inexperienced in how to deal with large riots.' Rozen's mother had rung him in Liverpool asking what it was like staying in a 'city of mobsters' – a rather tendentious enquiry, he felt. 'Everyone here has been very sympathetic about the deaths of the Belgians in the riots. You can't say the city belongs to mobsters. They are very human and very kind, except for a mad, small minority.'

Many foreign tourists (including a party of Russians from Odessa) were in Liverpool, and it had not taken them long, after watching television in their rooms, to become aware of the rapidly circumnavigating grief tangling with their innocent sightseeing. Wilbur Irvine, a retired engineer from New York and an all-American football fan, was in the Adelphi cocktail bar having a last nightcap, and reliving his own experiences of hooliganism on the rocks: 'It's all down to drink. I was staying in Ostend and the Liverpool fans tried to get into our hotel. But the owner would not allow them entry.'

The next evening brought these curious sightseers out in force to watch a special Requiem Mass 'to pray for the dead' at Liverpool's Metropolitan Roman Catholic Cathedral. A tense Archbishop Derek Warlock was chief celebrant in a packed congregation attended en masse by the Anfield club.

Eight years before, almost to the day, I had sat in a piazza café near the Tiber, in company with Frank Keating of *The Guardian*, watching shirtless, happy Liverpool fans celebrating their team's first European Cup victory in Rome against the West Germans, Borussia Münchengladbach, the night before. That had been the night of manager Bob Paisley's greatest triumph, the night that the wily, former 'Desert Rat' had tried in vain to find a Guinness at the Holiday Inn Anfield knees-up. Now Paisley was one of the mourners in the steep confines of a home cathedral.

Did he, I wonder, look back to those days of balmy sunshine when the Liverpool fans had swept joyfully and peacefully out of the Olympic Stadium calling out the names of Paisley, Kevin Keegan, Tommy Smith, Steve Heighway and the other architects of that thrilling 3–1 victory against the West German champions? It was there in Rome that Keating and I could hardly fail to applaud the behaviour of the world's best football fans at the time, and one which had deeply moved a Liverpool priest, named Father Tony Hitchens, whose parish was in one of the poorer parts of Liverpool. 'Wonderful, wonderful,' Father Hitchens beamed, on his way to sightsee at the Vatican. 'Haven't our fans been good?'

So they had, Father, but that seemed long ago now and there was a different tone under the banner headlines of the Italian press, a press which had been almost pious in their praise of the Liverpool fans in Rome. We could turn them over our aperitifs to odes such as this one in the Rome newspaper, *Il Messaggero*:

'The Liverpool fans did not devastate, pillage, profane sanctu-
aries or churches, or pillage wine and salami from shop shelves.'

Uncle Claudius would not have penned it better, wack, but
now it was 1985, and the mood of friendship that existed then
along the Tiber had turned bitter. Somehow the magic of the
previous years had gone, and for English clubs, it would be
'finis' in Europe.

21
The Hand of God

A short bus trip out from the 1986 World Cup finals in Mexico had brought me west of Guadalajara, to a sweltering port by the Pacific Ocean, revealing a stocky grey member of the home fleet beside a long, looping quayside where no human activity disturbed the peace of a lone resident donkey chewing a carrot under the shade of a palm tree.

If the Mexican fleet was in, it was very much in, but then this was lunch hour, when only mad Englishmen like myself ventured about in bouts of random sightseeing.

Both Mexico and England had recently been jostled out of the quarter finals by West Germany and Argentina, the former on penalties, the latter assisted by a blatant handball when Diego Maradona punched the ball past England's distinguished and durable goalkeeper, Peter Shilton. The defeat of Mexico in a close-run game at Monterrey had dampened the fiesta atmosphere prevailing across this mysterious land. The posters on the walls hailing their most precious striker, Hugo Sanchez, seemed almost superfluous now. They peeled at the corners under the rays of the Pacific sun; Sanchez's exulting bicycle leaps already fading under constant assault from the fumes of passing traffic.

After buying some random T-shirts for the children back home, I made for what seemed the port's only hotel, an old colonial building in the built-up centre. Its interior was very much pre-Revolution with a smoking room bar, basket chairs, high ceilings, profuse plants in tubs, a jangling of hotel keys and, fortuitously, a spacious restaurant with tables laid for lunch.

The expansive, shirt-sleeved patron ambled over, suggesting that as lobster was on the menu would I consider accepting his challenge, for, by taking up his offer, I would be indulging in one of the very best lobsters in Mexico. And caught that very morning as well! It was an offer I could hardly refuse. An electric fan whirred overhead, as the occasional businessman sat reading the sports pages.

It was easy to indulge in the relative peace offered by this backs to the ocean, out of the smart guide book, ensnarer of fruit and vegetable haven. After days and days of being endlessly searched before entering the Aztec Stadium in Mexico City before the canorous chants of the home country's fans threatened one's tingling eardrums; after grey afternoons in the slumlands of Neza, straying in shanty misery for miles outside the nation's capital, and ultimately to be the stadium site where Scotland's ambitions withered away against Uruguay; after days on the road with David Miller surviving hurricane-force electric storms, and feeling the odd tremor of an earthquake while queueing for tickets in the new hi-tec communications Press office – there was something to be said for relaxing and minding one's own business. This was just what the silent businessmen, scattered around me, seemed to have in mind as well.

Yet ports, as the late Kenneth Tynan once reflected, have a special excitement of their own, and the narrow street outside the restaurant windows offered the odd flutter of a seedier side to our nautical whereabouts. A bulbous whore on spiked heels, dressed in heavy black leather and straining tight mini-skirt, which in the heat must have stuck to her flesh like Super Glue, was escorting a Mexican matelot half her size to some nearby *chambre-de-lit*. As they disappeared from view, my lobster arrived, proudly born by the owner who proceeded to watch me imbibe this swollen king of the deep. I had to mutter 'magnifico' once or twice before he departed, beaming. In truth, the lobster's flesh would not have been out of place in the second-hand car dump down the road. Still, it was a change from cod.

'The lobsters are not quite what they seem to be,' said a voice suddenly from above me. 'I'll swear you are eating a crayfish.'

An elderly man in a faded, lightweight beige suit had appeared from nowhere, and much to my alarm, he lumped his way down into the basket chair opposite.

'I hear you are English,' he reflected, a large pair of jowls adding lustre to obvious corpulence. 'And so am I, if truth be known. We do not see very many of our countrymen around these parts.' The man had an ebony cane which he hung on to as he accepted my invitation to have an odd ceveza. A thin bead of perspiration intruded from an aperture which divided one side of his mouth from a plump cheek. 'I come from Worthing originally,' he said. 'But my banana boat reservation to this unholy dump booked no return. And from what I read in the odd newspaper I pick up from home, there is no reason to return. I fear our nation is in sad decline despite the Prime Minister's undoubted ability.'

The man, who called himself Fred Cuthbert, caught my gaze lingering away towards another outrageously painted woman of the port passing by, almost breaking into a jog to join her client.

'Do not indulge, dear boy,' warned Fred. 'They are not without something unquestionable. Be warned.'

It was when he got round to interrogating me about my motives for being in Mexico that he began to get restless. Taking a long sip of his beer, he suddenly whacked the edge of the table with his cane. Other diners at nearby tables were visibly disturbed by such a cantankerous act. 'I read of the hand of God,' he thundered. 'Trust a filthy little dago to resort to such tactics. What a stinking cheat! He should be disqualified from the World Cup. Dirty little Diego Whatshisname. Shoot him, I say.'

Such a sudden eruption brought peace to an end in the dining room – though the congregation were obviously used to such behaviour from a resident Englishman employed, I gathered later, as some kind of packet line liaison-man.

'The hand of God indeed. What an insult to our Britannic majesty! What a foul snub to the laws of Association Football! When I watched this lout on television flapping his hand and hitting the ball with it like a tennis racket at Wimbledon, I threw my beer glass across the room in contempt. The Argies behaved just as they did in the Falklands.'

England's defeat, brought about by Maradona's cynical act, which could not be absolved by a magical second goal, had obviously stirred up the old feelings of Empire gunboat patriotism in ageing Fred Cuthbert. If he could have hired a Mexican gunboat to bombard the Argentine training quarters, he would have done. Diego Maradona, the finest player in those World Cup finals and the player who did far more than any other Argentine player to win the Cup for his country, had thrown a pot of grease on the Union Jack.

Maradona employing unorthodox tactics against Shilton, Mexico City, 1986.

'I remember the days when players had manners,' growled Fred. 'It was often considered disrespectful to save a penalty when you knew the other fellow had been wrongly fouled. Now that filthy dago comes up with the act of gross indecency – the hand of God indeed.'

'Would you like another beer, Fred?'

'Of course I'll take another beer. Are you staying long?'

I was somewhat relieved to tell him my bus was scheduled to leave shortly.

'It's a bloody awful road. I know it well. Sometimes you have forest fires on it.'

'There's a small one now.'

'Take care, old boy, take care. Never pays to be fried. And that reminds me, the possessor of the hand of God should be fried at the stake. I suggest the offending hand should be put in boiling oil. Do you happen to know if the Queen is sending an envoy to sort out this grave scandal? It does seem to me to be worth another ear, you know. That little street urchin from Buenos Aires has a lot coming to him. He is a grotesque insult to his miserable nation.'

'But all the same, he's a very gifted footballer,' I offered.

'He's not a patch on Stanley Matthews or Raich Carter. He's a tubby conman if you ask me.'

It was eventually time to break free from Fred's thunderous tumultuations aimed at the hand of God. Like so many brief meetings during World Cups, I would have liked to have found out a bit more about him; but like so many foreign settlers in strange parts of the world, he hardly kept a biographical introduction clipped to a frayed top pocket. His farewell was effusive, perspiration sprinkly despite the presence of the fan. 'Goodbye, old boy, goodbye. And give that Diego one from me if you see him.'

Fred's anger, after all, was only about a doubtful goal in a football match, I thought as the bus trailed through the baked hills on the way back to base. But Maradona's action had undoubtedly stirred up a hornet's nest back in jolly old Blighty, and in every mad dog Englishman's foreign outpost overseas as well.

Not long ago, I read Bobby Robson's own thoughts on Maradona's volleyball goal in his World Cup diary, which, in retrospect, was much more subdued than Fred's. 'Five minutes before half-time against Argentina, our dreams were ended and my worst fears about both Maradona and the referee were real-ised. The first goal happened in such a flash but no one in the dug-out had any doubts at all. I immediately knew that it was handball and I waited for the officials to sort it out. Almost as quickly I realised that nothing was going to happen. Maradona had looked at the referee and seen him give the goal and was now celebrating the all-important breakthrough.

'Our normally passive players were going crazy. Hodge, who had played the ball back to Shilton, Hoddle, Sansom and Shilton himself were chasing the referee back towards the centre circle. Shilton, more than anyone, knew he had been cheated for the only way Maradona could have beaten him in that type of situation was by using his hand. I remained outwardly calm but there was a hollow feeling in the bottom of my stomach.'

Diego's hand of God had really done for our Land of Hope and Glory. Fred's nightmare said it all.

Burnley – a Journey to the Brink

For the three reporters who travelled in a creaky old London taxi from Preston station to Turf Moor, Burnley on May 9, 1987, the assignment ahead offered rather more than a routine League match for their offices. There was a suggestion of an early summer's day on the green banks of the motorway as the taxi lumbered reluctantly on, the driver hanging mournfully over his steering wheel like a tugboat commander riding into a tempest.

'That Burnley have only themselves to blame,' he muttered to any ear that would listen. 'They were a great crowd once. I supported them through thick and thin before moving to Preston. You remember the days of McIlroy and Pointer, Adamson and Blacklaw – they were a decent side then. We went potty when they won the First Division. Now they could be slung out of the Fourth if they lose today. A bloody disgrace! Bob Lord would turn in his grave.'

The young reporter from an East London newspaper sitting opposite me looked particularly twitchy, as a regular traveller with Orient on away days. The reason he was twitchy, which was suggested by the way he regularly rung his hands together, was that Orient had Burnley to beat if they had a chance of taking part in the Fourth Division promotion play-offs, while Burnley had to win to survive a drop into the hidden labyrinths of the GM Vauxhall Conference – a confrontation that spelt gripping tension in every sense.

The East End boy did not have the same sense of a great club dying away as myself. Steve, who was seated beside him, had put on a slightly puzzled expression to disguise the nervousness he undoubtedly felt. 'I remember Burnley in the good old days when I was at school,' said Steve. 'We used to see them winning matches galore on the box, with Kenny Wolstenholme going potty about Connelly dancing through and booting the ball into the net.'

'They must have been good,' the young reporter said. 'But I don't give a sod for them today. Orient have really got to walk all over 'em – get goals, and then we will be laughing all the way to the play-offs and the Third. Frank Clark will be shitting himself, I'm sure. But he's the kind of manager to get the best out of the lads on a big occasion.'

'The crowd will be behind Burnley,' Steve reflected. 'It will be hell in that piddley little Press Box too – and you won't be able to hear yourself speak. I feel this could be a dodgy afternoon.'

There is nothing more unnerving for a reporter on duty than the prospect of having one's lines of communication disrupted by mayhem and confusion, noise and hysteria, intolerant copy-takers and sudden squeaks when a line goes dead, or the sheer malice of a foreign-looking scribe trying to pirate a phone which is your sole property.

'Keith McNee will have a nightmare today. His livelihood at Burnley will be blown to pieces if Burnley go down.'

McNee was a stringer who had covered all Burnley's matches, going back to the days when they were in the First Division. Reports of GM Vauxhall Conference matches would not be regarded with much interest in Fleet Street.

A signpost on the left as we slid by indicated Whalley, a town my own father had been posted to in 1941 while serving in the Royal Artillery. He was trained to ride a Norton motorbike on these very same rambling hills in the distance; my mother, who had been living in digs to be near Rodrigo, spending her time painting Lancashire landscapes linked to cows munching grass in some very beautiful countryside spotted with urban souvenirs of the Victorian industrial chimney revolution. The memory of those blacked-out, often gloomy, tense days of war took my mind away for a while from the job in hand, but memories of better times at Turf Moor came alive again when the taxi bounced up outside the Bob Lord Stand in Brunshaw Road.

It was back in 1974 when I had been given a personal, private viewing of the extravagances of its VIP section, the Burnley chairman and bluff butcher, obviously highly proud of the gar-ish colours that dazzled the eyes, the polished cigar boxes, the pungent mod cons atmosphere where visiting directors' wives could murmur gossip to each other over tinkling teacups at half-time. Now in Burnley's tensest day in their League history, a plaque reminded the few of us who had arrived early that Edward Heath, a friend of Bob Lord, had opened the stand on September 14, 1974.

Tom, Steve and I made for the director's lounge, there not being many people about as yet, the tension of the lunch hour no doubt being eased in Burnley's watering-holes. But as we stepped into the lounge which had a bar at the far end, one of those official little men who do their best to make life uncomfortable for people on Saturday afternoons pounced on us.

'What you doing here, sirs? This is private, directors only.'

'We've come a long way, and we feel thirsty.'

'There's space downstairs for Press, if you're Press that is.'

'Come on, be a sport,' said Steve. 'There's nobody about, and this might be the last time we come here anyway if you drop out of the League.'

The official little man seemed to brood on these words of doom, and his expression began to change, like a funeral parlour attendant who has just been told that after one more service his services are no longer required.

Freed of the frightening aura of the late Burnley butcher, he began to relent, eyeing us in close proximity with a certain benevolence, as if his own job might indeed be on the line, if there were staff cuts at Turf Moor, especially in view of Burnley's horrible financial state.

'Well, go on in then – but don't put theeselves about too much. There's no substitute for discretion, you know, sirs.'

We slid past his wiry frame and sat down on three flame-coloured chairs, Tom's increasing anxiety beginning to wend its way into the nervous systems of his two companions. They say that on occasions like these, Guinness is good for you, and the barman was happy to oblige.

It was in this same lounge in 1974 that I had chatted to a most optimistic Burnley commercial manager, Jack Butterfield, who had predicted that the Turf Moor club was going to forge into the 1980s with a successful vigour that would make them one of the most modern football outfits in the country.

Only 12 years had elapsed, then, since Burnley had travelled to Wembley to meet and lose to Spurs in the FA Cup final, only 13 had elapsed since Burnley had taken part in the European Cup competition, and only 14 since they had sent the citizens of Burnley wild with joy by winning the

Football League championship. The victorious captain then, Jimmy Adamson, was now the manager; Butterfield, another former Burnley manager, had the task of raising funds for the club, in what was called a club development scheme blessed by Bob Lord.

Burnley was then a reasonably successful First Division club in a smallish Lancashire town, with near neighbours in big-time football over the hill in Yorkshire. Sitting here, all those years ago, had produced little to disturb a feeling of well-being and security fanned by the warmth of Butterfield's enthusiasm. He and his wife, Eileen, had started the development association in a small hut in a corner of the Turf Moor ground and the enterprise had grown large enough to give substantial help in financing the new Bob Lord Stand, where we were sitting, on the brink of a cliff. Butterfield had told me that the source of income provided by the development association would be important to Burnley if the retain and transfer system was abolished because the club had sold £1 million worth of playing staff in five years – a lot of money in those days. Burnley were so optimistic at that time that they had put up new floodlights in preparation for European competition which would surely arrive in a year or two, rallied by their manager, Adamson's war-cry: 'The main thing here is success on the field – but our facilities must be made to run as well. Burnley is a seven-day-a-week place.'

The confidence exuded by Butterfield and, to a more cautious degree, by Adamson back in 1974 was quickly sabotaged because of the team's failure to get results. The bright young side which had played well before losing an FA Cup semi final against Newcastle at Hillsborough in 1974, fell apart as Second Division football returned to Turf Moor two years later. From then on, the slide into the depths quickened, as the club fell into the Third in 1980, and after a brief return later to the Second, went all the way down to the Fourth, with the gasp of a man sliding uncontrollably down a precipice. Now the scene was set for their last dig at salvation and the television cameras were massed at Turf Moor to record what was to become a distinctly bizarre afternoon.

I left Tom fiddling nervously with his lemonade and Steve buried deep into his programme background notes and went up to the Press Box to find Keith. In the more scabrous atmosphere underneath the stand, Ian Wooldridge, the *Daily Mail*'s chief sports columnist, was perusing the scene like a machine gunner hanging over the side of a First World War fighter, searching the skies for enemy raiders. It was good to see Ian, though you could tell Turf Moor was not a place he frequently visited, his spruce appearance geared to St Andrews or Lords', providing the first real clue to the cliffhanging importance on offer now on this sunny Lancashire afternoon. Ian, like me, was looking for Keith, and we made our way up into the stand, up steep steps toward the Press Box, where McNee was to be seen battling with telephone flexes and looking thoroughly miserable.

'Not many people about,' Ian reflected. The terraces round the ground did look surprisingly bare, considering the momentous event to come, small groups of fans in claret and blue favours, chatting to each other like so many puffins on a rock, undisturbed by the thunder of waves. Keith talked fast, his mind already set on deadlines, commotion, confusion, chaos, nervous digs in the stomach, the bedlam of a goal being scored, the lack of friendship offered by a wrist watch on a sweaty wrist . . . But somehow he managed to sort out our queries, and Ian had many, concerning Burnley's plight. I envied him for having until Sunday morning to weigh it all up. My own phone by now looked more like my own executioner.

Down in the Press room, underneath the stand, a large group of scribes were chatting round a large table filled with teacups and the odd whisky glass. Brian Miller, the Burnley manager, put his head round the door and wished us well. 'Wish us luck,' he said, his outward joviality disguising the hideous tensions zinging electrically through his powerful frame. This was the same Miller once remembered as a young wing half playing for Burnley in the FA Cup quarter final against West Ham in 1964, who had kicked the ball off his own goal-line with an almighty swipe, the leg movement vividly captured by an *Observer* photographer. West Ham had won that thrilling match 3–2 and gone on to win the Cup. Miller had already played for Burnley in the Cup final of 1962, which Spurs won. Now an older, more mellowed Miller had arrived at Turf Moor for the toughest afternoon of his life, his notes in the club programme parading the earnestness of the hour and near pleading for added support from the town.

In another part of the programme, the precarious nature of Burnley's financial position was starkly laid out – the board demanding to know if the Burnley public really wanted to support a football side in the town. If there was any doubt about this almost wounded consideration, it was quickly laid to rest when I returned to my claustrophobic seat near Keith McNee. As in some far-off silent movie epic miracle, the neglected terraces of Turf Moor had suddenly been taken over by the fans who had long lost their desire to spend their afternoons standing on the banks of the Long Side cover. It was extraordinary, this sudden show of loyalty, so fanatical, in fact, that the game ultimately would be held up for 15 minutes while thousands queued outside to get in. The final register from the turnstiles revealed that 15,781 fans were on duty when George Courtney, the World Cup referee from County Durham, blew his whistle for the kick-off.

Everyone, for a brief time, apart from nearby Tom, seemed to have forgotten all about dear old Orient. In the ensuing pandemonium, grown men gibbered and crowed in praise of a team they had long grown disillusioned by – their Lancastrian accents betrayed the rough and ready nature of their total concern for the right result. And down there on the pitch, running and puffing, puffing and running, was Leighton James, the Welsh international, who had first played on the wing for Burnley back in 1968, before moving away to several other clubs including Swansea, returning to Turf Moor in the ebbtide of his career. For a time, Leighton looked as if he was willing to play Orient on his own. 'The tension was terrible,' he told me later.

Before the wise old owl James, winner of 54 full Welsh caps, had visibly calmed his team's tottering early nerves, the Cockney challenge almost proved fatal, as far as the Lancashire homesters were concerned. In the very first minute, with the reporters trying desperately to catch a glimpse of the action over rows of bobbing heads in front of the Press Box, Howard of Orient put in a startling delivery which completely foxed the knee-knocking Neenan in Burnley's goal. Orient were about to rejoice at making such an audacious start, when Leebrook, the Burnley right back, climbed up off the turf and nodded away the approaching missile, a deed which must have given him a splitting headache later.

Now, with James conducting proceedings chiefly up the left flank on a pair of ancient but still sprightly pins, Burnley began to press forward with the crowd screaming their heads off. Keith's nearby voice on one of his three phones almost screamed forth his recollections of this tingling Lancashire hotpot. There was James, racing away to put over a centre, which should have been put away by Gallagher but the tall defender, born in Liverpool, headed past the far post.

James changed his tactics by harassing both Orient flanks. Despite his enthusiasm, Burnley didn't score a goal until the injury time George Courtney had added on to the first half. It was a real beauty, and must have reminded the referee of the scenes of joy which surrounded Mexico's goal against Paraguay at the Aztec Stadium, Mexico City, a game he had been given the unenviable task of officiating. Grewcock was the scorer at Turf Moor, firing a sweeping shot from long distance to beat Cass in the Orient goal. Somehow Mr Courtney managed to make it clear to the players that half-time refreshments were on hand, the crowd baying out their pleasure as the players loped back to the dressing-rooms. Phew! – time for a pause, a stretch of the legs, a quick dash of tea downstairs – 45 minutes lay ahead for Burnley to balance their books, but Orient were not making the passage easy.

On the way back from the tearoom, I ran into Keith, half-slumped against a pillar by the stairs leading to the stand. He looked pale and uncomfortable, and clearly in distress.

'I've had a bit of a turn. Must be the tension,' he said, breathlessly.

'Do you want me to call a doctor?'

'No, I'll be okay. I'll hang around here for a bit. Tell Jim to take over my stuff. He knows the form. Thanks, anyway.'

I left Keith suffering below, not aware that his attack was a warning shot for the coronary that would kill him only weeks later. So the game of Burnley games went on without him up in his beloved Press Box, the ball whizzing backwards and forwards; Burnley trying desperately to add to their lead and Orient trying everything they knew to score two shock goals that could be their passport to the play-offs. The player who looked most likely to score was Burnley's stocky Ian Britton, who had laid on his team's first goal. Britton was in the veteran class, a Dundee-born player who had spent mixed seasons with Chelsea at Stamford Bridge, a player of the terrier type, with a clouting shot when he chose to aim at the bull's eye. This he did eventually, with a well-struck shot to put Burnley two ahead. It looked as if Burnley's troubles were over now, although there

Ian Britton, 'a well struck shot put Burnley two ahead'. . .

was a good deal of mathematical work to do with teams like Torquay and Lincoln jostling elsewhere to avoid the embarrassment of the big drop.

Orient were still determined to get back into the game, a determination that brought them the relief of a goal by Comfort, making life decidedly uncomfortable for the home team in the agonising final minutes. Rumours and counter-rumours swept the Bob Lord Stand about the progress of the other matches – but when Mr Courtney did blow the final whistle, the less-informed members of Burnley's fan club ran on to the pitch and started a victory celebration. But Burnley's future still remained in the balance until the news came through to us that Lincoln were for the drop, Burnley were safe, and Orient had blown the play-offs. 'Keith's gone home,' one of his colleagues said. 'He looked awful – couldn't stand watching the second half. What an afternoon! Almost fainted myself.'

Brian Miller almost ran down the corridor, accepting back-slaps with a frail smile. 'We should never have got into this situation in the first place,' he snapped. And one and all could thoroughly agree with him.

The losing manager, Frank Clark, emerged on the edge of the noisy throng in the Press Room, looking remarkably calm, despite the hideous pressures he had been forced to put up with in the visitors' dug-out. 'So we've blown the play-offs – but good luck to Burnley. They fought magnificently. And good luck to them. This was a great football celebration.'

What Clark did not say was something he kept to himself for a long time afterwards and only revealed to me a year or two later. 'I was dead scared that afternoon, I can tell you. A police superintendent had come up to me before the match and told me he could not guarantee the safety of my Orient players if we won the game. He hadn't enough officers on duty to protect us if the going got nasty – as it could have done.

'I kept the matter a secret from the players, it would have upset them to know. But all through the game I kept looking at the dressing-room exit and thinking there's one hell of a long way for us to run from the dug-out if the fans decide to make us scapegoats. In the end though, all was sweetness and light, and the Burnley fans could not have been more friendly.'

It was all a bit of an anti-climax, with everyone looking too stunned to whoop things up. We had a few beers upstairs and ordered a taxi back to Preston. I remember the evening turning grey, rain clouds threatening and Steve saying reflectively: 'That's one to tell your grandchildren. You couldn't beat that one for drama.'

Epilogue

The week ending April 15, 1989 had begun for me on a dazzling Saturday morning at Anfield, Liverpool, only a few hours before the start of the Grand National at nearby Aintree. As a London punter had used a bunch of banana-shaped fingers to make off with my raincoat the night before, during a torrential rainstorm, the prospects of an even wetter following morning seemed daunting. Instead, glorious sunshine reigned as the Liverpool players took it in turns themselves to sparkle like tiny rainbows sprouting over a lake following a savage thunderstorm. Sheffield Wednesday, near humiliated by five goals to one, could scarcely have had a more uncomfortable journey through 90 minutes, albeit after missing two easy chances early in the game.

There was a feeling of total supremacy about Liverpool's performance, with John Barnes, 'zPeter Beardsley, Steve McMahon and John Aldridge weaving ringlets of passes until this viewer began to feel decidedly dizzy. Memories sprang of the push-and-run formula used by Arthur Rowe's Spurs in the early 1950s, and their later double-winning successors at White Hart Lane managed by Bill Nicholson.

With their often reticent manager, Kenny Dalglish, offering a cautious smile afterwards, the Anfield factory looked in great shape, with Liverpool poised to catch Arsenal at the top of the First Division. So the Liverpool punters went off racing with joy in their hearts, as beholders of a wonderful football team in form.

Back at Wembley the next afternoon, it was time to admire Liverpool's FA Cup semi final opponents at the end of the week in which they won the Littlewoods Cup against Luton Town,

Dalglish – in celebratory mood. A traumatic April was to follow.

two of the goals coming from the Nottingham Forest manager's son, Nigel. Brian Clough had run out of the Wembley arena before the trophy was presented to his Forest players, presumably to leave the limelight to his squad members.

Clough has always had a penchant for the dramatic, choosing moments to either exit quickly or linger on for hours of discussion. I remember seeing him in 1973, blessing the crowd at the Baseball Ground, Derby, during one last farewell after he and his assistant, Peter Taylor, had resigned from the club during great controversy. The manner of his going was theatrical and certainly embarrassed the red-faced chairman, Sam Longson, who staged a Pope-like entreaty for loyalty from his own directors' box. But Clough, before departing in a large Rolls Royce for a television interview, clearly won the day's burlesque contest.

On another occasion, a social one this time, at the City Ground, Nottingham, Clough would dearly have loved to have prolonged a lunchtime meeting with a small team of journalists, ebulliently abandoning his sometimes bullying, macho attitude at Press conferences. On this occasion, Clough wanted to talk through a cold, frosty Nottinghamshire evening on a wide range of soccer subjects, going back to the days when he and Jimmy Greaves used to drive to play for England in a battered old Morris Minor, and more recent times when he was up there in the manager's ring, making himself unpopular with every soccer Colonel Blimp. 'You've got to be on the ball as a manager. It's no good keeping in the shallow end. You'll get bloody cold.'

Clough's afternoon in the City restaurant would have lasted much longer but for the presence of his wife, Barbara, who rarely turns up on these occasions, and eschews all contact with the Press if she can possibly help it. An elegant, no-nonsense family woman, her biddings are not taken highly seriously by Yorkshire's football firebrand, but as it happened on this occasion, she was positively obeyed. 'Brian, it is time to leave, *now*.' Clough got up with a wry smile and sheepishly left the room.

When Clough and Kenny Dalglish led their squads to Hillsborough on the Saturday following the Littlewoods Cup final, the prospects of a great match built up on a glorious afternoon. There was nothing to suggest the horrors to come as the two teams stripped in their dressing-rooms. But at 3.06 pm, shortly after the teams kicked off and Beardsley hit the bar for Liverpool, *the clock stopped suddenly on football*. A happy week had gone by full of anticipation; now with 95 fans from Liverpool crushed to death against the fences in their section of the terracing, the lights went out on our national game.

The resultant memorial services on Merseyside, the funerals, the tears of players, officials and fans alike, the inquiries, the post mortems, the floral tributes at the Anfield Kop, produced a very different emotional feeling in Liverpool than the guilty remorse stirred by the Heysel Stadium disaster four years before. The way in which Dalglish and his team united with the fans in a common bond was a sanguine lesson, a triumph if you like, over a game which had become manifestly sick and corrupt over recent years, governed by donkeys and hosted by stadiums not fit to entertain the cast of George Orwell's *Animal Farm*.

The days following the disaster in which the nation argued and debated, sometimes hysterically, the true reasons for the disaster, as they had after the Bradford fire, no one emerged more all-embracingly than Kenny Dalglish. The tragedy had cast aside the abrasive suspicion you felt he held for less informed, less privileged, and less gifted people involved with the game.

The agonies he went through with the club's chairman, John Smith, and chief executive, Peter Robinson, while debating when Liverpool should get their show on the road again, if indeed they could, in view of the disenchanted feelings of some of the Liverpool players like Barnes and Aldridge, ran in conjunction with his public appearances at hospitals in Sheffield and Liverpool, reading the lesson at the Anglican Cathedral from the Epistle to the Romans, Chapter 8 – 'What are we to say? If God is on our side, who is against us?'

Bobby Charlton, who remembered the grim days following the Munich air crash when he recovered from the ordeal to play for Manchester United in the FA Cup final, thought the Liverpool players should get back into action as quickly as possible. After two weeks of mourning, this is exactly what they did. Should they have come back so soon? I think they were right to play again, despite the feelings of many that they should have called off their season there and then, when the clock stopped at 3.06 on April 15.

Their League return against Everton at Goodison Park re-kindled memories of the match Manchester United played against Sheffield Wednesday after the Munich air crash disaster. David Lacey, of *The Guardian*, was there to record it: 'Football was a trivial reason for 95 people to die but football will help the city learn to live with the sorrow . . .'

Liverpool reached Wembley, beating Nottingham Forest 3–1 at Old Trafford very conclusively with two goals from Aldridge, three weeks and a day after the tragedy. 'They had,' wrote Lacey, 'come through the storm with heads held high and no one was any longer afraid of the dark.'

I had been at Villa Park on the afternoon of the tragedy, watching Everton beat Norwich to reach what was to become a Merseyside final. I don't think many people thought very much about the events of that semi final afterwards. Colin Harvey, the Everton manager, summed up what would soon horrify the nation after seeing explicit scenes of the carnage on their television sets and too graphic photographs in their national newspapers: 'We came off feeling full of the joys of spring and then we heard about the disaster. It takes the edge off everything and our thoughts are with all the families of the people who have died.'

Will football recover from its worst disaster within these shores? In view of Liverpool's own recovery, there is a will to keep going – added to a burning need to restructure antiquated attitudes to ground safety and spectator discomforts; all those pressing matters which have been lost in swollen files in numerous cellars round the country.

The idea of this book was to reflect in flickering images the state of a game, which in many cases had gone so disastrously downhill in two decades. It is sad and rather horrific that I should find myself typing the conclusion at the time of the Hillsborough tragedy, when it has been difficult to imagine the game surviving as an entertainment. But it will.

It will – because if some of the stunning contests played at the end of the 1988–1989 season in our domestic and European football are to be judged as antidotes for the future of a game reeling from various disorders, then the groggy old patient deserves some kind of revival.

Once Liverpool had emerged from a period of harrowing mourning after the Hillsborough disaster, they forged ahead with such professional zeal that the Double looked a formality, once they had beaten Everton 3–2 in the all-Merseyside FA Cup final. Two of Liverpool's goals came in extra time, both exquisite efforts from substitute Ian Rush. It was a quicksand period of ridiculously late goals with Everton's substitute, Stuart McCall, forcing extra time for Everton with an equaliser five seconds from the end, and scoring another to make the score 2–2. All this after Rush had hooked his Anfield team once more into the lead, originally given them by John Aldridge after only four minutes.

There was further drama yet to come the following Friday, if that was possible, with Arsenal visiting Anfield needing to win by two clear goals if they were to win the League Championship. But first there had been time to savour two vibrant performances conjured up by Napoli against Stuttgart in the second leg of the UEFA Cup final when Diego Maradona showed in one supreme moment in which he set up a goal for Careca why one is prepared to forgive some of the seedier aspects of his nature.

If Maradona's vision rivalled Pele's and Di Stefano's for that spellbinding ability to know precisely when to pull the trigger, the performances of the two Dutchmen, Ruud Gullit and Marco van Basten in scoring two goals apiece for AC Milan in the 4–0 victory over Steaua Bucharest in the final of the European Cup in Barcelona, revealed a joint genius which should honour the game of world soccer way into the 1990s. It is easy to look back into the past at hallowed heroes – but there is nothing like having them playing so well in the present and near future.

Gullit, van Basten and that marvellous motivator, freewheeling from defence, Frank Rijkaard, made one imagine, after watching their powers of destruction against Real Madrid, and then against the Romanians, an impromptu jam session with Charlie Parker (alto sax), Miles Davis (trumpet) and a burly bass player straying in from some nearby downtown bar. With the tall Gullit filling the role of 'Bird' Parker, van Basten a triumphant Davis and the moody Rijkaard, the bassist, they were all capable of merging together into magical improvisations. Van Basten's ability to achieve solo crescendos like Davis was reinforced by Gullit's impersonation of 'Bird' blowing lengthy, considered tornadoes on his horn.

Two nights after AC Milan's Nou Camp conquest in Catalonia, Liverpool's longest season came to an end, in a fashion few would have expected, or been brave enough to forecast. One of the exceptions was Arsenal's manager, George Graham, who remained convinced that his young team could do the trick. It was outrageously bold optimism by a former distinguished First Division professional with Aston Villa, Chelsea

and Arsenal. His team had not won at Anfield for seven years,
while Liverpool had not lost by two goals there in three. What
was more off-putting, as far as Arsenal were concerned, was
the limp way they had been performing in recent matches,
which had deprived them finally of top place to Liverpool. I
had seen Graham's team in a state of fear against a modest
Derby County side, losing 1–2, and playing so badly that some
of their loyalist rag-trade supporters stubbed out their cigars
and walked out long before the end. But in Derby's case,
their salvation was the 39-year-old Peter Shilton in goal, the
most durable of durable's, and on his way to beating Bobby
Moore's 108 international caps for England. Shilton on that
sunny afternoon was in a mood to fill his goal like a giant bear
– and he did.

I dropped into a Chelsea pub near my apartment to watch the
televised match. It was full of Chelsea supporters who normally
have no love of Arsenal, but on this occasion were prepared
to give another London club a cheer. 'It sticks in my mouth,
mate, but you've got to give George's lads a cheer tonight. It's
natural. After all, we won the Second Division championship.
We'll murder 'em next season, but that comes later. Come on
you Yellows!'

We were inside a saloon bar, recently modernised, with no
sign of sawdust or nicotined paintwork or tables set for domi-
noes but, instead, a mock library interior with shelves stacked
with books which must have come from various jumble sales
down the Fulham Road. Not that the Chelsea fans were prepared
to pick up such masterpieces as Jane Austen's *Northanger Abbey*
or Barbara Cartland's *A Virgin in Paris*; all eyes, some decidedly
blotchy, were focused at the television screen as the Arsenal
lads set out on a mission which required guts, power in the
tackle, and a will to win.

If there was any need to feel anxious about being late for a
dinner date, there seemed no need because Kenny Dalglish's
team's containing operation looked in no jeopardy. Then in the
53rd minute, the Chelsea fans hollered their appreciation of a
disputed goal by Alan Smith. 'Come on, you Gunners, walk all
over 'em.'

Time ticked on, with every Arsenal sally towards the Liverpool
goal greeted by wild cheers – I had heard Mexicans cheering
Brazilians, I had heard Spaniards cheering Argentinians, but
in 40 years of watching professional football never had I heard

A dramatic shot. Michael Thomas gives Arsenal their first League title since 1971.

Chelsea fans cheering Arsenal. It was almost as if Rangers and Celtic had decided to amalgamate.

Time was almost up now, with Liverpool playing out time and the Barclays League presentation table inside the players' tunnel, containing the victor's trophy festooned with red. Then it happened, the unbelievable, in six minutes of injury time. It was then that Michael Thomas decided the time was ripe for Arsenal to win their first League title since 1971, and he romped through to beat Bruce Grobbelaar for Arsenal's triumphant second goal. Now it was time for the Chelsea fans to dance with joy as the Arsenal players took a major salute from an applauding Kop and, for a time, West London became North London in a rare display of sporting unity.

Soon afterwards, I made my way up the Fulham Road, away from the Stamford Bridge stadium where I had happily spent a good part of my life watching the local team, haunted by the abounding memory of John Barnes sitting on the Anfield turf, fagged out and emotionally shattered. Often in the past, the eternal game had produced similar scenes of personal despair – but in Barnes's case, he had also been through the hell of Hillsborough.

Could there have been more poignancy in such a gesture of drained emotion? And all for what some people call only a game.

List of Books Consulted

The following books proved invaluable for jogging my memory of matters concerning the game over the past two decades.

Charlton, Bobby (with Ken Jones). *Bobby Charlton's Most Memorable Matches*. Stanley Paul, 1984.

Evans, Philip. *World Cup '82* and *World Cup '86*. Knight Books, 1982 and 1986.

Gallacher, Ken. *Jock Stein – The Authorised Biography*. Stanley Paul, 1988.

Glanville, Brian (ed.). *The Joy of Football*. Hodder and Stoughton, 1986.

Glanville, Brian. *The History of the World Cup*. Faber, 1982.

Green, Geoffrey. *Pardon Me for Living*. Allen and Unwin, 1985.

Inglis, Simon. *The Football Grounds of Great Britain*. Collins Willow, 1987.

Keating, Frank (illustrated by John Jensen). *Long Days – Late Nights*. Robson Books, 1984.

Korr, Charles. *West Ham United*. Duckworth, 1986.

McIlvanney, Hugh and Hopcraft, Arthur (eds.). *World Cup '70*. Eyre and Spottiswoode, 1970.

Malam, Colin. *World Cup Argentina*. Collins, 1978.

Miller, David. *World Cup 1970*. Heinemann, 1970.

Miller, David. *Father of Football*. Stanley Paul, 1970.

Pawson, Tony. *The Goalscorers*. Cassell, 1978.

Powell, Jeff. *Bobby Moore*. Everest Books, 1976.

Robson, Bobby (with Bob Harris). *Bobby Robson's World Cup Diary*. Collins Willow, 1986.

Rollin, Jack. *The Guinness Book of Soccer Facts and Feats*. Guinness, 1978, 1979, 1981, 1983.

Rollin, Jack (ed.). *Rothmans Football Yearbook – 1988–89*. 19th edition, Queen Anne Press, 1988.